The Serpent's Tongue:

The Spirit of Deception

La Wanda Blackmon

Copyright © 2023 La Wanda Blackmon

All rights reserved.

No part of this book may be reproduced, stored in a retrieval system, or transmitted in any form or by any means—electronic, mechanical, photocopying, recording, or otherwise—without prior written permission of the publisher and copyright owner, except for the inclusion of brief quotations in a review. This includes information stored on public, school, and personal computers, as well as software storage and retrieval systems. All use requires written permission from the copyright owner or publisher, except by a reviewer who may quote brief passages in a review or use quotations in a book review. Contact the publisher for information about this title or to order other books or electronic media. Contact the publisher below for bulk book sales to support sales promotions, fundraising, or educational programs.

HFT PUBLISHING Inc

HFT Publishing, Inc.
P. O. Box 1863
Brewton, AL 36427-1863
Email: HFT-Publishing@post.com

Paperback ISBN—978-1-953239-83-9

eBook ISBN—978-1-953239-87-7

Exterior and Interior Design of the book by:
HFT Publishing, Inc.
limited AI text research and assistance with extensive editing
eBook conversion by:
HFT Publishing, Inc.
Paperback Book Cover and eBook cover designed by:
HFT Publishing, Inc.
The Cover Photo—Fotor AI Generated by Author

Printed in the United States of America

DEDICATION

To the steadfast believers who cherish the Bible and stand as vigilant sentinels against the tide of spiritual deception that seeks to engulf the Church in these perilous times. May this book serve as a clarion call to deeper study, unwavering faith, and courageous discernment.

The Serpent's Tongue: The Spirit of Deception

TABLE OF CONTENTS

Dedication	iii
Table of Contents	iv
Acknowledgments	vii
Introduction	9
Chapter 1: The Unseen Architecture of Deception	13
Chapter 2: The Seeds of Deception	29
Chapter 3: Counterfeit Truths and Deceptive Tactics	57
Chapter 4: The Signs of Deception	77
Chapter 5: Strategies for Liberation from Deception	95
Chapter 6: The Gift of Discernment—Necessary for the Last Days	133
Chapter 7: The Spiritual Fortification Defense	151
Chapter 8: Restoring Truth and Mending What is Broken	181
Chapter 9: Readiness for His Coming: Eradicating Deceit	197
Conclusion	213
About Author	219
Books by this Author	223
References	231

ACKNOWLEDGMENTS

To all my followers and faithful prayer warriors whose unwavering support, insightful counsel, and prayerful partnership have been an indispensable strength, and to our ministry. Your prayers are worth more than gold!

Thank you, Momma, for helping proofread so much over the last three years!

La Wanda Blackmon

INTRODUCTION

In this modern, high-tech 21st Century, we are faced with a generation where truth is often malleable and spiritual discernment is increasingly elusive. The Bible stands as a formidable bulwark against the insidious forces of deception. This book is born out of a profound concern for the spiritual welfare of God's people, particularly those who hold the Bible in high esteem, recognizing its unique place as a divine book written by men as the Holy Spirit inspired them. These powerful words of God outline the principles necessary for us to live a victorious life. However, the landscape of modern faith is fraught with subtle distortions, outright falsehoods, and cleverly disguised errors that can lead even the most devout believers astray. From the pervasive influence of secular humanism and relativistic philosophies to the more overt manipulations of false teachers and aberrant movements, the enemy's strategies are varied and relentless.

When I felt led by the Holy Spirit to address this topic of deception, I initially ignored it. To write on all of the accounts of deception in the Bible and explain the particulars would result in a 500-600-page book. There are numerous aspects of deception, and many ways it can impact our lives and churches. So, I began to fast and pray over this topic. Ultimately, the best approach to this subject was to start with an overview of deception. Knowing that I could later write about the specific incidents in the Bible that show the various strategies of deception. In other words, I would be writing this overview like a sermon that I would preach on a Sunday morning and conclude it with the Sunday night service. Later, other topics could be covered, like preaching a series.

Note that my intention in writing this book is not to induce fear, but to equip each reader and believer with the tools needed to combat Satan. I want to provide a biblically grounded framework for understanding the nature, origins, and manifestations of spiritual deception, and to offer practical, actionable strategies for identifying and resisting it. We will trace the historical and theological roots of deceit, from the very beginning of humanity's rebellion to its contemporary expressions. Then you can read my book, which will be released before the end of 2024, titled *'The Gift of Discernment."* That is the ultimate tool for the Spiritual Warrior, guaranteeing success in combating this spirit—early recognition.

If you want to know more about living a victorious life, having answered prayers, and seeing revival in your church, or if you are on the leadership team of your church, then this book will provide you with the spiritual tools and sound theological understanding that will be your greatest defense. We will delve into the scriptural knowledge of Satan's role as the 'father of lies,' examine the internal vulnerabilities that make us susceptible to deception, and highlight the external influences that seek to pervert truth. Furthermore, we will learn to recognize the subtle signs of error, both in our personal lives and within the broader Church community, and equip ourselves with the biblical tools necessary for liberation and spiritual fortification. I pray that this book empowers you and serves as a guide to help you stand firm on the bedrock of God's truth, shielded by faith, and armed with the Sword of the Spirit, ensuring you are ready for His glorious appearing. We must recognize that a pervasive spirit of deception is increasingly taking control of the secular world in which we live. From the grand narratives of secular ideologies to the intimate whispers of doubt that assail the believing heart, falsehood has become a dominant force, often cloaked in the guise of progress, enlightenment, or even spirituality. Satan delights in the fact that he has been invited into most churches and granted a seat at the leadership table.

He no longer has to "cloaked" to deceive—he operates in the open now—in our faces with his deceptions, and so many do not even recognize his evil tools, because they are so concerned with things, money, power, fame, and "being in control" that they cannot see his counterfeit anointing and demonstrations. Recognizing and resisting these deceptive currents is not merely an intellectual exercise but a vital spiritual imperative. The Bible serves as a crucial anchor in an ocean of shifting truths and manufactured realities. We must read and study it daily to be able to receive the "Gift of Discernment" needed to survive the magnificent power of Satan in these last days to deceive, even the very elect, if possible.

I will start with the definition of deception and establish a theological framework for understanding deception, tracing its origins from the Fall in Eden to its sophisticated manifestations in our contemporary context, and understanding the enemy's methods–the subtle counterfeiting of the truth, fake news, exploitation of ignorance, and a fake anointing that is his greatest counterfeiting tool. Remember, the 'father of lies' is a master strategist, and his primary objective is to alienate humanity from the immutable truth of God. He does not care if you sin or not—if he can keep you from living victoriously, he can prevent you from helping others and being a threat to his kingdom. Then, if he can deceive you into believing a lie and be damned, that is icing on the cake for Satan. He will feel that he has been super effective!

Finally, we will discuss pride, self-deception, and spiritual apathy, which are fertile ground for the seeds of falsehood. We will investigate how the world system, with its competing philosophies and cultural indoctrination, seeks to redefine truth and undermine divine authority, often infiltrating the very fabric of religious discourse.

We will conclude with practical strategies for building one's spiritual defenses—from the helmet of salvation to the shield of faith and the sword of the Spirit. We will explore the indispensable role of prayer, the necessity of community, and the critical gift of discernment, particularly in these 'last days' foretold in prophecy.

Ultimately, this book is a call to action: a call to embrace truth with unwavering commitment, to actively participate in mending what deception has broken, and to live in such a way that we are ready for the imminent return of our Lord and Savior Jesus Christ. May the insights you glean from these pages equip you to stand firm, to speak truth in love, and to shine as a beacon of uncompromised faith in a world desperately in need of God's unchanging Word.

La Wanda Blackmon

CHAPTER ONE:
The Unseen Architecture of Deception

The very foundation of our faith, and indeed, of all reality as revealed in Scripture, is built upon the bedrock of truth. Deception in all of the forms that it takes on is here for one purpose—to discredit and stop God's divine purpose for our lives and his plans for our churches. To navigate the treacherous landscape of spiritual warfare, where the enemy's primary weapon is misdirection, it is imperative that we first establish a robust, biblically grounded definition of what constitutes deception. It is essential to identify all the ways deception can occur. The more knowledge we have, the more power we have to stop Satan's counterfeit operations. Remember, Satan is a master counterfeiter. He has never had an original idea. He counterfeits the true anointing, God's miracles, and the power of the Holy Spirit in an effort to deceive church members who are not filled with the Holy Ghost, strong spiritual warriors, or blessed with the gift of discernment. Without a clear understanding of the enemy's tactics, we are like soldiers marching into battle without knowing the face of their foe and without the proper armor to defeat that foe.

Definition of Deception

Deception, at its most fundamental level, is the act of causing someone else to believe something that is not true. The Merriam-Webster online dictionary (2023) defines deception as follows:

The act of causing someone to accept as true or valid what is false or invalid. The act of deceiving, resorting to falsehood and *deception*. Used *deception* to leak the classified information; the fact or condition of being deceived; something that deceives; tricks, fools by a scam artist's clever deception—synonyms: Deception, fraud, double-dealing, subterfuge, and trickery.

According to the Bible, deception is not limited to outright lies, although those are certainly included. Spiritual deception encompasses the subtle distortion of truth, the twisting of God's Word, the manipulation of emotions, and the perversion of sound doctrine. It is any deviation from the revealed, immutable truth of God, designed to lead individuals astray from His path and His purposes. The Bible consistently presents a stark dichotomy: truth versus falsehood, light versus darkness, God versus Satan. There is no middle ground, no neutral territory when it comes to the nature of reality and divine revelation. As our Lord Jesus Christ declared, **John 14:6,** "*I am the way, the truth, and the life*" (KJV, 2023). In this statement, Jesus identifies himself not merely as a bearer of truth, but as truth personified. To deviate from Him, or the truth found in his word, is to step into the realm of deception. In **John 8:44,** Jesus confronts the Jews who opposed Him, stating, "*Ye are of your father the devil; and the lusts of your father ye will do. He was a murderer from the beginning, and abode not in the truth, because there is no truth in him. When he speaketh a lie, he speaketh of his own: for he is a liar, and the father of it.*" (KJV, 2023).

This powerful declaration immediately establishes Satan as the originator of deception, a being whose very nature is antithetical to truth. He is not merely a purveyor of falsehoods; he *is* a liar, and lying is his native tongue. This understanding is foundational because it reveals that deception is not a random or accidental phenomenon in the spiritual realm; it is a deliberate, orchestrated assault by a sentient, malevolent intelligence. The pervasive nature of deception is also evident from the very beginning of human history, as chronicled in the book of Genesis. The serpent's encounter with Eve in the Garden of Eden serves as the archetypal instance of deception. The serpent did not outright deny God's command; instead, he subtly twisted it. In Genesis 3:1, "*Hath God said, Ye shall not eat of every tree of the garden?*" (KJV, 2023). This seemingly innocent question plants a seed of doubt. He then proceeds to contradict God's warning about death flatly: **Genesis 3:4-5** "*And the serpent said unto the woman, Ye shall not surely die: For God doth know that in the day ye eat thereof, then your eyes shall be opened, and ye shall be as gods, knowing good and evil*" (KJV, 2023).

This is a classic deceptive maneuver: presenting a falsehood as a more appealing or enlightening alternative to divine truth. The serpent capitalizes on Eve's desire for knowledge and empowerment, making disobedience to God seem like a pathway to greater understanding and godlikeness. This instance reveals that deception often appeals to our desires, pride, and perceived limitations, promising liberation while ultimately leading to bondage. However, the consequences of this initial deception were catastrophic, resulting in the fall of humanity and the introduction of sin, death, and separation from God into the world. This historical event serves as a profound theological lesson: ***deception is not a trivial matter.*** It has eternal ramifications. It is the **primary tool** the enemy uses to separate individuals and communities from the life-giving presence of God. Therefore, when we speak of deception from a theological standpoint, we are not merely discussing a matter of intellectual error; we are addressing a spiritual force that seeks to corrupt, enslave, and ultimately destroy.

Deception is often characterized by its subtlety. It rarely announces itself as a falsehood. Instead, it frequently masquerades as truth, wisdom, or even piety. The Bible warns us about this deceptive camouflage. In **II Corinthians 11:14**, the Apostle Paul writes, *"And no marvel; for Satan himself is transformed into an angel of light."* (KJV, 2023). This is a stark warning that the enemy can appear righteous, even divine, to draw unsuspecting souls into his snare. He does not always appear as a roaring lion, but often as a gentle lamb, or a wise counselor, or a charismatic leader. This transformation is achieved through the distortion of truth, the manipulation of scripture, and the exploitation of sincere desires for spiritual experience. The deceiver excels at presenting a counterfeit that is almost indistinguishable from the genuine article, making discernment an absolutely critical skill for every believer.

The scope of deception extends beyond individual belief and into the very fabric of our understanding of God, His Word, and His will. Satan's deceptive tool can manifest as a subtle downplaying of sin's severity, a distortion of God's character to make Him seem less holy or less just, or a perversion of His promises to encourage presumption rather than faith. For instance, a deceptive teaching might suggest that God's love means He overlooks sin without repentance, thereby undermining the necessity of the atoning sacrifice of Christ. Deception might twist the promise of answered prayer to imply that God is obligated to grant our every desire, irrespective of His will or our spiritual condition. These are not outright denials of God, but rather subtle manipulations that shift the focus from God's sovereignty and holiness to human desires and autonomy.

To equip ourselves against such insidious attacks, we must anchor our understanding of deception firmly in the unchanging Word of God. The Bible provides an unparalleled clarity and authority in this regard. Its translators, guided by the Holy Spirit and working from the most reliable ancient manuscripts available at the time, delivered an English translation that has stood the test of centuries. This translation is not merely a linguistic rendering; it is a theological bulwark. Its precise vocabulary and grammatical structures, rooted in the King James tradition, convey theological truths with an accuracy that is often diluted or obscured in more modern translations that rely on different textual bases.

Our understanding of God's nature, His plan of salvation, and the requirements of discipleship hinges upon our commitment to truth.

Deception leads us down paths of error that result in alienation from God, and ultimately, spiritual death. Deception is the subtle poison that can cripple even the most earnest believer, turning vibrant faith into a hollow imitation. Therefore, to engage in deception, no matter how insignificant it is, is to engage with a power or force that can destroy the very core of our Christian identity and our eternal destiny. We must study and prepare ourselves with the spiritual warrior tools needed to discern truth from falsehood. Without this tool (the gift of discernment), we cannot experience the fullness of God's blessing. The Bible is a lamp unto our feet and a light unto our path (**Psalm 119:105**). In an age where truth is increasingly subjective and relativized, the KJV stands as a steadfast beacon of objective, unchanging divine revelation. It is a testament to God's faithfulness in preserving His Word for every generation. By grounding our definition of deception in scriptural support from the Bible, I aim to help you build robust defenses, enabling you to recognize the enemy's insidious strategies.

Although I use other translations from time to time to provide extra help and understanding of synonyms, which aids the reader, I found that other translations altered the meaning of various topics related to deception. These subtle changes were deceptive themselves. I recommend sticking with the King James Version of the Bible for this study. The stark contrast between truth and deception, as presented throughout Scripture, underscores the critical importance of this foundational understanding. Deception is not merely a minor infraction; it is a direct assault on the character of God, who *is* truth. It is a rebellion against His revealed will and a pathway to spiritual destruction. Satan's goal is to corrupt God's creation and His people, and deception is his most effective weapon in this endeavor. By understanding deception as an active, intelligent force, originating with Satan and seeking to mislead humanity from God's truth, we can begin to appreciate the depth of the spiritual battle we are engaged in. This understanding equips us not only to identify falsehood but also to actively stand for and defend the truth.

The Apostle Paul admonishes us in **I Thessalonians 5:21**: *"Prove all things; hold fast that which is good."* (KJV, 2023). This is the essence of sound discernment and the most potent weapon against the onslaught of falsehood. Check and double-check everything we hear and read. Do not accept something just because the pastor says it is true. We need to verify everything we hear preached with the word of God. I do all verification checks with the King James Version only.

Spiritual Discernment:

Spiritual discernment is about recognizing that every deviation from God's revealed truth, every twisting of His Word, every manipulation of His character, is a manifestation of this pervasive force. Know that the Bible provides us with the essential framework for discerning the genuine from the counterfeit and for standing firm on the unassailable rock of God's truth. This foundational understanding is the first crucial step in fortifying our defenses and emerging victorious in the ongoing spiritual battle for truth.

Scripture repeatedly contrasts God's faithfulness and truthfulness with the deceitfulness of the adversary. For example, **Psalm 31:5** states, *"I have set the LORD always before me: because he is at my right hand, I shall not be moved. Therefore, my heart greatly rejoiceth; and with my song will I praise him."* (KJV, 2023). This confidence is rooted in the stability of God's character, which is entirely truthful and unchanging. Proverbs presents wisdom, which embodies truth, as a guiding force, while deception leads to destruction. (**Proverbs 15:9** says, *"The way of the wicked is an abomination unto the LORD: but he loveth him that followeth after righteousness"* (KJV, 2023). This verse starkly delineates the two paths: **one of righteousness and divine favor**, the other of wickedness and divine abhorrence, with deception often being a hallmark of the latter.

The pervasiveness of deception is not merely a matter of historical curiosity but a present reality that requires constant vigilance. The enemy, as described in the previous sections, is actively engaged in a spiritual war, and his primary strategy is to mislead. This makes the meticulous definition and understanding of deception absolutely paramount. The serpent's (Satan's) subtle questioning in the Garden of Eden marked the genesis of a profound spiritual warfare that continues to this day. This primal act of deception, meticulously recorded in the Bible, serves as an example of how falsehood infiltrates and corrupts God's perfect creation. The serpent, identified by our Lord Jesus Christ as the devil himself in **John 8:44**, did not approach Eve with a blatant denial of God's command. Instead, he employed a stratagem of doubt and insinuation. His opening salvo, *"Hath God said, Ye shall not eat of every tree of the garden?"* (**Genesis 3:1**, JKV, 2023), was designed to create a fissure in Eve's certainty about God's spoken word. This is the hallmark of deceptive tactics: to plant seeds of suspicion, to make the believer question the clear, authoritative pronouncements of the Almighty.

The serpent directly contradicted God's warning of death: *"And the serpent said unto the woman, Ye shall not surely die"* (**Genesis 3:4**, KJV, 2023). This was a direct assault on divine truth, an attempt to invalidate the very essence of God's covenant with humanity. However, the deception was not merely a negation of God's decree; it was also a sophisticated perversion of God's character and a tantalizing presentation of a false promise. The serpent continued, *"For God doth know that in the day ye eat thereof, then your eyes shall be opened, and ye shall be as gods, knowing good and evil"* (**Genesis 3:5**). This was a masterful stroke of manipulation by Satan to appeal to Eve's desire for knowledge, autonomy, and a god-like status. Satan framed disobedience not as rebellion, but as enlightenment and empowerment. This seductive narrative, promising ultimate understanding and freedom, was the very essence of the lie, cloaked in the guise of superior wisdom.

Consequences of Deception

The consequences of this monumental deception, as history and theology attest, were catastrophic. Eve, swayed by the serpent's words, partook of the forbidden fruit and gave it to Adam, who also ate. The immediate aftermath was not the promised enlightenment, but a profound sense of shame and fear. Their eyes were indeed opened, but to their nakedness, a realization that brought with it guilt and a desperate attempt to hide from the very presence of God. The direct communion they had enjoyed was broken, replaced by alienation and the introduction of sin, death, and all its attendant miseries into the human experience.

This original sin, born of deception, fundamentally altered the trajectory of human history, establishing a pattern of distrust toward God and a susceptibility to falsehood that has plagued mankind ever since. From the Garden of Eden, the narrative of deception weaves its way through the entirety of Scripture, demonstrating its pervasive and persistent nature. The Old Testament is a recurring theme of stories about individuals and nations succumbing to deceptive influences, resulting in spiritual decline and national catastrophe. The Israelites, despite witnessing God's miraculous deliverance from Egypt, frequently turned to idolatry, lured by the false promises of pagan deities and the deceptive whispers of the enemy. The prophets repeatedly warned them against hearkening to false prophets, whose smooth words and enticing visions were mere fabrications designed to lead the people astray from God's covenant and His truth.

Consider the story of King Saul. Initially chosen by God and filled with the Holy Spirit, Saul eventually succumbed to pride, envy, and disobedience. His later years were marked by a profound spiritual delusion, where he consulted with a medium at Endor, seeking guidance from the dead rather than from God. This act of using a medium was a clear manifestation of his rejection of God's appointed means of communication and his willingness to embrace the forbidden and deceptive in his desperation. The narrative of Saul's downfall illustrates how even those chosen by God can be ensnared by deception when they allow their pride and their fear to override their obedience to God's Word. The New Testament further amplifies the understanding of deception, particularly through the teachings of Jesus and the Apostles. Jesus was constantly confronted by those who sought to deceive Him or deceive the people with twisted interpretations of what Jesus said or what the law stated.

Jesus rebuked the Pharisees and Sadducees, calling them a "generation of vipers" and accusing them of making the Word of God of no effect through their traditions and their hypocritical piety. He warned His disciples explicitly about the dangers of false Christs and false prophets who would arise in the last days, performing signs and wonders to deceive, if possible, even the very elect (**Matthew 24:24**). This prophecy underscores the escalating intensity of spiritual deception as the end times approach.

The Apostle Paul, in his epistles, frequently addressed the issue of false teachings and the deceptive tactics employed by the enemy. In **II Corinthians 11:3**, he writes, *"But I fear, lest by any means, as the serpent beguiled Eve through his subtilty, so your minds should be corrupted from the simplicity that is in Christ."* (KJV, 2023). In this verse, Paul compares the primal deception in the Garden of Eden and the spiritual dangers facing the Corinthian church. He recognized that the enemy's methods remained consistent:

1) Subtle manipulation
2) Pride
3) Distorting the pure message of the Gospel.

Paul warned the Ephesian elders in **Acts 20:30**, *"Also of your own selves shall men arise, speaking perverse things, to draw away disciples after them."* (KJV, 2023). Deception can manifest not only from external sources but also from within the very fellowship of believers, emphasizing the need for constant spiritual discernment by pastoral and leadership teams in our churches. Deception can sometimes slip in and affect even the most faithful members in our churches. IT does not mean that the person is evil or that they are demonized. They have just fallen prey to Satan's oldest trick, deception. The Apostle John, in his first epistle, places a strong emphasis on testing the spirits. He exhorts believers, as stated in **I John 4:1**, *"Beloved, believe not every spirit, but try the spirits whether they are of God: because many false prophets are gone out into the world"* (KJV, 2023). To "try the spirits" is a direct command to exercise spiritual discernment, which means to critically evaluate teachings and spiritual experiences against the unchanging standard of God's Word. The historical trajectory of deception is not merely a series of isolated incidents but a continuous thread woven through human civilization. From ancient pagan mythologies that offered distorted views of the divine and the human condition to the philosophical systems that have elevated human reason above divine revelation, deception has often been presented as a form of wisdom.

The Enlightenment, for instance, with its emphasis on human autonomy and rationalism, while contributing to scientific advancement, also paved the way for a secular worldview that often sidelined or outright rejected biblical truths. This intellectual shift has, in many ways, mirrored the serpent's initial offer to Eve: a path of self-sufficiency and intellectual pride, leading away from dependence on God. In the 21st century, with modern technology and groundbreaking inventions (such as robots and artificial intelligence), the pervasive influence of social media, news networks, entertainment, and increasingly sophisticated forms of communication has created fertile ground for deception on an unprecedented scale.

False narratives, propaganda, and the deliberate manipulation of information are commonplace, including fake news, scams, and the promotion of products by celebrities who have never even heard of the products they are supposedly endorsing. These external forces often reinforce the internal susceptibility to deception that originated in the fall in the Garden of Eden. With our schools and colleges indoctrinating our young people to question authority, embrace relativism, and prioritize personal feelings over objective truth, they become increasingly vulnerable to the subtle and not-so-subtle lies that permeate society. The enemy's tactics have adapted to the technological landscape, employing digital platforms to spread misinformation and to sow discord with unparalleled speed and reach.

The theological significance of tracing deception back to its genesis in Eden cannot be overstated. It reveals that deception is not a superficial problem but a deeply ingrained aspect of the fallen human condition. It is not merely a matter of being mistaken; it is a spiritual warfare strategy employed by an intelligent, malevolent adversary who seeks to pervert God's creation and alienate humanity from its Creator. Understanding this origin story helps us to recognize the enemy's ancient patterns of attack: the subtle twisting of God's Word, the appeal to pride and forbidden knowledge, and the promise of liberation that ultimately leads to bondage.

The celestial narrative, stretching from the ancient dust of Eden to the intricate digital landscapes of today, consistently points to a singular, formidable adversary orchestrating the grand theater of spiritual deception. This adversary, known by numerous appellations—Satan, Lucifer, the Devil, the Serpent, the Accuser, Beelzebub—is not a mere abstract force of negativity, but a distinct, intelligent, and malevolent personality. The Bible unequivocally identifies him as the prime mover behind falsehood, the architect of spiritual warfare, and the ultimate progenitor of lies that seek to estrange humanity from its Creator and its intended purpose. Understanding this entity's nature is a critical component of spiritual survival and discernment in a world saturated with deceit.

Jesus Christ Himself provided a stark and definitive assessment of Satan's character and his relationship with truth when He declared to the Jewish leaders in **John 8:44**, *"Ye are of your father the devil, and the lusts of your father ye will do. He was a murderer from the beginning, and abode not in the truth, because there is no truth in him. When he speaketh a lie, he speaketh of his own: for he is a liar, and the father of lies."* (KJV, 2023).

This inherent untruthfulness is intrinsically linked to his initial rebellion against God. Scriptural and theological tradition points to Satan as originally being Lucifer, a high-ranking, beautiful, and mighty angel, created by God. **Isaiah 14:12-15 and Ezekiel 28:12-17**, though often interpreted in different contexts, are widely understood to allude to his fall. The descriptions speak of pride, a desire to ascend above God, to be like the Most High. This aspiration was rooted in a perversion of his giftedness and a rejection of his created status. His fall was an act of cosmic deception, convincing a third of the angelic host to join him in his rebellion (**Revelation 12:4**). This demonstrates that his deceitful nature was present from the very beginning of his existence, even before the creation of humanity. His opposition to God is not merely a matter of differing opinions; it is an existential war against the very nature of truth and order that God represents.

Satan's primary motivation is to seek ways to thwart God's redemptive plan for humanity and to usurp God's authority. His deception serves this **ultimate** goal. By corrupting truth, he corrupts the minds and hearts of individuals, turning them away from God's grace and fellowship. He aims to isolate humanity from its source of life and truth, plunging it into spiritual darkness and death. His actions are not random acts of malice; they are strategic maneuvers designed to achieve a specific outcome: the destruction and damnation of as many souls as possible, and the ultimate overthrow of God's reign. The "modus operandi" of this deceiver is as varied as it is consistent in its underlying principles. His methods are often subtle and insidious. He does not typically appear with horns and a pitchfork, openly advocating for evil. Instead, he insinuates doubt, distorts divine truth, appeals to human pride and desire, and offers alluring but ultimately destructive alternatives to God's way. He masters the art of the half-truth, the twisting of scripture, and the exploitation of human weakness and desire. He presents sin not as sin, but as freedom, enlightenment, or self-fulfillment.

In the Book of Job, Satan appears before God, not as an open adversary but as an accuser and a tempter. He questions Job's righteousness, attributing his faithfulness to God's blessings rather than to genuine devotion (**Job 1:9-11**). Here, Satan acts as an accuser, seeking to undermine Job's integrity and, by extension, to discredit God's character and the sincerity of His followers. This role as the *"Accuser of the brethren"* (**Revelation 12:10**) is a consistent theme. Satan seeks to find fault, to highlight imperfections, and to create a narrative of condemnation. This is a profound form of deception, presenting a distorted reality that focuses solely on flaws and failures, ignoring God's grace and forgiveness. He seeks to foster a spirit of discouragement and self-condemnation among believers, making them ineffective for God's kingdom.

The Apostle Paul, deeply aware of Satan's schemes, warned believers in **Ephesians 6:11** to "*put on the whole armour of God, that ye may be able to stand* *against the wiles of the devil."* (KJV, 2023). The word translated as "wiles" (Greek: *methodeia*) implies craftiness, a planned strategy, a scheme. Satan's deception is not haphazard; it is calculated and deliberate. He understands human psychology, including our desires, fears, and vulnerabilities. He crafts his lies to exploit these very aspects of our being. Satan can mimic righteousness, even appearing as an *"angel of light"* (**II Corinthians 11:14**), a testament to his cunning ability to masquerade as something holy and good while harboring malicious and murderous intent. This is a critical insight: the most dangerous deceptions or deceivers are often those that appear most virtuous. Throughout the Old and New Testaments, this pattern is repeated. False prophets in ancient Israel, described by Jeremiah as speaking *"visions out of their own heart, and not that which cometh forth out of the mouth of the LORD"* (**Jeremiah 23:16**), were instruments of Satanic deception. They offered smooth words and promises of peace, but their message led to destruction.

    Jesus warned of these individuals, stating that they would perform signs and wonders to deceive, if possible, even the elect (**Matthew 24:24**). This underscores the sophisticated nature of Satan's deception; it can even mimic divine power and truth to mislead the most devout. In the New Testament epistles, particularly those of Paul, the emphasis on discerning truth from falsehood is paramount. He speaks of being protected from *"the snares of the devil"* (**I Timothy 3:7**). He urges believers to *"stand fast in one spirit, with one mind striving together for the faith of the gospel"* (**Philippians 1:27**), implying a unified front against a divisive enemy.

    The very nature of spiritual warfare is the battle for the truth, and Satan's primary weapon in this war is deception. He seeks to corrupt the Gospel message itself, to sow discord within the church, and to lead believers into error, thereby neutralizing their witness and effectiveness. Consider the temptation of Jesus in the wilderness (**Matthew 4:1-11; Luke 4:1-13**). Here, Satan directly confronts Jesus, attempting to exploit His hunger, His divine identity, and His mission. Each temptation is a calculated assault of deception, presenting a distorted version of God's truth and an alternative path to achieving God's purposes.

    The first temptation, *"If thou be the Son of God, command that these stones be made bread,"* questions Jesus' identity and offers a shortcut to meeting His needs, bypassing reliance on God's provision. The second temptation, to cast Himself down from the temple, appeals to pride and a desire for a spectacular, self-serving display of divine power. The third temptation, offering all the kingdoms of the world in exchange for worship, is the ultimate temptation: to achieve the redemptive purpose through ungodly means, a direct echo of Satan's original rebellion. Jesus' responses, consistently rooted in quoting Scripture (*"It is written..."*), demonstrate the power of God's Word as the ultimate defense against Satanic lies.

The Apostle John, in his first epistle, provides a crucial directive for navigating this deceptive landscape: *"Beloved, believe not every spirit, but try the spirits whether they are of God: because many false prophets are gone out into the world"* (**I John 4:1**). This is not a suggestion but a command. It requires active engagement, critical thinking, and a constant comparison of teachings and spiritual experiences against the established, unchanging truth of God's Word. The "spirits" here refer to the underlying spiritual influence behind pronouncements and teachings. Satan seeks to infiltrate and corrupt even the spiritual realm, leading people to embrace false doctrines and practices that are antithetical to the true God.

The pervasive nature of deception means that it can manifest in countless ways, from outright denial of biblical truths to subtle perversions of doctrine, from the promotion of worldly philosophies that contradict God's nature to the fostering of personal pride and rebellion. Satan's objective is always to distance us from God, to weaken our faith, and to condemn us ultimately. He operates by creating illusions, distorting reality, and manufacturing falsehoods that appear plausible, even desirable. He is the master illusionist, skilled at making the wrong seem right and the destructive seem beneficial. Therefore, recognizing Satan's role as the active orchestrator of deception is not about succumbing to paranoia, but about exercising spiritual vigilance. It is about understanding that we are engaged in a genuine spiritual conflict, a war for truth and for the human soul. The Bible provides the essential tools for this discernment. It lays bare the enemy's strategies, his motivations, and his ultimate defeat. By understanding the nature of the deceiver, we can better identify his subtle whispers in our lives and in the world around us. With the power of God's truth, we can stand firm against his lies, anchoring our faith in the immutable reality of God's Word. His lies, however sophisticated, are ultimately unsustainable against the eternal truth of the Almighty. The battle is real, and understanding the nature of our adversary is the first crucial step in winning it.

Deception's insidious nature lies not only in its origin but in its remarkable adaptability and pervasive presence. It is not a monolithic entity; rather, it is a chameleon, capable of shifting its form to exploit the vulnerabilities of every age and every individual. To effectively counter its influence, we must train ourselves to recognize its manifold manifestations, both in the grand narratives of history and in the quiet corners of our daily lives. This section aims to illuminate these varied footprints, offering a practical framework for discerning truth from the myriad forms of falsehood that seek to obscure it.

One of the most common and potentially dangerous forms of deception is the subtle distortion of truth. This is not outright fabrication, but rather the artful twisting of facts, the careful omission of crucial details, or the presentation of information in a context that leads to a fundamentally false conclusion. Imagine a historical account that meticulously details the triumphs of a particular leader while conveniently overlooking their tyrannical decisions or the suffering they inflicted. The facts presented might be technically accurate, but the overall impression conveyed is one of unblemished virtue, a deliberate omission that paints a misleading picture.

This technique relies on the principle that a half-truth, artfully presented, can be more persuasive than a blatant lie. It appeals to our natural inclination to accept presented information at face value, especially when it aligns with our pre-existing biases or desires. The deceiver understands that building a case on a foundation of partial truths makes the entire structure appear more credible and, thus, harder to dismantle. This approach is frequently employed in political rhetoric, marketing campaigns, and even in interpersonal relationships where individuals seek to present themselves in a more favorable light. It requires a discerning mind to probe beneath the surface, to question what is *not* being said, and to seek out the broader context that might reframe the presented narrative.

Beyond distortion, outright lies form a more blatant, yet equally destructive, manifestation of deception. These are direct fabrications, assertions of falsehood intended to mislead. In the spiritual realm, this can range from outright denials of fundamental biblical doctrines—such as the resurrection of Christ or the existence of God—to fabricated testimonies or claims of divine revelation that contradict established scripture.

> The deceiver's aim here is often to erode foundational beliefs, creating an environment of doubt and uncertainty. Consider the historical phenomenon of Gnostic teachings, which, in the early centuries of Christianity, introduced complex philosophical ideas that often demoted or denied the physical world and the humanity of Christ, offering instead secret knowledge as a means of salvation.

These were not subtle distortions but radical departures from the apostolic message, a clear example of outright falsehood masquerading as higher truth. On a personal level, lies erode trust—the very foundation of healthy relationships. When a friend, family member, or spiritual leader intentionally deceives us, the damage can be profound, creating fissures that are difficult to mend. The impact of repeated dishonesty is cumulative; each lie, however small, erodes the integrity of the relationship, making future trust increasingly improbable. **Manipulation** is another potent tool in the deceiver's arsenal. This involves exploiting a person's emotions, fears, desires, or vulnerabilities to steer them toward a particular action or belief, often against their own best interests or judgment. This can be subtle, employing flattery or guilt to elicit compliance, or overt, using threats or coercion.

In religious contexts, manipulative tactics might include invoking divine wrath to instill fear and obedience, or promising extravagant blessings in exchange for unquestioning loyalty or financial contributions. The "prosperity gospel," for instance, can sometimes verge on manipulation when it presents faith as a transactional commodity, implying that material wealth is a guaranteed reward for those who give enough or believe with sufficient fervor, thereby preying on people's desire for security and comfort. Jesus Himself warned against those who "*devour widows' houses, and for a pretense make long prayers*" (**Mark 12:40**). This is a clear indictment of those who use the pulpit or television programs for personal gain and manipulation. We need to be able to recognize religious manipulations from the pulpit. However, this requires an awareness of our own emotional triggers and a critical evaluation of the motivations behind the preachers and their appeals that we are listening to. We must ask ourselves whether the call to action is based on genuine truth and love or an attempt to control our thoughts and behaviors through emotional manipulation. The Apostle Paul passionately warned against such perversions, referring to those who "*corrupt the word of God*" (**II Corinthians 2:17**). False teachers, often described as wolves in sheep's clothing, are adept at presenting their distorted messages in ways that sound plausible, even scriptural. They might misinterpret scripture, take verses out of context, or invent new theological frameworks that subtly undermine core tenets of faith. For example, a teaching that diminishes the absolute authority of scripture, suggesting it is merely a guide or a collection of ancient myths, perverts the doctrine of biblical inspiration and authority. Similarly, teachings that promote salvation through works or personal merit, rather than through grace by faith in Christ, fundamentally pervert the doctrine of salvation.

The distinguishing mark of this perversion is often its gradual nature; it does not necessarily announce itself as heresy but creeps in, subtly reshaping understanding over time, until the original truth is obscured or lost. Staying grounded in the foundational teachings of scripture and comparing new doctrines against this established standard is crucial to resisting this form of deception. The allure of exclusivity and hidden knowledge is another common deceptive tactic. This appeals to a sense of intellectual or spiritual superiority, suggesting that salvation or enlightenment is available only to a select few who possess remarkable insights or belong to a particular group. This was a hallmark of many Gnostic systems, which claimed esoteric knowledge as the key to salvation. Such claims often create an "us versus them" mentality, fostering pride in the initiated and alienation from those deemed "unenlightened." These types of claims also gained popularity among southern Pentecostals, who were extremely legalistic in their control of their churches and members.

This tactic is effective because it taps into our innate desire to be special, to possess something valuable that others lack. It can lead individuals to forsake the clear, accessible message of the Gospel for complex, often unbiblical, doctrines that promise greater spiritual rewards. The true Gospel, however, is characterized by its inclusivity and its universal accessibility through faith in Christ, not by secret passwords or exclusive knowledge. The Bible emphasizes that the way of salvation is open to all who believe, not just to a privileged elite. This same type of "special group" can extend past the confines of salvation and include any behavior or bias. Including but not limited to dress codes, events, church name, schools, cultural events, etc.

Artificial Intelligence:

This modern era of artificial intelligence has introduced new avenues for deception, particularly through the influence of social media and digital communication. The ease with which information—and misinformation—can be disseminated online allows for the rapid spread of news and information, often with little to no verification. Social media platforms are designed with algorithms. These algorithms are designed to promote engagement amongst the users. However, the way these are programmed can create echo chambers, where individuals are primarily exposed to information that confirms their existing beliefs. These algorithms help artificial intelligence (AI) learn your patterns, beliefs, and preferences by tracking what you like, click on, search for, and read. This AI is designed to send you links, videos, and other websites that contain information similar to what you are currently viewing. This process prevents you from receiving other information that would make you question or evaluate the news you have just read. These algorithms basically regurgitate what they think you already believe.

The primary disadvantage for the Christian who wants to research the scriptures and learn precisely what the Bible says, as well as understand the etymology of the King James Version of the Bible, is that these algorithms can sometimes block access, hoping to prevent you from encountering things you do not believe in. Hopefully, you can see where I am going with this—if it can manipulate what we get exposed to, what will happen with the anti-Christ gains control of all of this technology? The inexperienced Christian will be much more susceptible to manipulation and less likely to recognize what is happening. For example, a teenager uses AI for 10 years (from high school through college), and they begin to trust everything that Google, Siri, and other AI online tools provide them. When they are given false information about God and the Bible, they will be drawn to it. Their search engines have never let them wrong or given them false information before. This is also another reason that we should be planting the word of God into the hearts and minds of our children. They will never recognize the "false religion" of the false prophet.

I pray we are out of here before the antichrist sets up his reign. However, we do not know how long-suffering God will be with the generations currently on earth. If he decides to let us go through the beginning years of the tribulation period before rapturing us out, many Christians will not make it. The younger generations, especially, will be deceived by the technology and the "cleverness" of the False Prophet.

There are other ways that the internet impacts the spread of deceptive information. It provides an anonymity that can embolden individuals to spread lies and engage in cyberbullying or character assassination with impunity. The very nature of online discourse, often characterized by brevity and emotional reactions rather than thoughtful deliberation, can make it difficult to discern truth from falsehood. It can also cause individuals to make "knee-jerk" or instant reactions to what they think was intended in the comments. I have seen so many people react with a hateful "comeback" to someone who posted a comment on their Facebook post without even reading the rest of the post. If they had read the entire post twice before responding, they would have kept their mouth shut!

Sophisticated propaganda campaigns, deepfakes, and conspiracy theories can all thrive in this environment, sowing discord and undermining trust in established institutions and sources of information. Guarding against this requires a healthy skepticism, a commitment to verifying information from multiple reputable sources, and a conscious effort to seek out diverse perspectives. I realize this may appear overwhelming to the "baby boomers" reading this book. If you do not understand how artificial intelligence works, let me recommend an article for you. This may provide you with more information than you want, but it does not hurt to broaden your horizons. Key search words you can type in to look for more details: *digital detox, AI algorithms, How does my phone know what to send to me, and How can I escape my devices from bombarding me with ads and suggestions.*

Europeanmedia | Blogs | Digital Detox Dilemma: Can You Escape the Algorithm Bubble? https://www.europianmedia.com/blogs/digital-detox-dilemma-can-you-escape-the-algorithm-bubble

---

Deception often manifests through the manipulation of language itself. The use of euphemisms, jargon, or deliberately vague terminology can obscure the true meaning of something, making it appear more palatable or less objectionable than it actually is. For instance, referring to abortion as "choice" or "reproductive freedom" can be a way of framing the issue to downplay the gravity of the act itself. Additionally, the use of complex academic or theological jargon can serve to intimidate and exclude those who lack specialized knowledge, thereby creating an artificial barrier to understanding. This is a powerful tool for those who wish to control narratives and avoid accountability. It requires an active engagement with language, a willingness to unpack ambiguous terms and to ask clarifying questions, to ensure that we are not being misled by the way words are used.

The deceiver also frequently exploits our inherent human biases, which predispose us to favor certain types of information or interpretations. **Confirmation bias**, the tendency to seek out and interpret data in a way that confirms our pre-existing beliefs, is a prime example. Suppose we are predisposed to believe a specific political ideology or a particular theological viewpoint. In that case, we are more likely to accept information that supports it and dismiss information that contradicts it, regardless of its factual accuracy. This makes us fertile ground for deceptive narratives that cater to our existing prejudices. Apostle Paul's admonition to "*think soberly*" (**1 Corinthians 14:29**) and to examine our own thoughts and beliefs is a call to be aware of these biases and to challenge them with the truth actively.

Finally, deception can manifest not only in what is said or believed but also in what is *done*. Actions that are presented as virtuous but are motivated by self-interest, pride, or malice are a form of deception. Hypocrisy—claiming to hold specific values while acting in ways that contradict those values is a manifestation of deception. This can be seen in individuals who profess deep piety but engage in exploitative behavior, or in organizations that promote charitable causes while enriching their leadership. The Apostle John warns us that "*love not in word, neither in tongue; but indeed and in truth*" (**I John 3:18**), highlighting the importance of aligning our actions with our professed beliefs. When actions are out of sync with words, especially when those words claim spiritual authority, it is a clear sign of deception at play. Recognizing this requires careful observation of patterns of behavior over time, looking for consistency between professed values and actual conduct.

In summary, **deception is a multifaceted phenomenon**. It manifests as subtle distortion, outright lies, manipulative tactics, perverted doctrines, appeals to exclusivity, the exploitation of modern media, linguistic obfuscation, the leveraging of cognitive biases, and the hypocrisy of actions contradicting words. By understanding these diverse manifestations, we equip ourselves with the necessary discernment to identify and resist the pervasive influence of falsehood, anchoring ourselves firmly in the unshakeable truth of God's Word and the reality of His unchanging character. This ongoing process of identification is not a passive endeavor but an active spiritual discipline, essential for maintaining clarity and integrity in a world often shrouded in illusion.

CHAPTER TWO:

The Seeds of Deception

In an era increasingly saturated with various forms of deception–the subtle distortions, the outright falsehoods, the insidious manipulations, the perversion of sound doctrine, and the allure of exclusivity–clarity and doctrinal integrity are a profound defense against the many ways truth can be obscured and corrupted. We must stay alert, prayerful, and constantly in God's word, so that we have the greatest tool available to us to combat Satan—quoting the scriptures to him, like Jesus did, and utilizing the gift of spiritual discernment.

The human heart, a complex and often contradictory vessel, carries within it an inherent susceptibility to deception. This vulnerability is not an external imposition, but a deeply rooted consequence of the Fall of man—a corruption that permeates our innermost being. To truly understand how deception takes hold and flourishes, we must first turn our gaze inward, examining the internal landscape of the human spirit, where the seeds of falsehood find fertile ground. This introspection is not merely an academic exercise; it is a vital component of personal spiritual growth, a prerequisite for building resilience against the myriad ways truth can be distorted.

One of the most insidious forms of internal susceptibility is the phenomenon of self-deception. We are, by nature, capable of constructing elaborate narratives that shield us from uncomfortable truths, both about ourselves and about the world around us. This is not always a conscious act of malice, but often a subconscious defense mechanism, a way of preserving our ego, our comfort, or our cherished illusions. The Apostle Paul touches upon this when he writes in **Romans 1:25** that humanity *"exchanged the truth of God for a lie."* (KJV, 2023).

This exchange is not always a dramatic capitulation to blatant falsehood; more often, it is a subtle, gradual shift, a quiet compromise with our own desires and preconceptions. We can, for instance, convince ourselves that a particular sin is not truly harmful, or that a deviation from God's clear commands is a necessary exception.

This **self-deception** can manifest in numerous ways: rationalizing ungodly behavior, minimizing the severity of our failings, or convincing ourselves that our motives are pure when, in reality, they are mixed with pride or self-interest. It is a dangerous path, for when we deceive ourselves, we erect the first and most formidable barrier against the truth. The internal architect of our own delusion becomes the most effective agent of deception.

Pride is that ancient and pervasive sin that has toppled dynasties, resulted in entire countries being captured and enslaved, destroyed economies, and destroyed nations. Pride will kill you as an individual. However, the "ripple effect" of our unchecked pride can cause problems for our families, churches, and communities. The reason pride has such a profound impact is related to self-sufficiency, our belief in our own abilities, wisdom, and understanding. If we are not careful, pride will cause us to feel that we know better than God what is best for us or our churches.

Proverbs 16:18 famously states, "*Pride goes before destruction, and a haughty spirit before a fall.*" (KJV, 2023). When we are proud, we are less likely to seek wisdom from God's Word or from mature believers because we already believe we know. We become resistant to correction, viewing it as criticism rather than counsel. This can lead us to dismiss biblical truths that challenge our worldview or our lifestyle, not because the truth itself is flawed, but because our pride rebels against being told what to think or do.

A proud heart is an unteachable heart, and an unteachable heart is uniquely vulnerable to the whispers of deception. It erects an internal fortress against genuine spiritual discernment, convinced that its own pronouncements are the only ones worth heeding. This internal arrogance creates a vacuum where objective truth ought to reside, a vacuum readily filled by whatever narrative best serves the inflated self-image.

Unconfessed sin acts as a dark and fertile breeding ground for deception. When we harbor sin in our lives, consciously or unconsciously, we create an internal dissonance. The Holy Spirit, who guides us into all truth, is grieved by unconfessed sin, and our spiritual senses become dulled. The very act of hiding sin from God and from ourselves can lead to a distortion of reality. We may begin to believe our own lies about the sin's harmlessness, or we may develop elaborate mental gymnastics to justify it. This creates a fertile psychological environment for deception to take root.

The author of **Hebrews warns in chapter 12, verse 15**, "See to it that no one falls short of the grace of God and that no bitter root grows up to cause trouble and defile many." Unconfessed sin is precisely this bitter root. It can twist our perception, making us susceptible to believing things that are contrary to God's nature and His Word, simply because those beliefs align with our desire to continue in sin. It opens a backdoor through which deceptive influences can enter, often masquerading as something beneficial or even righteous, precisely because our own complicity has prepared the internal ground. The weight of unconfessed sin can lead to a desperate search for answers. In that desperation, one might embrace a deceptive "truth" that offers solace or justification, rather than the difficult path of confession and repentance.

Our innate desires, when left unchecked and unaligned with God's will, also contribute significantly to our internal susceptibility. The human heart is a desiring entity. We crave security, love, acceptance, purpose, and comfort. When these legitimate desires are pursued outside of God's framework, they can become powerful conduits for deception.

For example, **a deep passion for financial security might lead someone to embrace a get-rich-quick scheme or a prosperity gospel that distorts biblical teaching**. A craving for acceptance might lead an individual to compromise their values or beliefs to fit in with a group that promotes unbiblical ideas. The allure of spiritual experiences, when sought without proper discernment and submission to Scripture, can also be a deceptive pathway. Many cults and false religious movements thrive by appealing to these fundamental human longings, offering simplistic answers, promised fulfillment, or a sense of belonging that the deceived person desperately seeks. These deceptive promises prey on genuine human needs, twisting them into a justification for embracing falsehood. The desire itself is not inherently evil, but its misdirection and its pursuit outside of God's provision can open the door to profound deception.

Furthermore, a lack of rigorous intellectual engagement with scripture and doctrine renders us more susceptible to error. While faith is not purely philosophical, it is undoubtedly not anti-intellectual. God has given us minds to understand and to discern. When we neglect to cultivate this faculty, when we accept spiritual teachings uncritically or rely solely on emotional experience, we leave ourselves open to deception. A shallow understanding of biblical truth means that we are less equipped to recognize subtle distortions or outright heresies. **Deceptive teachers often exploit this lack of grounding**, introducing novel interpretations or teachings that sound plausible on the surface but unravel upon closer examination against the bedrock of established biblical doctrine.

The exhortation in **II Timothy 2:15**, *"Do your best to present yourself to God as one approved, a worker who does not need to be ashamed and who correctly handles the word of truth,"* (KJV, 2023), underscores the importance of diligent study and careful handling of God's Word. Those who do not invest in diligent research, content with a superficial grasp of faith, are like soldiers without adequate training, easily overwhelmed by the sophisticated tactics of deception.

The emotional landscape of the heart also plays a crucial role in our susceptibility to emotional influences. Fear, doubt, and disillusionment can create openings for deceptive ideas. When individuals feel abandoned, misunderstood, or overwhelmed by life's difficulties, they may become receptive to philosophies or teachings that offer an easy way out, a sense of control, or a simplistic explanation for complex problems.

For instance, **a person grappling with fear of the future might be drawn to deterministic prophecies that promise certainty**, even if those prophecies are not biblically sound. Doubt, if not addressed with faith and seeking, can also be a fertile ground. It can lead individuals to question foundational truths, making them susceptible to alternative explanations that seem to offer more intellectual satisfaction or emotional comfort. The enemy of our souls is adept at exploiting these emotional vulnerabilities, whispering doubts and fears that can erode faith and pave the way for deception. The emotional climate of the heart, therefore, is not a neutral space; it can either fortify our faith or leave us exposed to insidious falsehoods.

The concept of **"spiritual laziness"** also contributes to internal susceptibility. In a world saturated with information and competing ideologies, discerning truth requires effort. It requires time spent in prayer, in study, and in fellowship with other believers. When we are unwilling to invest this effort, when we opt for convenience over diligence, we become susceptible to accepting facile answers or trendy spiritual ideas without proper scrutiny. This laziness can manifest as a passive consumption of religious content, a reliance on sound bites and slogans rather than deep engagement with the text. It is a subtle form of spiritual apathy that allows deception to creep in unnoticed, much like weeds in an untended garden. The spiritual disciplines, when neglected, leave the soul vulnerable, its defenses lowered, and its capacity for discernment weakened.

Ultimately, recognizing our own internal susceptibility is the first and most crucial step in overcoming deception. It is an act of profound humility to acknowledge that we, the cherished creation of God, are inherently prone to error and self-deception. This recognition is not a cause for despair, but an invitation to embrace God's provision for our weakness. Through prayer, we can ask for wisdom and discernment. Through diligent study of Scripture, we can arm ourselves with the truth that exposes falsehood.

Through fellowship with other believers, we can hold one another accountable and gain diverse perspectives that enrich our understanding of God's word. By addressing the pride, the unconfessed sin, the unchecked desires, and the intellectual or spiritual laziness within our own hearts, we strengthen our inner defenses, making ourselves less susceptible to the external forces that seek to lead us astray. This inward journey of purification and preparation is indispensable in the ongoing battle for truth. It is in understanding the terrain of our own hearts that we can most effectively stand firm against the seeds of deception that are so often sown within.

In our pursuit of understanding the subtle and pervasive nature of deception, we have explored the internal vulnerabilities of the human heart. We have recognized how self-deception, pride, unconfessed sin, unchecked desires, intellectual complacency, emotional fragility, and spiritual laziness create fertile ground for falsehood to take root within us. However, the human experience is not lived in a vacuum. The internal predispositions we have examined are constantly being amplified and directed by external influences, particularly by the pervasive and often insidious "world system." This vast, interconnected network of philosophies, ideologies, cultural norms, and societal structures presents a compelling, and frequently deceptive, alternative narrative to the truth of God. Ignoring this external dimension would be like diagnosing a disease without considering the environmental factors that contribute to its spread. The seeds of deception not only find internal receptivity but also external advocates who actively cultivate their growth, often with a sophistication that can be disarmingly appealing.

The "**world system**" is not a monolithic entity with a single, unified agenda, but rather a complex tapestry woven from diverse threads of thought and practice that, collectively, often operate in opposition to divine revelation. At its core, this system consistently champions a human-centered worldview, prioritizing humanity and its capabilities as the foundation of understanding and authority. This is in stark contrast to the biblical perspective, which places God as the ultimate source of truth, wisdom, and authority, with humanity created in His image and accountable to Him.

When we examine the dominant philosophies and ideologies that shape contemporary thought, we see this humanistic tendency writ large. **Secular humanism**, for instance, extols human reason, ethics, and justice as sufficient without recourse to the divine. While advocating for noble ideals like compassion and progress, its foundational premise inherently displaces God from the equation of meaning and morality. This leads to a subtle but profound shift: instead of seeking to understand and align with God's truth, the focus becomes on creating and validating human-derived truths. The danger here lies not in the pursuit of reason or ethical behavior, but in elevating human autonomy to the point where it becomes the ultimate arbiter of reality, often dismissing or reinterpreting divine revelation through a purely human lens. This can manifest as a subtle devaluation of biblical authority, where scriptures are viewed as ancient literature or moral guides, rather than as inspired and infallible truth.

Another pervasive element of the world system that serves as a potent agent of deception is the pervasive embrace of **relativism**. In its various forms — moral relativism, epistemological relativism, and even ontological relativism — it posits that truth is not absolute but subjective, dependent on individual perspectives, cultural contexts, or historical periods. This stands in direct opposition to the biblical assertion of an unchanging, objective God and His absolute truth. When everything is relative, there is no fixed standard against which to measure truth or falsehood. This creates an environment where deceptive ideologies can flourish, as they are not held accountable to any ultimate reality.

For example, if **"truth"** is simply what an individual or a society believes it to be at a given moment, then deeply damaging falsehoods can be embraced and propagated without challenge, provided they gain enough adherents or cultural traction. This erosion of objective truth makes it incredibly difficult to discern the authenticity of spiritual claims, as the very framework for evaluation is dissolved. The world system, by promoting this relativistic mindset, actively undermines the Christian claim of a singular, authoritative truth found in Jesus Christ and the Scriptures. It encourages a spiritual buffet, where individuals pick and choose what resonates with them, discarding anything that requires personal cost or intellectual rigor to embrace.

The cultural narratives that saturate our modern landscape are another critical avenue through which the world system operates. From entertainment media and advertising to popular literature and social discourse, these narratives often subtly, and sometimes overtly, promote worldviews that are against our evangelical biblical principles.

Consider the prevalent emphasis on self-fulfillment and personal happiness as the ultimate goals of life, constantly promoted in sitcoms, cartoons, and secular music. While positive psychological well-being is essential, presenting it as the sole or primary measure of a life well-lived can lead to a disregard for self-denial, sacrifice, and obedience to God's commands. When society and our schools are constantly telling us that we are "perfect the way we are" or that there is no reason to "assess your selves in comparison to the scriptures" as our pastors tell us to—we are being fed a false narrative that can lead us to align our thinking with "personal pleasure" than the self-sacrifice that Jesus taught.

The allure of a life with everything we want, when we want it, and how we like it, is more exciting than the option of sacrificing to help carry the gospel around the world or sacrificing to spend time with others in our church and community who need help.

Additionally, these types of conversations on social media can quickly spiral out of control, creating tension for believers, mainly when the allure of a life centered on personal satisfaction clashes with the biblical call to follow Christ, which often involves carrying a cross and denying oneself.

Furthermore, many cultural narratives normalize or even celebrate behaviors that scripture explicitly condemns. The constant exposure to such content can desensitize individuals to the gravity of sin, gradually shifting their moral compass and making them more receptive to deceptive ideas that rationalize or justify such behaviors.

With the constant echo of particular worldviews reinforcing behaviors or disseminating deceptive information into our news feeds and minds, the sheer volume with which we are bombarded can cause people to be deceived. It is almost as if Satan is whispering into our ears constantly, "Let me show you how to evolve into a God. Let me lead you to better things, more money, fame, recognition, and all the pleasures you desire."

Many people believe that newer is better. If they see a new vacuum cleaner advertised on TV, they must get it, even if they already have three vacuums that all work great. They need the latest one—no matter the price, it has to be better! This was the first lie that Satan began to feed us in the 1980s and 1990s when the prosperity gospel began to be preached.

I have watched so many fellow pastors and preachers walk away from their churches and ministries since the COVID-19 pandemic ended. It is amazing to me that not only did the government close our churches, but Satan closed our hearts! In the area where I live in south Alabama, I know more than 20 ministers who have walked away from their churches and turned their minister's licenses into their denomination because they do not want to carry the load of pastoring this "woke generation" or have to deal with the drama of the aging "baby boomers."

However, what is more alarming than that is the five ministers that I know who were pastoring Evangelical churches and decided not only to tolerate or accept "same-sex" couples/marriages in their churches in leadership positions, but they have "come out of the closet" themselves and left their spouses for a same sex partner. No, these five have not given up their churches or licenses. They have pulled their churches out of the organizations they were a part of and have opened their doors to help young people "accept who they are with pride!"

This relentless pursuit of money, happiness, acceptance, and "woke" ideals will serve as an avenue for deception to enter our hearts. This new "One World Order" will utilize deception to the maximum, influencing the uneducated, the young, those without the education to research or critically evaluate what they are hearing, and the elderly who are afraid that if they do not accept their grandchildren, they will be left alone.

Within the world systems, there is a cultural inclination to equate the new with the better and the ancient with the outdated. This can lead to a dismissal of timeless biblical truths and established theological doctrines in favor of emerging spiritual trends or "**fresh revelations.**" Many deceptive movements gain traction by presenting themselves as a more evolved, enlightened, or advanced understanding of spirituality, implicitly positioning traditional faith as primitive or insufficient. This appeal to the cutting edge can be beautiful to those seeking deeper meaning or who feel their current spiritual understanding is lacking. The groups promoting "tolerance" and acceptance of lifestyles contrary to the Bible have used this "fresh revelation" concept to deceive many.

This past month, I was talking with someone I know personally who is in a same-sex relationship. She and her "spouse" both know that I am Evangelical and that I do not promote their lifestyle. They are friends and I pray for them daily. I love them and I want them to be rapture-ready. There is not a time when I talk to them or see them that I do not remind them to pray and know that they are rapture-ready, because the tribulation period is going to be worse than they can imagine.

One of these friends was raised a Southern Baptist, and the other was Catholic. They have attended Assembly of God churches over the years, and they have even gone to church with my husband and me. We do not apologize for what we believe, nor do we compromise, but we also know that we must love them and show them the "love of God," or we will never reach them.

However, the rate of deception that has taken them has been astonishing to me. They were living together before same-sex marriages were legalized. I would talk to them, and many times they would cry and say, We are going to change. We know we need to be ready. One of them had a grandmother filled with the Holy Spirit, who instilled a great deal of the Bible into her life. I have prayed many times over the past 10 years that those words would take root.

However, the spirit of deception has gotten so strong here in the United States that I am seeing people who were reachable 10 years ago appear to be unreachable, possibly even "turned over to a reprobate mind, to believe a lie and be damned" as Paul taught in the New Testament. When I talked with them last month, they informed me that they had been attending this Assembly of God church. "You know our pastor, La Wanda, he is Bro. X." Sure enough, I have known him since I was in my twenties. He and my father were licensed in the same denomination at one time. We have always kept in touch through the years. I was shocked at what they told me next.

"Oh, La Wanda, I do not understand why you cannot accept the fact that there will be gay people in Heaven. God made us this way. There is nothing that we can do about it, except embrace it. Bro. X has accepted this fact. He asked us if we were saved. We told him yes. He said that was all he needed to hear. If we were reading our Bible every day, praying, and we had a relationship with Jesus, that was all that the New Testament required. All of this other stuff is just legalism left over by the 'old heads' of the church world!"

I will not bore you with all of the conversation. In defense of this pastor, I tried to think of what he could have said that they might have misunderstood. I could not believe that he would endorse this lifestyle. When I left their presence, I felt a strong pull on my heart. I could not imagine a fellow Assembly of God minister, while still pastoring, making this statement. So, I grabbed my phone after getting into my Jeep and looked up his number. It had been about five years since I had talked with him. I called him.

I shared with him the conversation I had just been in with these two friends. I was not ready for what he said to me! "Oh, Sister La Wanda, dear, I remember you being this strong, energetic evangelist and missionary. You were always idealistic. Even in your nursing career, you held up these idealistic expectations of yourself as a nurse. I realize I am now in my 70s, and you are much younger, but even I have come to realize that we must do what Jesus said. We let the wheat and the tares grow together. On the day of the harvest, Jesus will let his angels sort out the tares."

I responded, "Bro. X, I fully understand the scripture you are quoting. I realize that we are not to go around judging people and excluding them from the church. However, you, of all people, stood with my dad, Bro. Trask and the Alabama District of the Assemblies of God officials for more than 20 years, standing for what was right, while trying to reach and keep the next generation in the church. I saw my dad compromise on outward appearance issues, etc. However, he never compromised on the 'works of the flesh.' If you had them in your life, you did not hold a position in the church. You could come to church, provided you understood that he would be preaching on those topics and they would not be specifically targeted at you. He would be teaching what God gave him and standing on the precepts of the gospel that Jesus taught!"

Then I went on to explain to him how I felt. I told him about a dream that God had given me with specific instructions not to judge, or belittle those that did not believe like me, but also not to compromise—no matter who changed around me—I was to stick with the truth of the Bible—the King James Version, not some of the newer versions. When I said that, he responded, "Well, Sis. La Wanda, that is part of your problem. When I got away from the old, legalistic King James translation, I began to see how wrong we had been about the love of God. He began quoting from the ESV, Urban, and other translations to me. Guess what—those translations are more tolerant—which lets the reader believe that those lifestyles were acceptable. Now, I have come to see that not all of the words of the King James are accurate. They used words that people would understand. However, those were not the words of Jesus. If you take those Aramaic and Hebrew words today and you translate them as these newer translations have, then you see that Jesus was loving and merciful. He did away with the Old Testament law for a reason—to eliminate legalism. See, Sis. La Wanda, you need to let go of the old and realize that we are in a new world—new technology, and a generation that is even more challenging to deal with than the millennials is coming of age now."

I was lost for words because I was in so much shock that my Dad's Church of God friend, whom he had been so close to over the years, was actually walking away from the Evangelical gospel and endorsing the "woke agenda." He was not endorsing it for financial gain or numbers. He was endorsing it because he had been deceived—he believed it was really not a sin!

Needless to say, when that conversation ended, I was not convinced to compromise, and he was so deceived that he was not going to change either. He was thoroughly convinced that he was "evolving" in God's will with his outreach. It was okay for this same-sex couple to teach a Sunday School class and work with the church's drug/alcohol program. It breaks my heart that a 70-year-old pastor, who has pastored for 48 years, could come down to the end—this close to the rapture—and be deceived!

If you do not remember anything else from this book, remember this: "To be rapture-ready, you must be consecrated before God to be his bride. You must be ready with your wedding garment on when he sounds the trumpet! There will not be time to get ready or to change. There definitely will not be time for a debate. If we are going to be a warrior bride for Christ, we must make the commitment necessary and be willing to consecrate ourselves (sacrifice and give up things) so that we can help others. We must be a consecrated warrior bride to be filled with the anointing of the Holy Ghost to minister, sing, pray, witness, etc. No one or nothing in this life is worth missing the rapture!"

However, this focus on novelty can be a deceptive trap, leading individuals away from the unchanging truth of God towards fleeting intellectual or experiential fads. The Bible itself warns against being tossed back and forth by the waves, carried here and there by the changing winds of human teaching (**Ephesians 4:14**). This warning is acutely relevant in an age where spiritual ideas are constantly being repackaged and marketed as the next big thing.

The commodification of spirituality and religion within the world system is another significant aspect of its deceptive influence. Faith and spiritual experiences are often packaged and sold, leading to a consumerist approach to religious truth. Books, seminars, retreats, and even online courses promise transformative experiences or profound insights, often with a focus on tangible outcomes like success, happiness, or personal power. While genuine spiritual growth and discipleship can involve investment, the danger lies in reducing faith to a transaction, where one seeks spiritual benefits without the corresponding commitment to the Source of all truth. This can lead to a superficial understanding of faith, divorced from the disciplines of repentance, prayer, and submission to divine authority. When spiritual insights are readily available for purchase, or when emotional highs are the primary measure of spiritual depth, individuals can become susceptible to believing they have achieved spiritual maturity without the rigorous work of character transformation that the Word of God demands. This approach can also foster a sense of entitlement, where individuals expect God to conform to their desires and plans, rather than aligning their lives with His.

Moreover, the **secularization of knowledge** and education within many societies contributes to the external whispers of deception. As academic disciplines increasingly operate under the assumption of methodological naturalism — that is, explaining phenomena solely through natural causes — supernatural realities and divine interventions are often relegated to the realm of myth or superstition. This pervasive worldview shapes curricula, research, and public discourse, subtly framing the biblical narrative as a product of human imagination rather than divine revelation. Consequently, individuals educated in such environments may find it challenging to reconcile their academic understanding with their faith, potentially leading to a compartmentalization of belief or a gradual erosion of conviction. When the dominant intellectual currents of society deny or ignore the possibility of the supernatural, it becomes harder to accept the biblical claims of miracles, divine judgment, or the personal, active involvement of God in human history. This creates a significant hurdle for authentic faith, requiring a deliberate act of intellectual courage and trust to affirm truths that are often deemed implausible or irrelevant by the prevailing academic consensus.

The influence of peer pressure and the desire for social acceptance also play a significant role in making individuals susceptible to the world system's deceptive narratives. In social circles, workplaces, or even within family structures that are not biblically grounded, there can be implicit or explicit pressure to conform to prevailing opinions and behaviors. Disagreement with the dominant worldview can lead to social ostracism, professional disadvantage, or personal conflict. To avoid these consequences, individuals may downplay their faith, adopt superficially appealing but unbiblical viewpoints, or remain silent when they should speak the truth. This conformity is a subtle form of deception, where the fear of man overrides the fear of God. It can lead to a gradual erosion of convictions, a willingness to accept or propagate deceptive ideas to maintain harmony or a sense of belonging. The desire to be accepted by the world system can override one's commitment to being set apart for God's truth, making them vulnerable to adopting the very ideologies that seek to undermine biblical authority.

In essence, the world system acts as a constant, powerful external force, shaping our perceptions, influencing our values, and providing an alternative framework for understanding reality. It does this by promoting human-centeredness, relativism, secularized knowledge, and culturally normalized behaviors that often contradict divine truth. It appeals to our innate desires for fulfillment, acceptance, and intellectual validation, often by offering superficial answers or distorted versions of reality.

Recognizing the pervasive nature of these external whispers is crucial. It requires a conscious and consistent effort to critically evaluate the messages we receive from our culture, our education, and our social environments against the unchanging standard of God's Word. Just as we examined the internal landscape of the heart to identify its vulnerabilities, we must now turn our attention to the external forces that seek to exploit those vulnerabilities, ensuring that our faith is not merely an internal conviction but a robust understanding grounded in truth, capable of discerning and resisting the pervasive deceptions of the world system. The battle for truth is fought both within the chambers of our own hearts and on the broader landscape of cultural and societal discourse.

The tapestry of human existence is not woven solely from threads of individual thought and internal disposition. While our hearts may harbor predispositions toward deception, the external world provides a rich and fertile ground for these seeds to germinate and flourish. Beyond the internal vulnerabilities we have explored, the social and cultural landscape in which we are immersed acts as a powerful, often unacknowledged, force in shaping our perceptions of reality and, consequently, our susceptibility to deception.

This chapter explores the intricate ways in which societal norms, educational systems, and omnipresent media platforms can consciously or unconsciously introduce, perpetuate, and normalize deceptive ideas, creating an environment where certain truths are not merely questioned but actively marginalized or dismissed. Understanding these ingrained societal influences is not simply an academic exercise; it is a vital component of developing robust critical thinking skills and maintaining an unwavering allegiance to biblical truth amidst prevailing cultural currents that may subtly or overtly advocate for ungodly perspectives.

The very fabric of society is woven with norms—unwritten rules and expectations that guide our behavior, shape our interactions, and define what is considered acceptable, desirable, or even normal. These norms are not static; they evolve and are perpetuated through countless social interactions, from family upbringing to peer group dynamics, and are reinforced by institutions that structure our lives. When these norms subtly or overtly deviate from biblical principles, they can act as a powerful conduit for deception.

Consider, for instance, the pervasive societal emphasis on individual autonomy and self-fulfillment as the ultimate measure of a successful life. While self-care and personal well-being are valid pursuits, when elevated to the supreme good, they can subtly undermine the biblical call to self-denial, service to others, and obedience to God, even when such obedience requires personal sacrifice. The cultural narrative champions the pursuit of happiness and personal satisfaction as paramount, creating a subtle pressure to align one's life choices with these values, even if they conflict with divine mandates. This can lead to the normalization of behaviors that Scripture clearly labels as sin, such as excessive materialism, casual sexual relationships, or a disregard for the sanctity of marriage. The constant exposure to these normalized behaviors, often presented as harmless or even aspirational, can gradually erode a believer's conviction, creating a cognitive dissonance that is resolved by subtly shifting one's moral framework to accommodate the prevailing cultural ethos. This is a form of social indoctrination, where belonging and acceptance are contingent upon adherence to the group's evolving moral code, which may subtly deviate from eternal truths.

Educational systems, from early childhood to higher learning, play a pivotal role in shaping the minds of future generations. While the primary purpose of education is to impart knowledge and critical thinking skills, the curriculum, pedagogical approaches, and the underlying philosophical assumptions embedded within educational institutions can inadvertently or intentionally foster deceptive worldviews. The rise of secular humanism as a dominant educational philosophy, for example, often emphasizes reason, empirical evidence, and human experience as the sole sources of knowledge and morality, frequently relegating religious or supernatural explanations to the realm of mythology or personal belief, rather than objective truth. This can lead to a systematic devaluation of biblical authority and historical accounts. When students are consistently taught that all knowledge must be verifiable through scientific methods and that any claims outside this purview are suspect, they may develop a cognitive bias against the supernatural, making it challenging for them to accept biblical accounts of miracles, divine intervention, or even the resurrection of Christ. This is not necessarily a malicious intent on the part of educators, but rather a consequence of operating within a philosophical framework that excludes the divine a priori.

The result is a generation that may be highly educated in secular subjects but ill-equipped to critically engage with or defend their faith, finding it increasingly difficult to reconcile their academic learning with their spiritual convictions. The very language used in educational discourse often reflects this bias; concepts like "faith" are frequently framed as irrational leaps, while "doubt" is presented as a mark of intellectual maturity. This subtly shapes the student's internal narrative, positioning doubt as a virtue and faith as a weakness, thereby opening the door to deceptive ideologies that claim intellectual superiority. The pervasive influence of media—television, film, music, social media, and the internet—cannot be overstated. These platforms are not neutral conduits of information; they are powerful cultural forces that actively shape our thoughts, values, and desires, often in ways that align with or promote the "world system" we have discussed. Entertainment media, in particular, frequently present narratives that subtly, and sometimes overtly, endorse lifestyles, values, and belief systems that are antithetical to biblical teachings.

The glorification of violence, the normalization of promiscuity, the celebration of materialism, and the portrayal of flawed or even evil characters as heroes can all contribute to a gradual desensitization to sin and a distortion of moral values. When these themes are consistently reinforced through engaging stories and relatable characters, they become ingrained in our cultural consciousness, making it easier to accept or even adopt these ungodly perspectives.

Social media, with its algorithms designed to maximize engagement, often creates echo chambers that reinforce existing beliefs and expose users primarily to content that aligns with their current worldview, whether that worldview is biblically sound or not. This can amplify deceptive narratives and insulate individuals from counterarguments or alternative perspectives, making them more susceptible to believing falsehoods that are constantly repeated and validated within their digital communities.

Advertising, too, plays a crucial role, often exploiting insecurities and desires by linking happiness and fulfillment to the acquisition of material goods or the adoption of certain lifestyles, thereby promoting a consumerist and materialistic worldview that is at odds with biblical contentment and stewardship. This constant barrage of media messages can create a dissonance with biblical truth, requiring a deliberate and disciplined effort to filter these messages through the lens of Scripture.

Furthermore, the nature of communication in the modern era has amplified the speed and reach of cultural indoctrination. Viral content, memes, and sound bites can encapsulate complex ideologies or deceptive arguments in easily digestible and highly shareable formats. These often bypass rational thought and appeal directly to emotions or pre-existing biases. A seemingly innocuous joke, a trending hashtag, or a viral video can subtly introduce or normalize a deceptive concept, which then spreads rapidly through social networks.

This phenomenon is particularly concerning when it involves spiritual or theological matters. Misinformation about biblical teachings, distorted interpretations of scriptures, or the promotion of syncretistic beliefs can gain widespread traction simply because they are popular or presented in a compelling manner, irrespective of their theological accuracy or biblical grounding. The speed at which information travels, coupled with the ease of sharing, means that deceptive ideas can saturate the cultural landscape before individuals have the opportunity to evaluate them or seek sound theological counsel critically.

This creates a challenging environment for discerning truth, as the sheer volume of information and the emotional resonance of popular narratives can overwhelm critical thinking and reasoned analysis. The very architecture of digital communication is, in many ways, optimized for the propagation of widely appealing, rather than necessarily truthful, content.

The secularization of public discourse is another potent force that contributes to social and cultural indoctrination. In many societies, particularly in Western cultures, there has been a discernible trend towards removing religious or spiritual considerations from public life, including politics, law, education, and even personal morality. This process often frames religious belief as a private matter, a matter of personal preference rather than a source of objective truth or a guiding principle for public life.

While this can be seen as a move toward tolerance, it can also lead to the marginalization and dismissal of religiously informed perspectives on societal issues. When discussions about ethics, justice, or societal well-being are conducted exclusively within a secular framework, biblical principles and values are often excluded from consideration. This can create a situation where deceptive ideas, framed in secular terms, are given greater weight and acceptance simply because they are presented within the accepted public discourse. For example, ideologies that promote radical individualism, deconstruct traditional family structures, or redefine fundamental moral concepts may gain traction because they are articulated using the language of progress, liberation, or human rights, without any critical engagement with the potential spiritual or societal consequences that biblical wisdom might highlight. This secularization process effectively sanitizes public discourse of any divine reference, making it harder for biblical truth to penetrate the prevailing cultural narratives and leaving society more vulnerable to deception presented under the guise of secular reason or modern advancement.

The pressure to conform, a deeply ingrained human need, is skillfully exploited by social and cultural indoctrination. In virtually every aspect of life—whether it is in the workplace, social gatherings, or even within family units—there exists an expectation to align with the prevailing opinions and behaviors of the group. This pressure is often subtle, manifested through social cues, unspoken agreements, or the simple observation of what is widely accepted. However, it can also be overt, involving explicit disapproval, ridicule, or even exclusion for those who deviate from the norm. When these norms are not aligned with biblical truth, this pressure to conform becomes a significant conduit for deception. Individuals may find themselves downplaying their faith, rationalizing ungodly behaviors, or remaining silent in the face of falsehoods to avoid conflict, maintain social standing, or gain acceptance.

This **fear of man**, as scripture warns, can become a snare, leading to a gradual erosion of conviction and a willingness to compromise on core beliefs. The desire to be accepted by the world, to be seen as relevant, modern, or intellectually sophisticated, can override the commitment to stand firm in biblical truth, making one susceptible to adopting and even propagating the very ideologies that seek to undermine divine authority and the trustworthiness of God's Word. This insidious form of indoctrination works by appealing to our innate desire for belonging, subtly coercing us into adopting a worldview that may be fundamentally deceptive.

The commodification of spirituality also plays a role in this external conditioning. In a consumerist culture, even matters of faith and spiritual growth can be packaged and sold. Books, seminars, workshops, and online courses promise transformative experiences, profound insights, or even supernatural power. While there is nothing inherently wrong with seeking spiritual growth through various means, the danger lies in reducing faith to a transaction, where spiritual benefits are sought without the corresponding commitment to the Source of all truth.

This approach fosters a superficial understanding of faith, divorced from the disciplines of repentance, prayer, humility, and submission to divine authority. When spiritual insights are readily available for purchase, or when emotional highs are the primary measure of spiritual depth, individuals can become susceptible to believing they have achieved spiritual maturity without the rigorous work of character transformation that the Word of God demands. This can lead to a form of spiritual deception where individuals are more enamored with the *idea* of spiritual experience or enlightenment than with the authentic, often costly, pursuit of Christ.

Moreover, this commodification can create a sense of entitlement, where individuals expect God to conform to their desires and plans, rather than aligning their lives with His. When spiritual narratives are shaped by market demands rather than by biblical faithfulness, the culture becomes susceptible to deceptive teachings that promise easy answers, quick fixes, or personal empowerment divorced from divine accountability.

Consider the subtle but pervasive influence of the "wellness" and "self-help" industries. While many of these resources offer genuine benefit, a significant portion of their messaging operates within a framework that implicitly or explicitly bypasses or contradicts biblical principles. The emphasis on positive thinking as a sole determinant of reality, the pursuit of personal happiness as the ultimate life goal, or the suggestion that individuals possess inherent divine spark that needs only to be "unlocked" can, in their extreme forms, foster a form of self-deification that is subtly at odds with the biblical understanding of humanity's need for redemption and God's sovereignty.

When the focus shifts from seeking God's will and conforming to His nature to unlocking one's own inner divinity or personal potential, the foundation of faith is subtly altered. This can lead individuals to adopt spiritual practices or ideologies that, while appearing beneficial on the surface, ultimately divert them from the unchanging truth found in Scripture. The language of empowerment and self-discovery, while appealing, can inadvertently displace the foundational biblical truths of dependence on God, the reality of sin, and the need for grace.

The very language we use is a vehicle for cultural indoctrination. Words carry connotations and frameworks that shape our understanding of the world. For instance, the framing of specific social issues through particular terminology can pre-determine how people think about them. When terms like "tolerance" are redefined to mean endorsement, or when "diversity" is presented as an absolute value that supersedes all other moral considerations, the underlying assumptions can lead to acceptance of ideologies that conflict with biblical morality.

The careful manipulation of language, a hallmark of sophisticated deception, can subtly influence public opinion and create a cultural climate where questioning these redefined terms is perceived as intolerant or outdated. This linguistic conditioning is a powerful tool in shaping thought without overt argumentation, making individuals susceptible to the underlying deceptive premises embedded within the favored vocabulary.

In conclusion, the social and cultural environment in which we live is a potent, pervasive force that actively shapes our perceptions and can lead us astray from biblical truth. From the ingrained norms of society and the philosophical underpinnings of our educational systems to the pervasive influence of media, the commodification of spirituality, and the subtle pressures of linguistic and social conformity, we are constantly bombarded with messages that can subtly advocate for ungodly perspectives.

Recognizing these external influences requires a vigilant and discerning mind, one that is grounded in the unchanging Word of God. It demands a conscious effort to critically evaluate the messages we receive, to question prevailing cultural narratives, and to anchor our understanding of reality in divine revelation rather than in the shifting sands of popular opinion or secular ideology. Without this critical engagement, we risk becoming unwitting participants in a grand deception, internalizing worldviews that, while seemingly benign or even positive on the surface, ultimately lead us away from the one trustworthy source of life and truth. The challenge for the believer is to navigate these cultural currents without being swept up by them, to engage with the world without being conformed to it, and to hold fast to the truth in a society that often seems to have forgotten its significance.

The tapestry of truth is not only threatened by the subtle currents of cultural influence and internal predisposition but also by the direct assaults of deliberate agents of deception. These are the false teachers, the architects of religious cults, and the proponents of aberrant movements who actively seek to mislead believers, twisting divine truth into something palatable yet poisonous. Their efforts are not accidental; they are calculated strategies designed to draw people away from sound doctrine and into their own carefully constructed systems of belief, often centered around a charismatic leader or a distorted interpretation of Scripture. Understanding their methods and motivations is not merely an academic exercise; it is a vital component of spiritual discernment and protection, a necessary fortification against the inroads they seek to make into the flock.

One of the primary weapons in the arsenal of false teachers is the distortion and manipulation of scripture. They do not necessarily discard the Bible outright; instead, they select verses out of context, reframe their meaning to suit their agenda, and often ignore or reinterpret passages that contradict their teachings. This selective approach allows them to build a façade of biblical legitimacy, making their aberrant doctrines appear to be grounded in divine revelation.

For instance, a teacher promoting a prosperity gospel might heavily emphasize verses about God's blessing and abundance, while downplaying or reinterpreting passages that speak of suffering, self-denial, or the transient nature of earthly riches. Similarly, those advocating for a particular eschatological interpretation might seize upon prophetic texts, weaving intricate timelines and predictions that stir excitement and fear, often at the expense of a balanced, historical-grammatical approach to biblical prophecy.

This practice is akin to a skilled surgeon who, instead of removing a tumor, meticulously carves away healthy tissue to create a grotesque mockery of the original form. By carefully selecting and reordering parts of God's Word, they can craft a narrative that, on the surface, seems compelling, but upon closer examination, reveals a profound disconnect from the overarching message and intent of scripture. This is a subtle yet devastating form of deception, as it leverages the very authority that believers trust to lead them astray.

Beyond textual manipulation, false teachers often rely heavily on appealing to emotions over truth. They understand that genuine spiritual understanding is usually accompanied by a sense of awe, peace, and conviction, and they skillfully mimic these spiritual experiences to foster a sense of divine approval.

Charismatic leaders may employ powerful oratory, dramatic testimonials, and emotionally charged music to create an atmosphere of heightened feeling. In such an environment, the emotional resonance of a message can be mistaken for its truthfulness. A profound emotional experience, however powerful, is not an infallible indicator of biblical accuracy. The Bible itself warns against being swayed by every wind of doctrine (**Ephesians 4:14**), including emotional influences.

Cultic groups, in particular, excel at fostering intense emotional bonds among their members. Through shared experiences, group affirmations, and often a deliberate isolation from dissenting voices, they create a powerful emotional reinforcement loop that makes questioning the group's teachings feel like a betrayal of deeply cherished relationships and a rejection of a shared spiritual reality.

This emotional entanglement can be so intense that even when presented with irrefutable evidence of error, individuals find it incredibly difficult to extricate themselves, as doing so would mean sacrificing not just a belief system but also their sense of belonging and emotional security.

A hallmark of many false teachers and cultic movements is the establishment of exclusive, authoritarian structures. Often, leaders position themselves as the sole interpreters of truth, the indispensable mediators between God and their followers, or even as divinely appointed individuals with unique access to spiritual knowledge.

This creates a hierarchy where questioning the leader or the established doctrine is not only discouraged but actively punished, often through ostracism, spiritual condemnation, or psychological manipulation. Such structures undermine the biblical principle that all believers have direct access to God through Christ and the Holy Spirit, and that Scripture itself is sufficient for guidance and doctrine.

When a single individual or a small, insular group becomes the ultimate authority, the foundation of faith shifts from the objective truth of God's Word to the subjective pronouncements of fallible human beings. This authoritarianism fosters an environment of dependence, stifles critical thinking, and makes followers vulnerable to the leader's every whim, whether it aligns with the Bible or not. In these systems, obedience to the leader often takes precedence over obedience to God as understood through clear biblical teaching. This creates a dangerous dynamic where spiritual discernment is replaced by unquestioning loyalty, a fertile ground for further deception.

Furthermore, false teachers often exploit the human desire for simple answers and immediate solutions to complex life problems. In a world filled with uncertainty, pain, and existential questions, the promise of a clear path to success, happiness, or spiritual enlightenment, free from struggle or doubt, can be incredibly alluring. They present their doctrines as the definitive "key" to unlocking one's potential, achieving a higher spiritual state, or securing divine favor, often implying that the established church has failed to provide these essential elements.

This can lead to a disdain for the often challenging and nuanced process of genuine spiritual growth, which the Bible portrays as a journey of perseverance, repentance, and reliance on God's grace through trials and tribulations. The allure of a shortcut or a secret knowledge can blind individuals to the superficiality and ultimate emptiness of such teachings. When spiritual progress is framed as a formula to be mastered rather than a relationship to be cultivated, the very essence of faith is perverted.

The language employed by these groups is often carefully crafted to subtly reinforce their distinct ideology and alienate followers from external influences. They may develop a unique jargon, using biblical terms with altered meanings or creating new terminology altogether. This linguistic inbreeding fosters a "us versus them" mentality, where those within the group possess an exceptional understanding, while outsiders are perceived as unenlightened or even spiritually lost.

This creates a barrier to objective evaluation, as the very language used to discuss concepts becomes colored by the group's specific dogma. It also fosters a sense of insider identity, making it harder for individuals to engage with outside perspectives or to articulate their beliefs in a way that can be understood or scrutinized by those not immersed in the group's worldview. This linguistic isolation is a powerful tool for maintaining control and preventing critical engagement with alternative viewpoints.

Moreover, these movements often present a distorted view of spiritual warfare. While the Bible clearly teaches that believers are engaged in a spiritual battle, false teachers frequently frame this warfare in ways that serve their own agendas. They might attribute all personal failures, illnesses, or financial struggles to demonic oppression, creating a constant state of spiritual anxiety and directing blame outward rather than encouraging individual responsibility and reliance on God's wisdom in navigating life's challenges.

Conversely, some may downplay or ignore the reality of spiritual opposition altogether, promoting a purely self-empowerment message that is devoid of the biblical understanding of spiritual adversaries and the need for God's strength and protection. This misrepresentation of spiritual warfare can leave believers either paralyzed by fear or misguided in their approach to spiritual battles, making them vulnerable to the very deceptions these teachers propagate.

The concept of "*testing all things*" (**I Thessalonians 5:21**) is therefore not merely an intellectual exercise but a fundamental aspect of discipleship in the face of deceptive influences. It requires a deep grounding in biblical truth, a reliance on the Holy Spirit for discernment, and a willingness to engage with truth even when it is uncomfortable or unpopular. The allure of charismatic personalities, the promise of easy answers, and the comfort of belonging to an exclusive group can all serve as powerful distractors from the unchanging, often challenging, truth of God's Word.

By understanding the tactics employed by false teachers and cultic movements—their manipulation of Scripture, their appeal to emotion, their authoritarian structures, their linguistic isolation, and their distorted views of spiritual realities—believers can be better equipped to recognize and resist these insidious forces, standing firm in the truth and safeguarding the purity of the faith. The church must remain vigilant, actively teaching biblical discernment and fostering an environment where questions are welcomed and truth is paramount, ensuring that the seeds of deception are identified and uprooted before they can choke out the good seed of God's Word.

The insidious nature of these external agents of deception lies in their ability to prey upon legitimate human needs and desires. Everyone yearns for belonging, for certainty, for purpose, and for a sense of divine favor. False teachers are adept at recognizing these inherent longings and offering counterfeit solutions. They often present themselves as more spiritual, more insightful, or more loving than mainstream religious communities, thereby attracting those who feel unfulfilled or alienated from traditional faiths. This creates a dangerous trap, where the pursuit of genuine spiritual fulfillment leads individuals into deeper deception.

The emphasis on a supposed "special revelation" or a "lost truth" is a common tactic, suggesting that the existing church has somehow failed to grasp the entirety of God's counsel. This appeal to exclusivity and hidden knowledge fosters a sense of superiority in the follower, isolating them from constructive critique and encouraging a dismissive attitude towards those outside the group. Such a mindset is a breeding ground for pride, a characteristic that Scripture warns is often a precursor to a fall.

Consider the tactic of leveraging spiritual gifts in a manipulative manner. While the Bible affirms the reality and importance of spiritual gifts such as prophecy, healing, and tongues, false teachers can pervert their purpose. They may claim to possess these gifts exclusively, using them to authenticate their authority and demand allegiance. Prophecies might be vague and open to interpretation, always seeming to confirm the leader's pronouncements or the group's agenda. Healing ministries can become spectacles, where miraculous cures are promoted to draw crowds and validate the teacher's perceived divine empowerment.

At the same time, genuine needs may go unmet or be attributed to a lack of faith on the part of the afflicted. The exercise of these gifts, when detached from a foundation of biblical doctrine and the fruit of the Spirit (love, joy, peace, patience, kindness, goodness, faithfulness, gentleness, self-control), becomes a performance designed to impress and control, rather than a means of edifying the body of Christ. The emphasis shifts from glorifying God to glorifying the individual or the movement, a subtle yet significant deviation that leads to spiritual idolatry.

Another common strategy is the creation of what might be termed "spiritual momentum." This involves building a narrative of constant progress and success, often marked by rapid growth, impressive outward achievements, or sensational spiritual experiences. This momentum is designed to create a sense of inevitability and divine blessing around the movement, making it difficult for individuals to question its trajectory or foundational tenets.

Doubts or concerns are often framed as personal failings or as evidence of spiritual immaturity, which, if left unchecked, will hinder this divinely orchestrated momentum. This pressure to maintain the illusion of unbroken success can lead to the suppression of honest feedback and the covering up of internal problems, further entrenching deception within the organization. The focus on external validation—numbers, buildings, influence—can overshadow the internal spiritual health and doctrinal purity of the community.

The manipulation of the concept of "love" is also a potent tool. False teachers often present themselves as embodying unconditional love and acceptance, drawing people in with warmth and affirmation. However, this "love" can be conditional, reserved only for those who remain loyal and compliant. Disagreement or departure from the group's ideology is often met with withdrawal of affection, accusations of spiritual rebellion, or outright condemnation.

This creates a psychological bind: to remain loved and accepted, one must conform; to seek truth elsewhere or express dissent is to risk losing love and a sense of belonging. This perversion of biblical love, which is steadfast and truth-oriented, can lead to deep emotional wounds and a distorted understanding of healthy relationships. True Christian love confronts error in love, but it does not compromise truth for the sake of maintaining superficial unity or avoiding conflict.

The formation of cults often involves a deliberate process of "brainwashing" or undue influence, a term that describes systematic psychological manipulation designed to alter an individual's beliefs, attitudes, and behaviors. This can include sleep deprivation, repetitive chanting or teachings, isolation from previous support networks, control over information, and the use of guilt and fear.

While the extent and nature of these techniques vary, the goal is consistently to dismantle a person's existing identity and worldview, replacing it with the ideology of the group. This process makes individuals highly susceptible to the leader's commands and the group's teachings, often leading them to abandon critical thinking and embrace even the most irrational or harmful doctrines. Understanding these coercive mechanisms is crucial for recognizing when a movement has crossed the line from a genuine religious community to a system of unhealthy control.

The Bible consistently calls believers to be discerning, comparing all teachings against the unchanging standard of God's Word. This is not an option but a command. The proliferation of deceptive teachers and movements is a testament to the ongoing spiritual battle for the minds and hearts of believers. It highlights the critical need for robust discipleship, consistent biblical education, and the cultivation of a community where truth is cherished, questions are encouraged, and reliance is placed on the Holy Spirit for discernment, rather than on the charismatic pronouncements of fallible human beings. The integrity of the faith and the spiritual well-being of individuals depend on our vigilance and our unwavering commitment to the foundational truths of the Gospel.

The tapestry of truth, as we have seen, is not merely threatened by overt falsehoods or the machinations of deliberate deceivers. It can also be subtly eroded, thread by almost imperceptible thread, in the seemingly ordinary fabric of our everyday interactions. These are not the grand pronouncements of false prophets or the calculated manipulations of cult leaders, but rather the quiet concessions, the minor embellishments, the casual dismissals that, over time, can significantly warp our collective and individual perception of what is real and what is right. This erosion of truth, often born from convenience, social pressure, or a desire to avoid discomfort, creates a fertile ground for more substantial deception to take root.

Consider the pervasive nature of what might be termed "casual misinformation." This is not necessarily born of malice, but rather a lack of diligence in verifying information before it is shared. Think about the proliferation of unverified anecdotes, sensationalized headlines passed along without critical examination, or even the casual sharing of rumors that can quickly morph into accepted "facts." In a social media landscape that amplifies speed over accuracy, this phenomenon is particularly rampant. A friend shares a seemingly alarming piece of news, such as a forwarded chain message that purports to reveal a hidden conspiracy or a meme that oversimplifies a complex issue.

Without pausing to consider the source, the evidence, or the potential for bias, we click "share." Each unverified piece of information we propagate, however minor it may seem, contributes to a broader cultural environment where truth is less valued than immediacy and sensationalism. This constant drip-feed of unverified data can desensitize us to the importance of accuracy, making us less likely to question information in the future, even when the stakes are higher. We begin to accept that "good enough" information is, well, good enough, and the meticulous pursuit of verified truth becomes an onerous task.

This casual disregard for accuracy can extend to our interpersonal relationships. We might find ourselves embellishing a story to make ourselves seem more impressive, exaggerating our achievements, or downplaying our failures. The motivation might be as simple as seeking approval or avoiding embarrassment. For instance, when recounting a professional experience, one might inflate one's role or the success of a project to impress colleagues or superiors. In personal conversations, we might exaggerate the details of a vacation to make it sound more adventurous or gloss over an individual's failing to avoid judgment.

While these might seem like harmless social lubricants, they are, in essence, small departures from the truth. They are admissions that the unvarnished reality of our lives is somehow insufficient, that it needs to be polished or altered to be acceptable. Over time, this habit of exaggeration can blur the lines between reality and fabrication in our own minds, making us less attuned to the nuances of truth in more significant matters. We begin to operate on a spectrum of "truthiness," where what feels true or what we want to be true takes precedence over objective reality.

Another insidious form of truth erosion occurs in the downplaying of sin. This is particularly dangerous within religious contexts, where a nuanced understanding of sin's gravity is fundamental to faith. We might hear phrases like, "It is just a little white lie," "Everyone does it," or "It is not that big of a deal." These statements, often uttered with a dismissive tone, serve to minimize the seriousness of wrongdoing. When confronted with a transgression, rather than acknowledging it for what it is—a violation of God's standards and a barrier to our relationship with Him—we find ourselves rationalizing, minimizing, or deflecting.

This can manifest in various ways: blaming circumstances, attributing negative behavior to external forces, or simply avoiding the conversation altogether. For instance, a spouse might downplay an act of infidelity by saying it was merely a momentary lapse in judgment, not a betrayal of their vows. A church member might excuse gossip by claiming they were "sharing concerns" about another, rather than admitting to slander.

This constant downplaying of sin has a desensitizing effect. It is like repeatedly exposing oneself to a mild irritant; eventually, the body's reaction diminishes. When minor transgressions are consistently excused or minimized, our spiritual sensitivity to sin is dulled. The internal alarm bells that should ring when we deviate from God's path become fainter.

Consequently, when more significant sins arise, we are less equipped to recognize their gravity and are more likely to fall prey to the same patterns of rationalization and minimization. The very concept of repentance, which requires a clear understanding of what we are repenting *from*, becomes muddled. If sin is consistently framed as a minor inconvenience rather than a grave offense against a holy God, the transformative power of forgiveness and the necessity of seeking God's grace are diminished.

The **social pressure to conform** also plays a significant role in this erosion of truth. In many social circles, honesty, particularly when it is inconvenient or potentially divisive, can be met with disapproval. We might avoid speaking a brutal truth for fear of alienating friends, damaging relationships, or appearing judgmental. This is the temptation to prioritize social harmony over objective reality.

For example, if a group of friends engages in a biblically questionable behavior, speaking up about it might lead to ostracism. The easier, and often socially rewarded, path is to remain silent, to nod along, or even to participate. This silence, however, is a form of complicity, a subtle concession that the desire for acceptance outweighs the commitment to truth. When we consistently choose the path of least resistance, we train ourselves to suppress our convictions when they conflict with group norms.

This can also extend to downplaying or ignoring aspects of Christian doctrine that are challenging or unpopular. While the core tenets of the Gospel are timeless, applying biblical principles in a modern, pluralistic society can be a complex task. There may be a temptation to "soften" biblical teachings on controversial topics, presenting a version of Christianity that is more palatable to a broader audience and thereby avoiding potential conflict or criticism. This is not about compromising core truths, but about carefully curating which aspects of Christian teaching are emphasized and which are discreetly omitted or reinterpreted to align with prevailing cultural sentiments. This selective presentation of truth can leave individuals with an incomplete or distorted understanding of God's Word, making them ill-equipped to navigate the complexities of faith in the real world.

The media we consume, both traditional and social, is a significant contributor to this subtle erosion. The relentless pursuit of clicks and engagement often leads to sensationalism, biased reporting, and the amplification of opinions masquerading as facts. We are bombarded with narratives that are designed to provoke an emotional response rather than to provide objective information. When we passively absorb this content without critical evaluation, we internalize its biases and its skewed perspectives. This can lead to a gradual shift in our understanding of complex issues, making us more susceptible to simplistic explanations and emotionally charged rhetoric. The constant exposure to biased framing can subtly alter our perception of reality, making it harder to discern the objective truth when it is presented. Furthermore, the very language we use can be a vehicle for this erosion. The adoption of euphemisms to soften harsh realities is a common linguistic trick. We might talk about "downsizing" a workforce instead of "firing" people, or "collateral damage" instead of "civilian casualties." While sometimes used to mitigate unnecessary offense, these euphemisms can also serve to obscure the true nature of events, distancing us from the uncomfortable realities they represent.

When applied to moral or spiritual issues, this linguistic sanitization can be particularly damaging. We might discuss "personal choices" instead of "sin," or "alternative lifestyles" instead of biblical prohibitions. While compassion and sensitivity are vital, the use of language that deliberately avoids acknowledging the moral implications of actions can lead to a collective desensitization to sin and its consequences. This constant exposure to softened truths and downplayed sins can lead to a gradual hardening of the heart. When the gravity of sin is diminished, the perceived need for divine intervention and the transformative power of grace are also lessened. This can foster a sense of spiritual complacency, where individuals may feel they are living a reasonably good life, without a deep understanding of their need for a Savior.

The urgency of the Gospel message, which hinges on the reality of human sin and the necessity of redemption, can be muted in such an environment. It is like a slow leak in a tire; the car might still run for a while, but it is inefficient, unstable, and eventually, it will break down. Similarly, a faith that minimizes the reality of sin is fundamentally weakened, less resilient, and less capable of leading individuals to actual spiritual vitality.

The cumulative effect of these seemingly minor departures from the truth is profound. They create an environment where our discernment faculties are dulled, our commitment to accuracy is weakened, and our sensitivity to sin is diminished. This makes us increasingly vulnerable to more overt forms of deception. Suppose we have become accustomed to accepting unverified information, exaggerating our own lives, and downplaying the significance of sin. In that case, we are less likely to recognize the red flags when larger deceptions emerge. The groundwork for susceptibility is laid through these everyday compromises.

Therefore, the call to "test all things, hold fast to what is good" (**I Thessalonians 5:21**) is not an abstract theological principle; it is a practical, daily discipline. It requires a conscious effort to verify information, to speak truthfully even when it is difficult, and to confront sin—both in ourselves and in others—with a clear understanding of its gravity, all within the framework of love and grace. It means cultivating a mindset that values accuracy and integrity above convenience and social acceptance. It involves actively seeking out reliable sources of information, practicing humility in our interactions, and refusing to participate in the casual dismissal or rationalization of wrongdoing.

This vigilance is not about adopting a suspicious or cynical outlook. Instead, it is about maintaining a discerning heart, one that is deeply rooted in the unchanging truth of God's Word. It is about recognizing that every interaction, every piece of information we consume and share, is an opportunity to either reinforce the integrity of truth or to contribute to its subtle erosion. By committing to truthfulness in the small things – the way we speak about others, the information we share, the way we acknowledge our own shortcomings – we build a foundation of integrity that will serve as a robust defense against the larger deceptions that seek to undermine our faith and our understanding of God's reality.

The battle for truth begins not on grand theological stages, but in the quiet moments of our daily lives, in the choices we make about what we believe, what we say, and how we present ourselves and the world around us. It is in these seemingly insignificant arenas that the seeds of deception, or the steadfastness of truth, are most effectively sown.

La Wanda Blackmon

CHAPTER THREE:

Counterfeit Truths and Deceptive Tactics

The adversary's most potent strategy, the one that has ensnared souls across millennia and continues to be his masterstroke, is not outright rebellion or blatant blasphemy. Instead, it is the insidious art of mimicry. Satan does not present himself as the bringer of chaos and despair, for such an overt display would be easily recognized and rejected by even the most naïve individuals. Instead, he disguises himself as an angel of light, as the Scriptures so powerfully reveal **(II Corinthians 11:14)**. This is his primary weapon: the creation of counterfeit realities that closely resemble divine truth, making them almost indistinguishable from it, and leading the unwary into spiritual shipwreck. He does not offer outright heresy; he offers a subtle distortion, a perversion of the pure and unadulterated Word of God.

This mimicry operates on multiple fronts, each designed to ensnare the target. One of the most effective methods is the twisting of biblical concepts. Satan takes sacred truths, the very foundations of our faith, and subtly alters their meaning or context, rendering them impotent or even dangerous. Consider, for instance, the concept of grace. The Bible teaches that God's grace is unmerited favor, a gift freely given that enables us to overcome sin and live righteously **(Ephesians 2:8-9)**. It is a grace that empowers transformation.

Satan, however, can twist this into a doctrine of cheap grace, suggesting that because God is merciful, our actions hold little consequence. This distorted view can lead to a relaxed attitude towards sin, where believers might feel they can indulge in ungodly behavior, secure in the belief that God's grace will cover it, without any need for repentance or a change of heart. This is not the grace that sets free; it is a perversion that shackles with complacency. The devil knows that the power of grace lies in its ability to liberate us from sin's dominion, and by divorcing it from the accompanying call to holiness and obedience, he neutralizes its life-changing force. It becomes a license to sin rather than a power to overcome sin.

Another area where Satan excels in mimicry is in distorting God's character. The God of Scripture is a God of love, yes, but He is also a God of justice, holiness, and righteous wrath against sin. Satan's tactic is to amplify one attribute while suppressing others, creating a caricature of the Almighty. He will present a God who is *only* love, relentlessly emphasizing His mercy and kindness while conveniently omitting His absolute holiness and His judgment against iniquity. This portrayal leads to a sentimentalized, domesticated version of God, one who would never truly condemn or punish. Such a distorted view makes the need for a Savior seem less urgent. If God is merely a benevolent grandfather figure who overlooks all flaws, why the necessity of the atoning sacrifice of Jesus Christ? Why the radical call to repentance? This distorted deity is far easier to accept, far less demanding, but ultimately, a deceptive fabrication that fails to prepare us for the true God. This is not the God who declared, "*Be holy, because I, the Lord your God, am holy*" (Leviticus 19:2). This is a fabrication designed to lull the soul into a false sense of security, one that bypasses the profound reality of sin and the profound solution offered in the Gospel.

Furthermore, Satan presents falsehoods in a package that appears righteous or beneficial. He is a master of packaging. He takes a kernel of truth and wraps it in layers of appealing, yet deceptive, half-truths and outright lies. Think of the prosperity gospel. It takes the biblical concept that God desires His children to prosper and twists it into an equation where faith equals wealth. If you have enough faith and give generously, God is obligated to bless you with abundance. This perverts the biblical understanding of prosperity, which encompasses not only material wealth but also spiritual well-being, peace, and the ability to serve God effectively. The enemy offers a gilded cage, a deceptive promise of earthly gain that distracts from the eternal riches found in Christ. The allure is powerful: who would not want a guaranteed path to financial security? However, this mimicry comes at a cost, often leading believers to question their faith when material blessings fail to materialize, or worse, to develop a transactional relationship with God, where love and obedience are reduced to means of personal gain. This is a far cry from the Biblical message of finding contentment in all things and seeking first the Kingdom of God.

Consider also the subtle shifts in the interpretation of biblical prophecy. While the Bible speaks of a future restoration and ultimate triumph of God's kingdom, Satan can sow seeds of confusion by promoting interpretations that are speculative, divisive, or focused on temporal, earthly power rather than the spiritual reign of Christ. These counterfeit prophecies can create anxiety, lead to misguided actions, or foster an unhealthy obsession with timing and earthly kingdoms, diverting attention from the fundamental call to live faithfully in the present. He does not need to invent entirely new scriptures; he can pervert the meaning of existing ones, twisting them to fit his narrative.

The devil's deception is often most effective when it appeals to our deepest desires and insecurities. He can mimic the promise of fulfillment, offering shortcuts to happiness, success, or spiritual enlightenment that bypass the disciplined, surrendered walk of faith. These paths may promise immediate results, exotic experiences, or profound insights, all while subtly drawing individuals away from the steady, foundational truths of the Gospel. It is the allure of the quick fix, the easy answer, the path of least resistance, all cloaked in the language of spirituality.

This mimicry extends to the very presentation of spiritual warfare. While the Bible clearly teaches that believers are engaged in a spiritual battle against demonic forces, Satan can distort this truth by either making believers overly fearful and paralyzed by the enemy's supposed power or by making them dismissive, suggesting that the concept of spiritual warfare is outdated or irrelevant. Both extremes serve his purpose. Excessive fear leads to incapacitation, while dismissiveness leaves individuals vulnerable and unprepared. The genuine truth is a balanced understanding: we are engaged in a spiritual battle, but we are equipped with divine armor and empowered by the Holy Spirit to stand firm (**Ephesians 6:10-18**).

The enemy's mimicry also manifests in the subtle distortion of Christian ethics. He can twist principles of love and acceptance into a relativism that negates biblical absolutes. For example, the call to love our neighbor is a cornerstone of Christian teaching. However, Satan can distort this into a belief that *all* behaviors are equally acceptable and that any statement affirming biblical morality is inherently unloving or judgmental. This creates a dilemma in which believers are told that speaking the truth that challenges a particular lifestyle is to violate the command to love. This is a sophisticated inversion of the truth, designed to silence the voice of biblical conviction. True love, as defined by God, often involves speaking truth, even when it is difficult, in the hope of guiding others towards righteousness.

Another powerful mimicry is found in the counterfeit of spiritual authority. The Bible speaks of God-ordained leadership and the authority vested in His Church. Satan can pervert this by promoting false apostles, manipulative leaders, or cultic structures that demand absolute loyalty to an individual rather than to Christ and His Word. These counterfeit authorities often demand unquestioning obedience, isolate followers from external counsel, and prioritize the leader's agenda over biblical fidelity. They mimic the structure of healthy spiritual leadership while undermining its true purpose, which is to build up believers in Christ and equip them for service.

The allure of spiritual knowledge without the accompanying spiritual transformation is another tool in Satan's arsenal. He can promote intellectualism that puffs up, encouraging a focus on theological debate and esoteric knowledge that disconnects from a humble, obedient heart. This creates individuals who are knowledgeable about God but have little personal intimacy with Him. They can be easily swayed by sophisticated arguments that sound biblical but lack the savor of true spiritual insight, which always points to Christ and fosters humility and love. Understanding this mimicry is not merely an academic exercise; it is essential for spiritual survival. The enemy's goal is not to make everyone an atheist. His aim is far more insidious: to deceive believers into accepting a diluted, distorted version of Christianity that effectively neutralizes their witness and leads them away from the true life and power found in Christ. It is like counterfeit currency that appears genuine but holds no real value, thereby debasing the economic system it infiltrates. The ability to discern the genuine from the counterfeit is a gift from God, nurtured through diligent study of His Word, prayerful reliance on the Holy Spirit, and the fellowship of a discerning community of faith. The Scriptures are our ultimate standard. By immersing ourselves in the unadulterated truth of the Bible, we develop an internal compass that can detect the subtle deviations and outright distortions of Satan's deceptive tactics. When we fill our minds with the pure doctrines of faith, the counterfeits become jarringly discordant.

This is why the Apostle Paul urged believers to "*test everything; hold firmly to what is good*" (**I Thessalonians 5:21**). This is not a call to suspicion, but to a discerning engagement with the world and its messages. It requires critical thinking, a willingness to question, and a deep commitment to the revealed truth of God. When we encounter teachings or ideas that seem plausible, even appealing, we must always measure them against the plumb line of Scripture. Does this teaching align with the character of God as revealed in Jesus Christ? Does it exalt Christ? Does it promote holiness and obedience? Does it lead to growth in love and truth, or does it foster division, pride, or a casual attitude toward sin?

The danger of Satan's mimicry lies in its subtlety. It is not a frontal assault but a creeping infiltration. It is a gradual erosion of truth, a slow poisoning of the wellspring of our faith. By understanding that the enemy's primary tactic is to create convincing falsehoods that masquerade as truth, we can begin to recognize his fingerprints. We can become more vigilant, more prayerful, and more grounded in the unchanging Word of God, guarding our hearts and minds against the elaborate deceptions that seek to lead us astray from the narrow yet life-giving path of true discipleship. This awareness is the first and most crucial step in rendering Satan's masterstroke ineffective in our own lives and in the life of the Church. It equips us to stand firm, anchored in the unshakeable truth of God.

Satan thrives on ignorance, particularly ignorance of God's Word. This is not an accidental consequence; it is a deliberate strategy. The adversary understands that waves of deceptive doctrines and manipulative ideologies can easily toss a mind unanchored in the solid rock of biblical truth. When individuals lack a robust understanding of Scripture, they become fertile ground for misinformation, susceptible to teachings that may sound plausible, even spiritual, but are ultimately hollow echoes of divine truth. This theological illiteracy is not merely a passive state of not knowing; it is an active vulnerability that Satan actively cultivates and exploits to gain a significant advantage in his spiritual warfare against humanity.

The power of misinformation lies in its ability to mimic truth. It is like a master forger who painstakingly replicates every detail of a valuable painting. If one is not intimately familiar with the original, the forgery can easily pass for authentic. In the spiritual realm, this means that teachings that subtly twist or omit key biblical doctrines can gain traction because the discernment needed to identify the error is absent. For instance, consider the concept of salvation. The clear biblical message is that salvation is by grace through faith in Jesus Christ alone (**Ephesians 2:8-9**). It is a gift, not something earned through works or ritual. However, Satan can introduce misinformation by subtly shifting the emphasis. He might promote ideas that suggest salvation can be achieved through good deeds alone, or through adherence to specific religious practices, or even through self-improvement programs presented as avenues to spiritual attainment. These alternative paths, while seemingly noble or empowering, bypass the central, essential role of Christ's atoning sacrifice. When individuals are ignorant of the biblical necessity of Christ's redemptive work, they can easily be led to believe that their own efforts are sufficient, thus rendering the Gospel's power inert in their lives. This does not require an outright denial of Christ; it simply requires a subtle redirection of focus away from His unique salvific role.

Another potent area where ignorance is exploited is in the understanding of God's nature and character. The Bible presents a comprehensive portrait of God: He is love, yet He is also righteous, just, holy, and sovereign. He is a God of mercy, but He is also a God of wrath against sin. Satan's strategy is to present a partial, distorted view, selectively highlighting specific attributes while omitting others to create a God that is palatable to human pride and sin.

For example, he might promote a narrative of a God who is solely defined by His love and forgiveness, to the exclusion of His justice and holiness. This creates a "sugar-coated" deity, one who is perpetually approving, never condemning, and whose standards are so low as to be almost non-existent. In such a distorted worldview, the concept of sin becomes trivialized, and the need for repentance, atonement, and a transformed life loses its urgency. When people are ignorant of God's absolute holiness and His righteous judgment against sin, they are less likely to perceive the depth of their own sinfulness and the absolute necessity of God's intervention through Christ. This breeds a false sense of security, where individuals feel spiritually "good enough" without the radical transformation that the Gospel demands. The biblical warning, "You must be holy, because I, the Lord your God, am holy" (**Leviticus 19:2**), is either ignored or reinterpreted to fit a more comfortable, less demanding theology.

The intentional dissemination of misinformation often exploits human desires for simple solutions and instant gratification. In a world that frequently feels complex and challenging, people yearn for simple solutions and definitive paths. Satan capitalizes on this by offering counterfeit spiritual insights that promise quick enlightenment or guaranteed success, often bypassing the disciplined, frequently arduous process of genuine spiritual growth that is rooted in Scripture and prayer.

For instance, the allure of instant spiritual gifts or prophetic pronouncements that promise future success can be incredibly tempting. When individuals are not grounded in biblical teachings about spiritual growth, which emphasize patience, perseverance, and the slow cultivation of character through the Holy Spirit, they become vulnerable to these shortcuts. These counterfeit promises often lead people down paths that appear to offer spiritual advancement but are, in reality, detours away from the true, Christ-centered journey. The Bible describes spiritual maturity as a process that develops over time, through trials and consistent engagement with God's Word and the community of faith. However, misinformation can present a narrative that suggests spiritual maturity is a commodity that can be acquired quickly through the proper techniques or associations, leaving individuals unaware of the foundational work required for genuine spiritual formation.

The enemy also leverages ignorance concerning spiritual warfare. The Bible clearly states that believers are in a spiritual battle against unseen forces **(Ephesians 6:12)**. However, Satan can manipulate this truth by creating two extreme, equally damaging responses: either paralyzing fear or dismissive indifference. If people are ignorant of the biblical strategies and protections available in Christ, they might be consumed by fear of demonic influence, leading to superstition or a sense of helplessness. Conversely, if they are taught to disregard or deny the reality of spiritual conflict, they become unprepared and vulnerable to it. Misinformation can paint the concept of spiritual warfare as outdated, irrelevant, or even a sign of psychological imbalance, thereby disarming believers and leaving them defenseless against the very real attacks of the adversary. When individuals are unaware of the provisions God has made for spiritual protection – the armor of God, the power of prayer, and the authority of Christ's name – they are left vulnerable. This ignorance allows Satan to sow discord, doubt, and despair without encountering meaningful resistance.

Furthermore, the deliberate spread of theological illiteracy is evident in the distortion of biblical prophecy. While the Bible offers a future hope and a sovereign God who is in control of history, Satan can inject confusion by promoting speculative, sensationalized, or self-serving interpretations of prophetic passages. This often leads to an unhealthy fixation on end-times timelines, a preoccupation with earthly political events as the sole fulfillment of prophecy, or the development of niche theories that create division within the body of Christ. When individuals lack a solid grounding in hermeneutics— the principles of biblical interpretation—and the overall narrative arc of Scripture, they are easily swayed by these misleading claims. Misinformation can present prophecy as a puzzle to be solved for personal gain or notoriety, rather than as a source of hope, a call to faithfulness, and a testament to God's ultimate sovereignty. This distracts believers from their present calling and can foster anxiety rather than faith.

The application of biblical knowledge is not merely an academic pursuit; it is a vital defense against this onslaught of misinformation. Diligent Bible study is the primary means by which individuals can equip themselves to discern truth from error. When believers are intimately familiar with the Scriptures, they develop an internal compass that can detect deviations from sound doctrine. The Word of God is the objective standard against which all claims must be measured. It is the very voice of God, revealing His will, His character, and His plan for humanity. To neglect its study is to willingly surrender one's spiritual discernment, leaving oneself open to deception.

The Apostle Paul's exhortation in **I Thessalonians 5:21**–"*Test everything; hold firmly to what is good*"–is a direct command to combat misinformation through informed discernment. This testing is not an act of cynical suspicion, but a necessary practice of spiritual diligence. It requires us to actively engage with teachings, ideas, and even personal experiences, comparing them against the unwavering standard of Scripture. Does a particular teaching align with the character of God as revealed in Jesus Christ? Does it point people to Christ, or to a person, a system, or a feeling? Does it promote holiness, humility, and love, or does it foster pride, division, and a casual attitude towards sin? These are the questions that must be asked, and they can only be answered with a foundational knowledge of God's Word.

Moreover, the ignorance that Satan exploits is often rooted in a lack of critical thinking skills applied to spiritual matters. The modern world bombards us with information from countless sources, and the spiritual realm is no exception. Without the ability to analyze claims, identify logical fallacies, and cross-reference information with authoritative sources, individuals can easily fall prey to persuasive but erroneous arguments. This is especially true when misinformation is presented with emotional appeals, personal anecdotes, or seemingly profound spiritual experiences that lack biblical substantiation. The enemy is adept at crafting narratives that resonate with our deepest desires and anxieties, and in the absence of informed discernment, these narratives can masquerade as divine revelation.

The importance of community in combating misinformation cannot be overstated. The New Testament frequently emphasizes the role of the church community in testing and confirming truth. When believers are part of a healthy, biblically grounded fellowship, they benefit from the collective wisdom and discernment of their fellow believers. False teachings are more easily identified and challenged when they are presented before a community committed to biblical orthodoxy. However, Satan can also exploit ignorance by isolating individuals, creating a sense of elitism where they believe they have received a "special revelation" that sets them apart from the ordinary teachings of the church. This isolation makes them even more vulnerable, as they lack the checks and balances that a community of faith provides. The enemy seeks to dismantle the communal discernment that acts as a bulwark against deception.

Therefore, the consistent, prayerful study of the Bible is not an optional add-on for the Christian life; it is the bedrock of spiritual defense. It is the process by which we are transformed by the renewing of our minds (**Romans 12:2**), becoming equipped to recognize and reject the counterfeits that Satan so artfully deploys. When our minds are saturated with the truth of God's Word, the deceptive whispers of misinformation become dissonant, jarring, and easily identifiable. This grounding in Scripture provides the clarity needed to see through the fog of deception, to stand firm against the subtle distortions, and to live out the genuine, life-transforming truth of the Gospel. Without this intentional pursuit of biblical knowledge, we remain vulnerable, susceptible to the adversary's most persistent and damaging tactic: exploiting our ignorance. The ongoing battle for truth is, in large part, a struggle against ignorance, and the weapon God has given us is His infallible Word.

Satan's arsenal is not limited to subtle distortions of doctrine or the exploitation of ignorance. He is a master strategist, and a significant part of his deception involves a direct assault on our senses and emotions, employing tactics designed to bypass critical thinking and genuine biblical understanding. These strategies create an immersive, often powerful, experience that can feel profoundly spiritual, even divine, yet ultimately lacks the solid foundation of God's Word. The adversary understands that truth is not solely an intellectual assent; it is also deeply felt, and he seeks to replicate, or rather, counterfeit, that feeling to draw individuals away from authentic spiritual engagement.

One of the most potent methods Satan employs is sensationalism. This involves presenting spiritual concepts or experiences in an exaggerated, overly dramatic, or intensely stimulating way. It is akin to a magician using smoke and mirrors to create an illusion that captivates the audience, drawing their attention away from the actual mechanics of the trick. In the spiritual realm, sensationalism might manifest as pronouncements of immediate, dramatic deliverance from all problems, miraculous financial windfalls guaranteed by a specific prayer or offering, or prophecies that predict imminent, earth-shattering events without the clear scriptural backing.

These messages are crafted to evoke a robust emotional response – excitement, awe, anticipation, or even fear – creating an experience that feels undeniably real and significant. The danger lies in the fact that the emotional intensity of the experience can be mistaken for divine approval or confirmation. When a message is delivered with great fervor, accompanied by dramatic music, awe-inspiring visuals, or testimonials of overwhelming emotional breakthroughs, the recipient can be persuaded that the message itself must be valid, simply because of the profound emotional impact it had. This bypasses the crucial step of evaluating the content against the unchanging truth of Scripture.

This sensationalism is often intertwined with sophisticated emotional manipulation. Satan knows our hearts are prone to desires for happiness, success, comfort, and acceptance. He crafts deceptive narratives that tap into these deep-seated longings, promising fulfillment through means that are subtly or overtly contrary to God's will. For example, a teaching might emphasize radical self-acceptance and unbridled personal fulfillment, downplaying the biblical call to self-denial, repentance, and crucifying the flesh.

While self-worth and joy are indeed aspects of the Christian life, they are to be found in Christ and through obedience, not as the primary end goal achieved through unchecked personal desires. When a message promises immediate emotional satisfaction or liberation from all struggle, it plays on our innate aversion to pain and difficulty. This can lead people to embrace teachings that offer an easy path, a "Christianity Lite," which avoids the challenging but ultimately rewarding process of spiritual growth that often involves suffering, perseverance, and dependence on God through trials. The emotional hook is powerful: who would not want an immediate resolution to their anxieties or a guarantee of perpetual happiness? This is where discernment becomes paramount. We must learn to distinguish between genuine spiritual joy that arises from a right relationship with God and a fleeting emotional high that is manufactured or misplaced.

The appeal to sensory experiences is another key component of Satan's deceptive arsenal. This can range from the use of potent imagery and evocative language to the creation of environments designed to induce specific emotional states. Think of rituals that employ incense, chanting, elaborate visual displays, or even physical sensations aimed at creating a mystical or transcendent atmosphere. While worship can and should engage our senses in a wholesome way, these sensory elements can be deliberately orchestrated to overwhelm our rational faculties and create an experience that feels divinely inspired, regardless of the theological soundness of the underlying message.

The goal is to create an overwhelming *feeling* of spirituality that can cloud judgment. For instance, a charismatic speaker might use highly emotional language, dramatic pauses, and direct, piercing eye contact to create a sense of personal connection and prophetic insight. This intense personal engagement can feel like God is speaking directly to the individual through the speaker, creating a powerful emotional bond and a willingness to accept whatever is being communicated. This is not to say that passionate preaching or the use of artistic elements in worship is inherently wrong. The Bible itself is rich with poetry, imagery, and calls to passionate worship. However, when these elements are used to bypass the mind and heart's critical engagement with the truth of God's Word, they become a tool of deception. The actual test is not how the message makes us feel in the moment, but whether it aligns with the enduring, objective truth of Scripture and leads us to a deeper, more Christ-like character.

Consider the power of music and atmospheric elements in spiritual gatherings. While worship music can uplift and inspire, music can also be used to manipulate emotions. A somber, melancholic melody can create a sense of reverence or sorrow, while an upbeat, powerful anthem can evoke feelings of triumph and exultation. Satan can exploit this by using music that creates an overwhelming emotional tidal wave, making people feel uplifted or deeply moved, and then associating that strong emotional experience with a teaching that is, in fact, unbiblical. The feeling becomes the validation, rather than the truth of the teaching itself. Similarly, the creation of a specific ambiance—such as dim lighting, incense, and repetitive sounds—can induce a trance-like state or a heightened sense of spiritual awareness that feels authentic but is, in reality, a manufactured experience. This reliance on external stimuli to generate spiritual feelings can lead to a superficial faith, one that is dependent on the "right" atmosphere or the "right" emotional trigger, rather than on a settled conviction of God's truth internalized through the study of His Word and the work of the Holy Spirit.

Furthermore, Satan can counterfeit the experience of spiritual breakthrough. Many deceptive teachings promise immediate transformation, rapid spiritual growth, or instant access to spiritual gifts. Intense emotional experiences often accompany these promises during the imparting of these supposed gifts or truths. Individuals may report feeling a jolt of energy, a surge of peace, or a sudden influx of insight. While genuine spiritual experiences can be powerful and transformative, they are typically characterized by the fruit of the Spirit – love, joy, peace, patience, kindness, goodness, faithfulness, gentleness, and self-control (**Galatians 5:22-23**)– which develops over time through consistent engagement with God. When these counterfeit experiences are presented as the pinnacle of spiritual attainment, they can lead individuals to believe they have arrived or possess a special spiritual authority, without the underlying character development and biblical grounding that God's Word requires. This fosters a dangerous sense of spiritual pride and complacency, where the genuine work of sanctification is neglected in favor of pursuing fleeting, sensational experiences.

The danger of mistaking emotional intensity for divine truth is particularly insidious because emotions are such a powerful part of the human experience. We are not purely rational beings; we feel, we react, and our feelings often inform our perceptions. Satan exploits this inherent human characteristic. A teaching that evokes strong feelings of love, acceptance, or even righteous anger can be very persuasive, especially if it seems to confirm our existing biases or desires. For example, a teaching that validates a particular lifestyle choice that is contrary to biblical teaching might be presented with language that emphasizes unconditional love and personal freedom. The emotional resonance of feeling loved and accepted can be so compelling that it overrides any internal alarm bells that might be ringing about the theological inconsistency. This is why the Apostle Paul's admonition to "*be transformed by the renewing of your mind*" (**Romans 12:2**) is so crucial. True spiritual transformation begins with a reorientation of our thinking, aligning our minds with God's truth, rather than allowing our emotions to dictate our theological conclusions.

The adversary also employs the tactic of creating a sense of urgent, exclusive revelation. He might whisper to individuals that they have received a special insight or a hidden truth that others do not possess. This often comes with an accompanying emotional charge of excitement and exclusivity. When this revelation is coupled with dramatic pronouncements or promises of great spiritual power, the individual can become convinced of its authenticity. This creates a feeling of being "in the know," which can be very appealing. However, this exclusive revelation often lacks the broad, consistent endorsement found in Scripture. It can lead to a form of spiritual elitism, where individuals who claim these remarkable insights view themselves as superior to or more enlightened than those who adhere to traditional, biblical teachings. This isolation, fueled by an emotional sense of superiority, makes them vulnerable to further deception, as they are less likely to submit their claims to the scrutiny of the wider Christian community, which is itself a safeguard against error.

It is vital to understand that God's Word is not only intellectually sound but also deeply fulfilling on an emotional and spiritual level, but in a way that is rooted in truth and aligns with the character of God. The joy that comes from genuine salvation, the peace that surpasses understanding, and the love that flows from a relationship with Christ are profound and lasting. However, these experiences are the *result* of being connected to the true vine, not the primary means of establishing that connection. Satan's counterfeit experiences often present the emotional payoff as the *means* to spiritual attainment, or as the definitive proof of it, divorced from the established truths of the faith. He wants us to feel our way into spiritual reality, rather than to believe our way into it, with belief firmly anchored in objective revelation.

Discerning these deceptive tactics requires a conscious effort to evaluate not just the feeling a teaching evokes, but its actual content and its conformity to the Bible. When a message, no matter how emotionally compelling or sensorially stimulating, contradicts or omits key biblical teachings about God's nature, salvation, sin, or the Christian life, it should be viewed with extreme caution. We must develop the discipline of bringing all spiritual experiences, all pronouncements, and all emotional highs and lows before the unchanging standard of God's Word. Is this teaching drawing me closer to Christ and His unchanging character? Does it foster humility, obedience, and love for God and neighbor, or does it promote pride, rebellion, and a focus on self? Does it equip me with the truth of Scripture, or does it bypass Scripture in favor of subjective experience? By consistently asking these questions and grounding our answers in biblical literacy, we can begin to recognize the counterfeit spiritual experiences that Satan so expertly crafts. This is not about suppressing emotions or dismissing the validity of genuine spiritual encounters, but about ensuring that our emotional and sensory experiences are rightly interpreted and validated by the objective truth of God's Word, rather than being used as a deceptive substitute for it. Our faith must be built on the bedrock of divine revelation, not the shifting sands of ephemeral feelings or sensory overload.

Satan's most insidious tactic in his arsenal of counterfeit truths is the systematic distortion of God's very being— His character and His promises. This is not merely a matter of misinterpreting a verse or two; it is a profound assault on the foundational understanding of who God is, how He relates to humanity, and what He has pledged to us. If the enemy can successfully warp our perception of God's nature, he can then effectively lead us astray in our faith, our obedience, and our very hope. This distortion is not always a blatant declaration that God is evil, but rather a subtle twisting of His attributes, a selective emphasis on certain aspects while downplaying or denying others, all designed to create a false image that cannot be truly trusted or faithfully followed.

One of the primary ways Satan corrupts our understanding of God's character is by portraying Him as capricious, unreliable, or even inherently unloving. The God of Scripture is unchanging, a bedrock of steadfastness in a world of flux. However, the adversary can sow seeds of doubt, suggesting that God's moods shift like the weather, that His favor can be withdrawn arbitrarily, or that His love is conditional upon our perfect performance. This creates an anxiety-ridden faith, where believers constantly fear they have done something to displease God, earning His silent disapproval. Such a distorted view can lead to paralysis, where individuals are too afraid to approach God, fearing rejection, or conversely, to an unhealthy pursuit of outward piety designed to placate an imagined, fickle deity. The Bible, however, presents a God who is eternally the same, whose love is not earned but freely given, and whose faithfulness is as sure as the sunrise. His promises are not dependent on our fleeting successes but on His enduring covenant. To present God as someone who randomly withdraws His presence or favor is to fundamentally misrepresent His revealed nature, which is characterized by immutable love and unwavering commitment.

Furthermore, the enemy may attempt to paint God as unjust or unfair, particularly when individuals are experiencing suffering or hardship. When trials persist, and prayers for relief seem unanswered, it is tempting for the human heart, especially in its pain, to question God's righteousness. Satan capitalizes on this vulnerability, whispering accusations that God is indifferent, that He plays favorites, or that He permits injustice without concern for His creation. This can lead to bitterness, resentment, and a rejection of faith altogether. The scriptures, however, consistently uphold God's perfect justice, even when that justice is difficult for us to comprehend in the midst of our pain. God's ways are higher than ours, and His reasons for permitting suffering are often beyond our immediate grasp. He promises to work all things for the good of those who love Him (Romans 8:28), a promise that assures us that even in perceived injustice, God is actively engaged in a righteous plan. To suggest God is fundamentally unjust is to deny the very essence of His holiness and ultimate sovereignty over all.

Another insidious distortion involves twisting God's promises to foster presumption or a perversion of faith. God's promises are abundant, offering hope, guidance, and assurance to His children. However, Satan can seize these promises and twist them into a license for recklessness or a basis for demanding God's intervention according to our own selfish desires. For example, the promise of answered prayer can be manipulated to imply that God is obligated to grant any request we make, regardless of its alignment with His will. This leads to a consumerist approach to faith, where God is seen as a cosmic vending machine, dispensing blessings upon demand. Such a perversion overlooks the biblical emphasis on praying according to God's will (**I John 5:14-15**) and the often patient, character-building process that accompanies genuine spiritual growth. The adversary can take verses about God's faithfulness and twist them into a guarantee that if we perform a particular ritual or have sufficient faith, God will deliver us from all earthly troubles, financial or otherwise, in a manner dictated by our preferences. This is not the faith of Scripture, but a form of magical thinking that places the believer in the driver's seat, dictating terms to the Almighty.

Consider the promise of eternal life. While this is a cornerstone of Christian hope, Satan can distort its implications. He might encourage a mindset that downplays the importance of present obedience and discipleship, suggesting that since salvation is assured, one need not strive for holiness or actively engage in living out the Gospel. This is a perversion of grace, turning it into an excuse for antinomianism—the belief that adherence to moral law is unnecessary for salvation. Conversely, he might twist the promise of eternal rewards into an incentive for self-serving actions, where good deeds are performed not out of love for God and neighbor, but for the promise of greater accolades in heaven. Steadfast faithfulness is motivated by gratitude and love for the Savior, not by a calculated pursuit of heavenly bonus points. The essence of God's promises is to secure our hope and guide our steps toward Him, not to provide loopholes for sin or justifications for self-aggrandizement.

The distortion of God's promises often hinges on presenting them in isolation from the context of His covenantal relationship and His call to obedience. God's promises are not empty pronouncements; they are made within the framework of His relationship with humanity, a relationship that calls for trust, faithfulness, and alignment with His revealed will. When Satan isolates a promise, he can strip it of its intended meaning and application. For instance, a promise of provision might be twisted to suggest God will provide *all* material comforts, regardless of whether one is actively working, stewarding resources wisely, or prioritizing God's kingdom. This can lead to a neglect of diligence and responsibility, with the expectation that God will miraculously intervene to compensate for a lack of effort or poor stewardship. The biblical perspective is one of partnership: God promises to bless the work of our hands and provide for our needs when we seek His kingdom first (**Matthew 6:33**), but this is not a blank check divorced from human responsibility and wisdom.

The immutability of God's character is a crucial defense against these distortions. The Bible repeatedly emphasizes that God does not change. **Malachi 3:6** states, "*For I, the LORD, do not change; therefore you, O children of Jacob, are not consumed.*" **Hebrews 13:8** echoes this sentiment: "*Jesus Christ is the same yesterday and today and forever.*" This unchanging nature means that God's love, His justice, His mercy, and His truth are constant. Circumstances do not sway him, nor is His disposition towards the faithful believer subject to arbitrary shifts. When we are tempted to view God as moody or inconsistent, we must anchor ourselves in the unshakeable truth of His unchanging nature. His promises are guaranteed not by our fluctuating feelings or our inconsistent efforts, but by His own steadfast character and unbreakable covenants.

Understanding God's character also involves recognizing His holiness and absolute opposition to sin. Satan often seeks to downplay the seriousness of sin and God's righteous judgment against it. He may promote a "niceness" theology, where God is portrayed as so loving and gentle that He would never truly condemn anyone, or that He overlooks sin in favor of universal acceptance. This is a dangerous distortion that removes the necessity of repentance and the transformative power of the cross. God's love is indeed profound, but it is a holy love, one that cannot coexist with unrepentant sin. His mercy is extended through the atoning sacrifice of Christ, which fully and justly addresses the problem of sin. To present God as a deity who tolerates or ignores sin is to rob humanity of the understanding of its own desperate need for a Savior and the immense cost of redemption.

The biblical narrative consistently portrays God as a God of covenant, and His promises are intrinsically linked to these covenants. From Abraham to Noah, to David, and ultimately to the new covenant established through Jesus Christ, God's promises are relational and rooted in His commitment to His people. Satan's distortions often seek to sever these promises from their relational context, turning them into transactional guarantees or abstract assurances. For example, the promise of the Holy Spirit as our comforter and guide is presented not as a gift to empower believers for a life of obedience and service, but as a means to achieve heightened spiritual experiences or personal empowerment for worldly success. This detachment from the covenantal framework—which implies mutual commitment and responsiveness—allows for the perversion of the promise's true intent, which is to draw us closer to God and conform us to the image of Christ.

To counteract these deceptive tactics, a robust understanding of God's attributes as revealed in Scripture is paramount. We must actively study and internalize the biblical descriptions of God's love, mercy, justice, sovereignty, faithfulness, and immutability. This is not merely an intellectual exercise; it is the cultivation of a proper knowledge of God that shapes our trust, our worship, and our response to life's challenges. When we encounter teachings that portray God as erratic, unloving, or unjust, we must bring them to the light of Scripture. Does this teaching align with the God who is described in **Exodus 34:6-7** as *"the LORD, the LORD, a God merciful and gracious, slow to anger, and abounding in steadfast love and faithfulness, keeping steadfast love for thousands, forgiving iniquity and transgression and sin, but who will by no means clear the guilty"* (KJV, 2023)? If a teaching contradicts this fundamental description, it is likely a counterfeit.

The distortion of God's promises also requires careful examination. Are the promises being presented in their full biblical context? Do they encourage a faith that is passive and demanding, or one that is active, hopeful, and obedient? Does the promise lead to a greater reliance on God, or to a presumption that bypasses the need for His wisdom and guidance? For instance, the promise of divine healing, while a legitimate aspect of God's care, can be distorted into an expectation that all sickness will be miraculously eradicated in this life, leading to despair when healing does not manifest as expected. The biblical perspective on healing is often nuanced, involving God's perfect timing, His purposes for sanctification through suffering, and the ultimate healing that awaits us in the resurrection. To present healing as an automatic, unconditional promise for the present age, divorced from these considerations, is to warp its intended meaning.

The spiritual discipline of prayer itself becomes a battleground for these distortions. Satan can whisper that if we pray with enough faith, or use the right words, or repeat a prayer a certain number of times, God is obligated to respond according to our wishes. This reduces prayer to a formula, a magical incantation, rather than a genuine communion with a loving Heavenly Father. The biblical model of prayer is one of humble petition, submission to God's will, and a deep trust in His perfect plan, even when it is not immediately apparent or desirable to us. When our prayers become demands rather than heartfelt conversations, we have strayed into deceptive territory.

Ultimately, the defense against these distortions lies in cultivating a deep and abiding knowledge of God's Word, coupled with a humble reliance on the Holy Spirit's guidance. The Holy Spirit illuminates the truth of God's character and His promises, helping us to discern the genuine from the counterfeit. When Satan attempts to paint God as capricious, we must remember His faithfulness. When he whispers that God is unjust, we must recall His righteous judgment and His merciful provision through Christ. When he twists promises to foster presumption, we must return to the biblical context of covenant and obedience. By grounding our faith in the unshakeable truth of God's unchanging character and His sure promises, we build our lives on a foundation that the enemy's deceptions cannot erode. Fleeting feelings or distorted whispers must not shape our understanding of God, but by the clear, consistent, and eternal revelation of His Word. This unwavering knowledge is the most potent weapon against the adversary's attempts to redefine the very nature of our Creator and Redeemer. It ensures that our hope is not built on shifting sand, but on the rock of God's eternal truth.

The enemy's strategy of deception is a masterclass in subtle subversion. While the previous discussion focused on distorting God's character and promises, a more foundational assault involves elevating human intellect and subjective experience above divine revelation. Satan, the archetypal tempter, seduces humanity with the promise of independent knowledge, a path that bypasses reliance on God's communicated truth. This is not an outright denial of God, but rather a sophisticated redirection of trust, urging us to become our own authorities and arbiters of what is true and proper.

The Genesis narrative provides the blueprint for this tactic. The serpent did not tell Eve that God's command was inherently wrong or that He was a malicious deceiver. Instead, he questioned God's motive and presented an alternative source of wisdom in **Genesis 3:5**: *"For God knows that when you eat from it your eyes will be opened, and you will be like God, knowing good and evil"* (KJV, 2023). This was a direct appeal to Eve's intellect and a veiled suggestion that God's authority was a restriction on her personal enlightenment. The implication was clear: God's word was one perspective, but human reason offered a superior, more liberating truth. By casting doubt on God's pronouncement and highlighting the perceived benefits of independent thought, Satan initiated a rebellion against divine authority, a rebellion that continues to echo through human history.

This insidious appeal to human reason has manifested in countless philosophical systems, ideologies, and personal belief structures throughout the ages. When human intellect, unaided by or in opposition to divine revelation, is placed on the throne, it inevitably leads to a distortion of truth. The limitations of the human mind are profound. We are finite beings, bound by our experiences, our cultural contexts, and the inherent biases that accompany our fallen nature. To assume that our reason alone is sufficient to grasp the infinite, to comprehend the divine, and to discern ultimate moral and spiritual realities is a form of intellectual hubris that echoes the original sin. As the Apostle Paul warns in **I Corinthians 1:21**, *"For since in the wisdom of God the world through its wisdom did not know God, it pleased God through the foolishness of preaching to save those who believe"* (KJV, 2023). The world's wisdom is ultimately insufficient to lead us to a proper knowledge of God.

The Enlightenment, with its emphasis on reason and scientific inquiry, while yielding significant advancements in various fields, also paved the way for a pervasive secular humanism that often positions human autonomy and rationalism as the supreme guides. In this framework, religious texts and divine pronouncements are frequently viewed as relics of a less enlightened age, to be critically examined, dissected, and often dismissed if they do not align with contemporary intellectual paradigms. The Bible, for instance, might be subjected to historical-critical analysis to the point where its divine inspiration and authority are effectively nullified, leaving behind a collection of ancient literature rather than the authoritative Word of God. Satan thrives in this environment, where an overreliance on human intellectual capacity undermines the very notion of divinely revealed truth.

This elevation of human reason often manifests in a subjective approach to truth. Instead of asking, "What does God's Word say?" the question becomes, "What makes sense to me?" or "What feels right?" Personal feelings, intuitions, and individual interpretations are then elevated to the status of divine revelation. This can lead to a highly personalized and fragmented understanding of faith, where each constructs their own version of reality, devoid of any objective, external standard. While proponents might champion this as a form of spiritual liberation or authentic self-discovery, it is, in fact, a dangerous pathway into deception. Consider the modern emphasis on "personal testimony" as a primary source of spiritual authority. While genuine testimonies of God's work in people's lives can be edifying, they can also be manipulated. When a personal experience is presented as having equal weight to, or even superior to, the clear teachings of Scripture, the foundation of faith begins to crumble. A feeling of peace, a compelling dream, or an unusual encounter might be interpreted as direct communication from God, even if it contradicts biblical principles. Satan delights in fostering this disconnect, encouraging individuals to trust their inner voice above the timeless wisdom of God's revealed Word. The danger lies in creating a feedback loop where subjective feelings validate subjective interpretations, leading to an increasingly entrenched, yet ultimately deceptive, worldview.

The Bible itself warns against this temptation. **Proverbs 3:5-6** urges, *"Trust in the LORD with all your heart and do not lean on your own understanding; in all your ways acknowledge him, and he will make straight your paths."* This passage explicitly cautions against relying solely on oneself in matters of spiritual truth. Our understanding is inherently flawed; our hearts are deceitful. True wisdom, the kind that leads to life and righteousness, comes from acknowledging God and submitting to His guidance as revealed in His Word. To lean on our own understanding is to risk being led astray by our own limited perspective. The enemy employs sophisticated philosophical arguments or scientific theories to challenge the validity of divine revelation. These are presented as irrefutable intellectual constructs that logically disprove biblical claims. A deeper examination typically reveals that these arguments are founded on unbiblical presuppositions, such as the denial of the supernatural, the absolute certainty of current scientific understanding (which is constantly evolving), or a materialistic worldview that excludes the possibility of God. When Christians uncritically accept such frameworks, they inadvertently elevate human reason and contemporary thought above the eternal truths of Scripture, effectively discrediting God's Word in favor of man's ever-changing wisdom.

The sufficiency of Scripture is a cornerstone of biblical faith. The Apostle Paul declares in **II Timothy 3:16-17**, *"All Scripture is breathed out by God and profitable for teaching, for reproof, for correction, and for training in righteousness, that the man of God may be complete, equipped for every good work."* This statement underscores the comprehensive nature of God's Word. It is not merely a historical document or a collection of moral guidelines; it is the very breath of God, fully adequate for every aspect of spiritual life and growth. When we supplement Scripture with human philosophies, psychological theories, or subjective experiences as equally valid or even superior sources of truth, we implicitly deny its sufficiency. We suggest that God's revelation is incomplete, and that humanity must fill in the gaps with its own intellectual constructs.

The temptation to intellectualize faith to the exclusion of its relational and volitional aspects is also a significant deception. While theological study and intellectual engagement with Scripture are vital, they can become a substitute for genuine faith and obedience. A person might become adept at debating theological points, quoting biblical verses out of context, and constructing intricate doctrinal systems. Their hearts remain distant from God, and a lack of love and obedience characterizes their lives. This is the equivalent of knowing all the ingredients for a meal but never tasting it, or understanding the mechanics of a car but never driving it. The enemy can foster a form of religious intellectualism that breeds pride and a false sense of security, all while the individual remains spiritually barren.

This **intellectual pride** can lead to a critical and judgmental spirit towards those who may not possess the same level of academic or philosophical understanding. Instead of employing Scripture for teaching, reproof, and correction in a spirit of love and humility, it can be wielded as a weapon to assert intellectual superiority. This misapplication of God's Word further serves Satan's purpose by creating division and alienating people from the truth. True wisdom, as James reminds us, in **James 3:17** is *"first pure, then peaceable, gentle, reasonable, full of mercy and good fruits, impartial and sincere"* (KJV, 2023). This is a wisdom that flows from God, not from man.

The enemy's tactic of exalting human reason also undermines the essential element of faith — trust in the unseen. The Bible defines faith in **Hebrews 11:1** as "the assurance of things hoped for, the conviction of things not seen" (KJV, 2023). When we insist on empirical evidence or logical proof for every aspect of our faith, we discard the very foundation upon which a relationship with God is built. Satan's appeal to the intellect is an attempt to reduce faith to a rationalistic calculation, to eliminate the element of trust and reliance on God's testimony. He wants us to believe only what we can see, touch, or logically deduce, thereby severing our connection to the spiritual realm and the ultimate reality of God's kingdom.

This reliance on human reason can also lead to a distortion of biblical interpretation. When individuals approach the Bible with preconceived philosophical notions or a commitment to a particular worldview that is antithetical to scripture, they will inevitably twist its meaning to fit their agenda. The allegorical or symbolic interpretations that detach passages from their literal or intended historical context are often employed to reconcile biblical narratives with secular viewpoints. For example, the creation account in Genesis might be reinterpreted as a mere metaphor to accommodate evolutionary theory, or the resurrection of Christ, the cornerstone of Christian faith, might be dismissed as a symbolic representation of hope rather than a historical event. This is not the pursuit of truth, but the imposition of a pre-determined conclusion onto the sacred text.

The Christian's response to this pervasive temptation must be a resolute commitment to the supremacy and authority of God's Word. We must cultivate a deep reverence for Scripture, recognizing it not as a human book, but as the divinely inspired, inerrant, and infallible revelation of God Himself. This means approaching the Bible with humility, acknowledging our need for the Holy Spirit's illumination to understand its truths. The Holy Spirit, who inspired the Scriptures, is also our guide into all truth (**John 16:13**). He enables us to discern the authentic from the counterfeit, to understand God's Word in its intended meaning and application.

Therefore, the task of discerning truth requires a diligent and prayerful study of the Bible, coupled with a rejection of any intellectual system or personal feeling that contradicts its clear teachings. It means prioritizing biblical authority over philosophical speculation, emotional experience, or popular opinion. When faced with intellectual challenges or personal doubts, the believer is called to return to the solid ground of God's Word, to anchor their understanding in its timeless truths. This is not to say that reason is to be discarded entirely. Indeed, God has given us minds to be used for His glory. However, our reason must be sanctified, submitted to, and illuminated by the light of divine revelation. The ultimate arbiter of truth is not the human mind, but the Word of the Living God.

By understanding Satan's strategy of exalting human reason above divine authority, we are better equipped to guard ourselves against his deceptions. Our faith is not a blind leap into the irrational, but a reasoned trust based on the reliable testimony of God's Word and the confirmed work of His Spirit in our lives. It is a faith that embraces truth, wherever it is found, but recognizes that ultimate, salvific truth originates from God alone and is faithfully preserved for us in the pages of Scripture. To reject this foundation is to build our spiritual house on the shifting sands of human opinion, a structure that is destined to crumble when the storms of doubt and deception arise. The KJV Bible, as the faithful preservation of God's inspired Word, remains our ultimate defense and guide in this ongoing spiritual warfare.

CHAPTER FOUR:
Recognizing the Spirit of Deception

The adversary's most insidious assaults are not always on the grand scale of societal movements or philosophical systems; often, his most devastating work occurs within the quiet, unseen chambers of the human heart and mind. Having established that deception seeks to undermine divine authority by exalting human reason, we must now examine how this grand strategy unfolds in the intimate landscape of our personal lives. The "spirit of error," as it is often termed, is not merely an abstract concept; it is a palpable force that infiltrates our thoughts, twists our perceptions, and erodes our spiritual vitality from within. Identifying its subtle manifestations in our own lives is not an exercise in morbid self-analysis, but rather a necessary act of spiritual vigilance—a critical precursor to repentance and the restoration of a clear spiritual vision.

One of the most pervasive signs of this personal deception is the insidious creep of rationalization, particularly in relation to one's own sins. We are all prone to err, and the spirit of error excels at presenting our transgressions not as deviations from God's path, but as understandable, even justifiable, responses to circumstances. When a particular sin – be it gossip, impatience, lust, dishonesty, or pride–becomes a recurring pattern. Instead of deep contrition and a fervent desire to change, we find ourselves crafting elaborate justifications; we must be on high alert. The spirit of error whispers, "It is not that bad," "Everyone does it," "I had no choice," or "They deserved it." This is not the honest self-reflection of a healthy conscience; it is the deceptive art of minimizing wrongdoing, of divorcing our actions from their spiritual consequences, and ultimately, of subtly absolving ourselves of responsibility before God. The truly repentant heart, however, acknowledges sin's ugliness and grieves over it, regardless of the external pressures or internal impulses that may have contributed. When the voice of justification begins to drown out the voice of conviction, it is a clear indicator that the spirit of error is at work, seeking to domesticate sin within our lives, making it an acceptable, albeit hidden, companion.

Closely linked to rationalization is the chilling phenomenon of spiritual apathy. When the fire of devotion begins to wane, when the once-cherished disciplines of prayer, Bible study, and corporate worship become burdensome chores rather than life-giving experiences, it is a significant warning sign. The spirit of error is content with a faith that is outwardly functional but inwardly barren. It whispers lies of contentment, suggesting that one's current spiritual state is sufficient, that there is no need for deeper hunger or greater exertion. This spiritual lethargy can manifest in a subtle disinterest in God's Word, a lack of urgency in pursuing righteousness, and a general dullness of spiritual sensitivity. The vibrant, active pursuit of God, characterized by a longing for His presence and a keen awareness of His will, is replaced by a comfortable mediocrity. The enemy thrives in this stagnant spiritual environment, where the soul becomes accustomed to a low level of spiritual nourishment, mistaking mere existence for genuine spiritual life. Apathy is not necessarily a sudden abandonment of faith, but a slow, drifting away, a quieting of the inner voice that calls us toward God.

Another potent manifestation of personal deception lies in a distorted view of God's grace. Grace is a cornerstone of the Christian faith, the unmeritorious, undeserved favor of God extended to sinners. However, the spirit of error can pervert this glorious truth into a license for continued sin. It twists grace from a power for transformation into an excuse for complacency. The lie is subtly woven: "*God's grace is so immense, it covers anything I do, so I do not need to worry too much about my actions.*" This perversion ignores the biblical teaching that God's grace not only forgives but also teaches and empowers us to live righteously (**Titus 2:11-12**). When God's grace is understood as a free pass to indulge in sin without consequence, it reveals a fundamental misunderstanding of God's character and the redemptive purpose of His grace. True grace leads to repentance and a transformed life, not to a perpetuation of the very sins from which it liberates us. The spirit of error seeks to create a cheapened version of grace, one that allows for sin to persist without genuine remorse or the striving for holiness.

A persistent, nagging sense of unease about one's spiritual state, when not accompanied by a genuine desire for repentance, can also be a sign of deception. This is not the Holy Spirit's gentle conviction, which leads to confession and restoration, but a form of spiritual anxiety that the enemy may use to paralyze or discourage. It can manifest as a constant feeling of not being "good enough," or a perpetual worry about one's salvation, often without clear biblical grounds. The spirit of error can magnify minor failings, twisting them into evidence of utter spiritual failure, thereby fostering despair rather than leading to reliance on God's faithfulness. This form of deception seeks to immobilize us with fear, to keep us focused on our own inadequacies rather than on God's all-sufficient power and love. It is a subtle attack on the peace that comes from assurance in Christ, aiming to replace it with a debilitating, unproductive anxiety.

Furthermore, consider the deceptive influence that can arise from an overemphasis on subjective spiritual experiences, detached from the bedrock of Scripture. While the Holy Spirit does speak to us in various ways, including through inner promptings, dreams, or feelings, the spirit of error excels at elevating these subjective impressions above the clear, objective truth of God's Word. When a personal feeling or an unusual experience takes precedence over biblical teaching, even when it contradicts it, it signifies a dangerous departure from a faith grounded in divine revelation. The enemy delights in fostering an environment where personal intuition reigns supreme, thereby creating a fractured and unstable foundation for belief. This can lead to highly individualized, idiosyncratic forms of spirituality that have little grounding in the historical, consistent witness of Scripture. The question shifts from "What does God say?" to "What do I feel or experience?" This is a classic tactic of the spirit of error, seeking to replace God's authoritative voice with the unreliable whispers of human subjectivity.

Another subtle but significant indicator is the perversion of spiritual gifts and the pursuit of spiritual experiences for personal validation or elevation. When gifts like prophecy, tongues, or even fervent prayer become more about self-promotion, attracting attention, or establishing spiritual superiority than about building up the body of Christ and glorifying God, the spirit of error is likely at play. This can foster a critical, judgmental attitude towards fellow believers who may not exhibit the same outward manifestations of spirituality. The enemy thrives on division and pride, and a misapplication of spiritual gifts is a potent tool for achieving both. True spiritual maturity is marked by humility, love, and a servant's heart, not by a display of charismatic prowess that isolates or diminishes others. When the pursuit of spiritual phenomena becomes an end in itself, or a means to personal exaltation, it is a sign that the spirit of error has distorted the true purpose of spiritual gifting.

The temptation to equate intellectual assent with genuine faith is another area where the spirit of error operates effectively within personal lives. One can become adept at articulating theological doctrines, quoting Scripture with precision, and engaging in sophisticated spiritual discourse, all while lacking a heart transformed by God's love and a life submitted to His will. This is a form of spiritual intellectualism that can breed pride and a false sense of security. The enemy can foster a Christianity that is rich in orthodoxy but impoverished in orthopraxy – correct belief without correct practice. The danger lies in mistaking knowledge for transformation, in believing that understanding the map is equivalent to walking the journey. True faith involves a relational commitment, a yielding of the will, and a life lived in obedience, not merely an intellectual agreement with a set of propositions. When our faith is primarily an intellectual exercise, devoid of genuine heart-transformation, it has been subtly compromised by deception.

The enemy can promote a skewed understanding of freedom in Christ, framing it as an excuse to disregard or minimize biblical guidelines and moral standards. While believers are indeed liberated from the bondage of sin and the Mosaic Law, this freedom is not a license for unbridled license. The spirit of error whispers that the old covenant rules are now irrelevant, or that the New Testament offers a vague, unfettered liberty that allows for a broad range of behaviors. This distortion ignores the fundamental principle that Christian freedom is expressed through love and is exercised in service to God and others. When we interpret freedom in Christ as permission to live according to our own desires, even when those desires contradict the clear teachings of Scripture, we are falling prey to a sophisticated deception. The apostle Paul in **Galatians 5:13** warned against this very temptation, stating, *"For you were called to freedom, brothers. Only do not use your freedom as an opportunity for the flesh, but through love serve one another"* (KJV, 2023).

A subtle indicator can also be found in the way we handle disappointment and adversity. When challenges arise, the spirit of error can whisper doubts about God's goodness, His sovereignty, or His promises. It can encourage bitterness, resentment, or a questioning of God's faithfulness when circumstances do not align with our expectations. Instead of clinging to God's character and trusting in His unfailing love, we may be tempted to accuse Him, to withdraw from Him, or to seek solace in earthly solutions that bypass His will. This form of deception seeks to erode our trust in God's plan, especially during difficult times, by suggesting that He is either incapable or unwilling to work for our good. A healthy, discerning faith, however, recognizes that God's purposes are not always immediately apparent and that His faithfulness remains constant even in the midst of trials.

Finally, consider the subtle erosion of discernment regarding media, entertainment, and cultural influences. In our information-saturated world, the spirit of error can present worldly values, philosophies, and lifestyles as harmless or even beneficial to our spiritual lives. When we uncritically consume content that promotes immorality, celebrates sin, or subtly undermines biblical truth, we are allowing deceptive influences to seep into our thinking and shape our worldview. The enemy does not always present outright falsehoods; often, he promotes half-truths, subtle distortions, or the normalization of what God calls sin. This can lead to a gradual desensitization to ungodliness and a compromised understanding of biblical morality. A discerning believer, guided by the Spirit and grounded in Scripture, will be cautious about what they allow to influence their minds and hearts, recognizing that not all that is popular or entertaining is also pure or righteous.

Recognizing these internal indicators—the rationalization of sin, spiritual apathy, a distorted view of grace, a nagging sense of unease, an overemphasis on subjective experience, the misuse of spiritual gifts, intellectual pride without transformed living, a perversion of Christian freedom, a questioning of God's faithfulness in adversity, and a lack of discernment in cultural engagement—is the vital first step in dismantling the spirit of error in our personal lives. These are not signs of inherent wickedness, but indicators of a spiritual battle that requires conscious engagement. The Holy Spirit is our ultimate guide in this discernment process, convicting us of sin and leading us into all truth. By prayerfully examining our hearts and minds in light of God's Word, we can identify these subtle deceptions and, through repentance and reliance on God's power, walk in the freedom and clarity that He offers.

The insidious nature of deception, as we have explored in its personal manifestations, does not confine itself solely to the individual believer. Its ambition is far greater, aiming to corrupt the very fabric of the Christian community. Within church bodies, the spirit of error can infiltrate doctrine, practice, and the delicate dynamics of communal life, often with devastating consequences for the spiritual well-being of the flock. Identifying these broader, communal signs is not an optional exercise for the passive observer but a vital responsibility for every member, particularly for those entrusted with leadership, ensuring the church remains a steadfast beacon of truth in a world saturated with confusion.

One of the most prevalent signs of communal deception is an overemphasis on sensationalism and novelty at the expense of foundational biblical truths. The enemy is adept at crafting experiences and teachings that capture attention, stir emotions, and create a buzz, often masking a departure from the unchanging Word of God. This can manifest in various ways: a fascination with the bizarre or extraordinary, a constant pursuit of new revelations or prophetic utterances that supersede or contradict established biblical teaching, or a focus on outward displays of spiritual power that lack the substance of biblical character and fruit. When a church body becomes more captivated by the extraordinary, the emotional, or the latest spiritual trend than by the unadulterated preaching of the Gospel, the faithful exposition of Scripture, and the cultivation of godly character, it signals a significant drift. The spirit of error excels at making the familiar seem dull and the outlandish seem profound, thereby subtly shifting the church's focus away from the enduring power of the cross and the wisdom of God's revealed Word. This can lead to a superficial faith, easily swayed by fleeting trends and lacking the deep roots necessary to withstand doctrinal storms.

A closely related indicator is a discernible drift from core biblical tenets. Deception rarely announces itself with a blatant rejection of fundamental doctrines. Instead, it operates through a gradual erosion, a subtle reinterpretation, or a quiet omission of essential truths. This can be seen in teachings that downplay the sovereignty of God, dilute the doctrine of salvation by grace alone through faith alone, minimize the reality of sin and the necessity of repentance, or redefine biblical morality in accordance with prevailing cultural norms. When a church's teaching becomes increasingly vague on matters of sin, judgment, and the exclusivity of Christ, or when it begins to embrace ideologies that are clearly at odds with biblical ethics, it is a warning sign. The spirit of error often seeks to make Christianity more palatable to the world by excising the challenging and counter-cultural aspects of the faith. This can result in a watered-down Gospel, a faith that offers comfort without challenge, and a community that struggles to discern truth from falsehood because its doctrinal foundation has been compromised. The pursuit of relevance can become a siren song, luring the church away from the timeless truths that equip it for its mission.

The phenomenon of unhealthy spiritual experiences also serves as a significant marker of deception within a church community. While the Holy Spirit is indeed active in bringing conviction, comfort, and empowerment, the spirit of error can distort these genuine workings into something sensationalized, manipulative, or even demonic. This might include manifestations that are unbiblical or demonstrably false, such as exaggerated emotional outbursts presented as divine encounters, claims of receiving secret knowledge or power apart from Scripture, or a pervasive emphasis on ecstatic experiences that lead to a neglect of daily discipleship and ethical living. When spiritual experiences are divorced from the fruit of the Spirit as described in **Galatians 5:22-23**—love, joy, peace, patience, kindness, goodness, faithfulness, gentleness, and self-control—or when they become the primary metric of spiritual vitality, the church is vulnerable. The enemy can mimic spiritual phenomena to deceive, leading believers into error and diverting them from the path of true spiritual growth. A discerning community will test all experiences by the plumb line of Scripture, prioritizing character and obedience over sensational displays.

Furthermore, the elevation of charismatic personalities over the authority of Scripture is a dangerous symptom of deception within church life. When a leader, due to their captivating speaking style, apparent spiritual gifts, or perceived success, gains a level of authority that places them above or on par with the clear teaching of the Bible, the church is treading on perilous ground. The spirit of error loves to establish figures who can bypass or reinterpret Scripture according to their own will or agenda. This can lead to doctrines being shaped by the pronouncements of a particular leader, rather than through careful and faithful exegesis of God's Word. Such personality-driven ministries often foster an environment where questioning the leader is seen as asking God, thereby stifling critical thought and doctrinal integrity. Loyalty to a person can supersede loyalty to Christ and His infallible Word, creating a cult of personality rather than a Christ-centered community. The church's ultimate authority rests in the inspired and authoritative Word of God, not in the pronouncements of any human leader, however gifted or popular they may be.

Unhealthy expectations regarding prosperity and personal well-being can also indicate a deceptive trajectory within a church. The so-called "prosperity gospel," which teaches that God desires all believers to be wealthy and healthy in this life and that faith is a means to unlock these blessings, is a prime example of this deceptive deviation. While God is indeed generous and His people are called to walk in faith, this distorted teaching often shifts the focus from God's glory and the eternal kingdom to material gain and personal comfort. It can lead to a transactional view of faith, where God is seen as a divine ATM whose blessings are contingent upon our giving or our level of faith. Such teachings can leave believers disillusioned and spiritually bankrupt when adversity strikes or their material needs are not met, undermining their trust in God's faithfulness beyond earthly circumstances. The true Gospel calls believers to a life of discipleship that often involves suffering and self-denial for the sake of Christ and His kingdom, not merely the pursuit of personal comfort and affluence.

A critical indicator of communal deception is a stifling of dissent or a prohibitive atmosphere towards questioning or critical examination of teachings and practices. In a truly healthy church, there should be an open invitation for members to engage with Scripture, ask clarifying questions, and voice concerns in a respectful manner, knowing that they intend to seek truth. When a church body creates an environment where such questioning is met with immediate rebuke, labeled as a lack of faith, or viewed as an act of rebellion, it suggests that the leadership may be guarding against scrutiny because their teachings are not fully aligned with God's Word. The spirit of error thrives in an environment of unquestioning obedience to human authority, as it prevents the community from discerning and rejecting deceptive influences. A church that fears questions rather than embracing them is likely hiding something, or perhaps, more tragically, is itself deceived.

Another significant sign is a warped understanding of spiritual warfare and the enemy's tactics. While the Bible clearly teaches that believers are engaged in spiritual warfare, the spirit of error can distort this truth by creating an unhealthy obsession with demonic forces, attributing every minor difficulty or personal failing to direct demonic influence. This can lead to a focus on exorcisms, deliverance ministries, or an excessive engagement with spiritual warfare terminology that eclipses the core message of the Gospel and the power of God's grace. Conversely, deception can also manifest as a denial or minimization of the reality of Satan and his influence, rendering the church ill-equipped to recognize and resist his subtle, pervasive strategies. A balanced, biblical understanding of spiritual warfare involves identifying both the pervasive, subtle deceptions and the ultimate victory of Christ, equipping believers to stand firm in God's strength, rather than being paralyzed by fear or consumed by an unhealthy fixation on the enemy.

The erosion of biblical disciplines within the corporate life of the church can also signal a move towards deception. This is not merely about a decline in attendance at Bible studies or prayer meetings, though that can be a symptom. It is about a subtle shift in emphasis, where these disciplines are no longer seen as vital means of grace and growth in Christ, but as optional extras or even relics of a bygone era. When preaching becomes more of an inspirational talk than an exposition of Scripture, when corporate prayer devolves into a superficial sharing of requests without genuine dependence on God, and when discipleship is reduced to outward conformity rather than inner transformation, the spirit of error is likely at work. It seeks to make faith comfortable and effortless, severing the connection between spiritual vitality and the diligent, faithful practice of biblical disciplines that nourish and strengthen the soul.

Furthermore, an unhealthy emphasis on unity at the expense of truth is a hallmark of deceptive movements. While Christian unity is a precious goal and a command from Scripture, it is not to be pursued by compromising biblical doctrine or condoning unbiblical practices. The spirit of error can promote a superficial unity, one that seeks to avoid any form of doctrinal disagreement or correction, often by appealing to love and acceptance while implicitly demanding silence on matters of truth. This can lead to a situation where false teachers are tolerated, or even celebrated, for fear of creating division. True unity, however, is rooted in shared truth and love for Christ, and it is strengthened through honest dialogue and, when necessary, corrective discipline exercised in love. A church that sacrifices truth on the altar of an enforced, superficial unity is ultimately undermining the very foundation of its identity and mission.

The manipulation of biblical texts to support pre-existing agendas or personal desires is another profound sign of deception that can permeate a church. This involves taking verses out of context, misinterpreting passages to fit a modern ideology, or selectively emphasizing certain scriptures while ignoring others that contradict the desired outcome. When biblical interpretation becomes driven by a desire to affirm what is already believed or wanted, rather than by a genuine attempt to understand what God is revealing, the spirit of error has gained a foothold. This can lead to a theology that is tailored to human preferences, creating a faith that is comfortable and affirming but ultimately devoid of the transformative power of God's unadulterated truth. The faithful church, conversely, approaches Scripture with humility, seeking to be conformed to its message, rather than reshaping it according to its own image.

A community that exhibits a pervasive spirit of judgment and self-righteousness, particularly directed towards those outside its immediate circle or towards dissenting voices within, can also be a manifestation of deception. While the church is called to uphold biblical standards and to speak truth in love, a spirit of harsh judgment, condemnation, and an exclusive claim to possess all truth, without a corresponding demonstration of Christ-like love and humility, is not of God. The enemy often uses a distorted sense of zeal to breed pride and isolation, creating a spiritual fortress rather than an open door of invitation. When a church becomes known more for its pronouncements of judgment than for its expressions of grace and compassion, and when its members exhibit an attitude of superiority towards other believers or those yet to embrace the faith, it is a strong indicator that the spirit of error may be at work, twisting God's truth into a weapon of self-exaltation.

The discipleship models that emerge within a church can also reveal deceptive influences. Suppose discipleship focuses primarily on outward behaviors and conformity to rules, without addressing the inner disposition of the heart and the transformative work of the Holy Spirit. In that case, it can become a form of legalism that is both deceptive and soul-crushing. Conversely, suppose discipleship minimizes the importance of godly character and obedience, reducing it to a passive reception of grace that requires no effort or surrender. In that case, it can lead to a form of antinomianism that is equally deceptive. A healthy discipleship model, rooted in Scripture, emphasizes the empowering grace of God that enables believers to live lives of increasing holiness and obedience, fostering a deep intimacy with Christ that is expressed through both faith and works. When the emphasis shifts to mere participation in activities or the adoption of a particular subculture rather than the profound, ongoing transformation of the individual, deception may be present.

Finally, a recurring pattern of internal conflict, disunity, and interpersonal strife that remains unresolved, despite attempts to address it, can be a significant indicator of a deceptive influence at work. While disagreements are inevitable in any human community, a persistent inability to foster reconciliation, a tendency for conflicts to fester and escalate, and a lack of demonstrable progress in applying biblical principles of forgiveness and unity can indicate a deeper issue. The spirit of error thrives on division, sowing discord, and creating factions that weaken the body of Christ. When a church struggles to maintain a healthy, unified fellowship, characterized by mutual love, respect, and a commitment to resolving differences according to biblical principles, it may be an environment where deceptive forces are actively undermining its spiritual cohesion and effectiveness. The ongoing presence of unresolved strife can be a clear signal that the adversary is successfully at work, fragmenting the community and hindering its witness to the world.

Recognizing these signs within church communities—the overemphasis on sensationalism, the drift from core biblical tenets, unhealthy spiritual experiences, the elevation of personality over Scripture, warped views on prosperity, the stifling of dissent, distorted understandings of spiritual warfare, the erosion of biblical disciplines, unity at the expense of truth, manipulative biblical interpretation, judgmentalism, flawed discipleship models, and unresolved internal conflict—is crucial. These are not indicators of inherent sinfulness in the members, but rather signals of a spiritual battle that requires diligent prayer, careful discernment, and a steadfast commitment to the unchanging truth of God's Word. By being vigilant and equipped with the wisdom that comes from above, the church can safeguard itself against deception, remaining a pure and powerful witness to the saving grace of Jesus Christ.

The internal landscape of the human spirit often serves as a crucial, albeit subtle, indicator in discerning truth from error. Deception, by its very nature, is a disruptive force, an intruder that seeks to unsettle the spiritual equilibrium of a believer. When one encounters teachings or experiences that originate from the spirit of falsehood, there is often a discernible internal dissonance —a nagging sense of unease that resists easy categorization. This is not the righteous conviction that arises from encountering God's holiness, which can be both awe-inspiring and convicting, but rather a disquiet that feels more like internal friction. It is a sense of things not quite fitting, of a spiritual disharmony that can manifest as anxiety, confusion, or a persistent lack of settled conviction. The smooth and persuasive language of deception can often mask an underlying spiritual emptiness or a subtle warping of truth that the discerning spirit picks up on. It might be the feeling that a teaching, while perhaps sounding good on the surface, leaves one feeling spiritually parched, or worse, subtly agitated. This inner turbulence can serve as an alarm bell, a quiet whisper from the Holy Spirit, urging caution and a deeper examination of one's thoughts and actions.

Biblical accounts offer poignant illustrations of this principle. Consider the reaction of the Ephesians to certain teachings that, while presented with oratorical flair, lacked the solid foundation of apostolic truth. Paul's instruction in Ephesians 4:14 speaks of being "no longer children, tossed to and fro by the waves and carried about by every wind of doctrine, by human cunning, by craftiness in deceitful scheming." The imagery here is of being unsettled, buffeted, and unable to find stable ground—a stark contrast to the steadfastness that genuine truth provides. This lack of stability, this feeling of being tossed about, is a spiritual symptom that indicates a departure from the anchoring truth of the Gospel. Similarly, when

Jesus spoke about false prophets, He warned His followers to beware of them, implying that their deceptive nature would be discernible, at least to those with spiritual discernment. The internal "feeling" associated with deception is rarely one of profound peace; it is more often characterized by a subtle but persistent disquiet, a sense that the spiritual waters are troubled.

In stark contrast, the genuine work of the Holy Spirit in confirming biblical truth brings an unparalleled sense of peace and settled assurance. This peace is not merely an absence of conflict or a fleeting emotional high; it is a deep, abiding calm that resonates from the core of one's being. When the Holy Spirit illuminates Scripture, or when a teaching aligns perfectly with the revealed Word of God, there is a profound sense of rightness, a spiritual "click" that confirms its authenticity. This is the peace that the Apostle Paul describes in **Philippians 4:7**: *"and the peace of God, which surpasses all understanding, will guard your hearts and your minds in Christ Jesus."* (KJV, 2023). This is a peace that transcends intellectual agreement; it is a spiritual confirmation that settles the soul. It is the feeling of coming home, of finding a truth that resonates with the very depths of one's renewed spirit.

The Holy Spirit acts as the ultimate spiritual barometer. He does not coerce but rather guides, illuminating the truth and bringing a settled conviction. When we encounter genuine biblical teaching, the Spirit bears witness with our spirit, affirming its divine origin. A chaotic emotional upheaval does not usually accompany this affirmation, but by a quiet certainty, a growing assurance that strengthens our faith. It is like the steady hum of a well-tuned instrument, producing a harmonious resonance within. This internal confirmation provides a stable foundation, enabling believers to stand firm against the shifting winds of false doctrine. It is a peace that provides clarity amidst confusion, strength amidst weakness, and unwavering conviction in the face of doubt. This inner peace is a divine endorsement, a testament to the life-giving and life-affirming nature of God's truth.

The contrast between the unsettling nature of deception and the peace that comes with truth is evident in various contexts. For instance, consider individuals who are drawn to teachings that promise immediate worldly success or secret spiritual knowledge. Often, while initially captivated by the allure of such promises, they may find themselves plagued by internal anxiety, a fear of failure, or a subtle pressure to perform. The focus shifts from God's sovereignty and grace to human effort and the manipulation of spiritual forces for personal gain. This can lead to a spiritual precariousness, where their confidence is tied to outward results rather than to an inward trust in God. The peace that such teachings offer is often superficial, brittle, and dependent on continued success, rather than being rooted in the unchanging character of God.

Conversely, those who engage with biblical teachings that emphasize God's grace, the pursuit of holiness, and the call to self-denial for Christ's sake, even when these teachings are challenging, often report a deep sense of inner peace and purpose. They may face external difficulties or internal struggles, but their core identity and hope remain anchored in Christ. The Holy Spirit's work is to confirm the truth of God's love and faithfulness, bringing a steady assurance that can sustain them through trials. This peace is not the absence of tribulation, but a deep-seated contentment that transcends circumstances, a quiet confidence that God is at work and that His promises are sure. It is a peace that guards the heart and mind, a sanctuary amidst life's storms.

The critical distinction lies in the source and the effect. Deception, originating from a spiritual adversary, aims to destabilize, to create confusion, and to lead away from God ultimately. Its internal "feeling" is therefore one of unease, of spiritual unrest, even if an outward show of excitement or power masks it. Truth, on the other hand, originating from God, aims to edify, to confirm, and to draw us closer to Him. Its internal confirmation is a profound peace, a settled assurance that strengthens and sanctifies. This inner resonance serves as a vital compass for navigating the complex spiritual landscape, guiding believers toward the steadfast truth that liberates and sustains. It is a discerning principle that, when honed through prayer and diligent study of Scripture, equips the faithful to recognize the distinct fingerprints of the divine upon genuine revelation.

The enduring adage, "*By their fruits you will know them*," originating from Jesus Himself in the Gospel of **Matthew 7:16-20**, offers a profound and practical lens through which to evaluate the authenticity of spiritual claims and movements. This principle transcends mere intellectual assent or charismatic appeal; it directs our attention to the tangible, observable results that flow from a particular teaching, ministry, or spiritual leader. While the internal resonance of peace, as previously discussed, serves as a crucial inner barometer, the test of fruit provides an external, verifiable confirmation—or refutation—of spiritual genuineness. Deception, despite its alluring style, presents itself as coming from God, but ultimately reveals its true nature by the quality and character of the "fruit" it produces in the lives of individuals and in the broader community of faith.

The nature of this fruit is multifaceted, encompassing not only individual transformation but also the relational dynamics and the ethical framework that emerge from a spiritual source. When we examine the results, we are looking for evidence of God's character being displayed and cultivated. The Apostle Paul, in his letter to the **Galatians 5:22-23**, enumerates the "fruit of the Spirit" as "love, joy, peace, patience, kindness, goodness, faithfulness, gentleness, and self-control." These are not merely abstract virtues; they are demonstrable qualities that should, in some measure, be evident in the lives of those who are genuinely walking with God and in alignment with His truth. Conversely, teachings or movements rooted in deception often yield a different harvest—one characterized by spiritual immaturity, relational discord, moral compromise, and an overall departure from the foundational tenets of Christian doctrine and practice.

One of the most telling indicators of deceptive spiritual influence is the fostering of **division**. True spiritual unity, while not necessarily uniformity of thought or expression on every minor issue, is marked by a binding love that overcomes differences. Deception, however, often thrives on creating schisms. It may manifest as an "us versus them" mentality, where those who adopt the new teaching are perceived as enlightened or superior. At the same time, those who adhere to established biblical truths are dismissed as unenlightened, legalistic, or even spiritually compromised. This creates an unhealthy separation within the body of Christ, undermining the very unity that Christ prayed for in **John 17**. Such divisiveness is often accompanied by judgmentalism, harsh criticism of dissenting views, and an unwillingness to engage in gracious dialogue. The fruit of division is inherently contrary to the fruit of love and gentleness that characterizes the Spirit's work. Consider, for instance, movements that isolate their followers from their families, former friends, or broader Christian communities, branding such connections as spiritual hindrances. While healthy boundaries are essential, complete estrangement, fueled by a sense of exclusive spiritual insight, is a red flag, a distinctly ungodly fruit.

Another significant fruit of deception is the cultivation of **pride**. True spirituality is marked by humility—a recognition of one's dependence on God and an acknowledgment of one's own sinfulness and limitations. Deceptive teachings, however, often appeal to the ego, promising special knowledge, elevated spiritual status, or unique insights that set the adherents apart from the masses. This can foster an arrogance, a sense of spiritual elitism, and a dismissiveness toward those who do not share their views. Leaders who promote such teachings often exhibit an unshakeable self-confidence, an unwillingness to admit error, and a demand for unquestioning loyalty. The "fruit" here is a spiritual puffiness, an inflated sense of self-importance that is antithetical to the self-emptying nature of Christ. This pride can manifest in boasting about spiritual experiences, achievements, or insights, rather than giving glory to God. It creates an environment where constructive criticism is seen as an attack and where accountability is rejected. The fruit of pride is a poison that corrodes the spiritual life, leading to a distorted view of oneself and one's relationship with God and others.

Furthermore, deception invariably leads to a **departure from or a distortion of biblical morality**. While true spiritual transformation involves a deepening commitment to righteousness and holiness, deceptive influences often subtly or overtly permit or encourage behaviors that are contrary to God's Word. This can range from a loosening of ethical standards in personal conduct to the justification of unbiblical practices in the name of spiritual advancement or a redefinition of biblical terms. For example, teachings that prioritize personal fulfillment or subjective experience over objective biblical commands, or those that seek to legitimize behaviors condemned by Scripture through creative reinterpretations, are bearing the fruit of moral compromise. The line between what is biblically acceptable and unacceptable becomes blurred, often catering to the desires of the flesh rather than the call to deny oneself and follow Christ. This fruit is particularly insidious because it can appear harmless to those who are not firmly rooted in biblical truth, allowing a slow drift away from established ethical moorings. It is a departure from the holiness that God calls us to, a substitution of His standards with man-made rationalizations.

Conversely, the genuine work of the Holy Spirit, as manifested in actual biblical teaching and authentic spiritual leadership, yields a predictable and positive harvest. The first and most significant fruit is **righteousness**. This is not merely the absence of sin but the active pursuit of God's will, a growing conformity to the character of Christ, and a life lived in obedience to Scripture. Those under the influence of accurate spiritual guidance will examine their lives, repent of sin, and seek to live lives that honor God. The focus is on cultivating a heart that loves God, desires to please Him, and is committed to justice and compassion toward others. Another hallmark of true spiritual influence is the cultivation of **love**. This is not merely a fleeting emotional affection but a deep, abiding, and active love for God and for others, including those who may differ from us. It is a love that is patient, kind, and seeks the best interests of the other person, even at personal cost.

Where actual spiritual influence is at work, relationships are characterized by grace, forgiveness, and mutual edification. Division and judgmentalism are replaced by a spirit of unity and acceptance, rooted in the shared identity believers have in Christ. This love extends beyond the immediate circle of believers to encompass the wider community and even those who are hostile or indifferent. It is the love that the world will recognize as evidence of Christ's presence in His followers. The fruit of **unity** is also a clear indicator of genuine spiritual work. While disagreements may arise on secondary matters, the core of a unified community lies in the shared commitment to the fundamental truths of the Gospel and the mutual respect and love that bind believers together. Teachings that foster genuine unity will lead to stronger, healthier relationships within the church and a shared purpose in ministry. Instead of creating schisms, they build bridges, encouraging collaboration and mutual support. This unity is not forced or artificial; it is a natural outgrowth of a shared life in Christ, where the Holy Spirit is binding people together in love and truth. It fosters a sense of belonging and shared responsibility, strengthening the collective witness of the church to the world.

Moreover, actual spiritual influence leads to **spiritual maturity**. This is a process of growth and deepening understanding, marked by a greater capacity to discern truth from error, a more robust faith, and an increased ability to apply biblical principles to all areas of life. Followers of genuinely spiritual teachings will be encouraged to engage in diligent study of Scripture, prayerful reflection, and thoughtful application of God's Word. They will be equipped to think critically about spiritual matters and to resist deceptive influences. This maturity is evidenced by a stable faith, a balanced perspective, and a consistent walk with God, rather than being swayed by every new trend or teaching. The fruit of maturity is a resilient faith that can withstand the storms of life and continue to grow in grace and knowledge.

When evaluating the fruit, it is crucial to consider the long-term impact, not just the initial excitement or emotional high. Deception can often generate a temporary surge of enthusiasm or a sense of immediate spiritual attainment, but this is usually unsustainable and ultimately leads to spiritual burnout or disillusionment. Actual spiritual growth, on the other hand, is a process that unfolds over time, characterized by steady progress, resilience in the face of challenges, and a deepening commitment to God's truth. The fruit of righteousness, love, unity, and maturity are not fleeting phenomena; they are the enduring results of a life truly transformed by the Holy Spirit.

In practice, this means we must be diligent in observing the outcomes of any teaching or spiritual movement we encounter. Are individuals becoming more Christlike, or more self-centered? Is there an increase in love and unity, or in division and judgmentalism? Are lives being transformed by righteousness and humility, or are pride and moral compromise creeping in? The test of fruit is an ongoing assessment, a constant application of Christ's directive to look beyond outward appearances and to discern the true spiritual character by its tangible results. It requires careful observation, biblical discernment, and a willingness to confront uncomfortable truths when the fruit does not align with the truth of God's Word. It is a vital tool in protecting ourselves and the broader Christian community from the inroads of deceptive spiritual forces. By diligently applying this principle, we can navigate the complexities of the spiritual landscape with greater confidence, discerning the genuine work of God from the counterfeit.

The preceding discussion has laid the groundwork for understanding the deceptive nature of spiritual error, highlighting how "by their fruits you will know them." This vital principle directs our attention to observable outcomes—the tangible results in individuals and communities. However, to effectively discern these fruits, we require an unassailable standard, a plumb line against which all spiritual claims must be measured. For the discerning Christian, this standard is, and must always be, the Holy Scripture is not merely an ancient text; it is considered by many to be the most faithful

English translation of the original Hebrew and Greek manuscripts, preserving the purity of God's revealed Word with remarkable clarity and authority.

To truly recognize the spirit of deception, one must engage in a rigorous comparison between external teachings and the unwavering truth found within the Bible. This is not an exercise in textual criticism for the sake of academic debate, but a vital spiritual discipline for safeguarding the soul. When a new doctrine emerges, a charismatic leader speaks with compelling rhetoric, or a seemingly miraculous experience is recounted, the immediate impulse should be to turn to the pages of Scripture for confirmation or refutation. Are the claims made consistent with what the Bible unequivocally teaches? Does the message align with the character and nature of God as revealed throughout the Bible? Suppose there is even a subtle deviation, a reinterpretation of established biblical truths, or the introduction of concepts not found within its sacred pages. In that case, it is a signal that demands scrutiny. Deceptive spirits are subtle; they do not always present outright blasphemy. Often, they weave their falsehoods by twisting or adding to God's Word, creating a narrative that sounds plausible on the surface but crumbles under the weight of biblical scrutiny.

Consider the teaching on salvation. The Bible is unequivocally clear on the foundational elements: salvation is by grace through faith in Jesus Christ, His atoning sacrifice, and His resurrection (Ephesians 2:8-9). It emphasizes repentance from sin and the new birth through the Holy Spirit (John 3:3-7). Now, imagine an external teaching that suggests salvation can be achieved through good works alone, or through adherence to a particular ritual not ordained by Scripture, or perhaps through a secret knowledge imparted only to a select few.

The comparison extends to the ethical and moral teachings of Scripture. The Bible consistently upholds a standard of holiness and righteousness that is rooted in God's unchanging character. It speaks of the importance of sexual purity, honesty in all dealings, love for one's neighbor, and the rejection of all forms of idolatry and occult practices. When external teachings begin to redefine these concepts, rationalize sinful behavior, or incorporate practices that the Bible condemns, the discerning believer can readily identify the deviation. For example, the Bible's explicit prohibitions against spiritualism, fortune-telling, and consulting mediums (**Deuteronomy 18:10-12**) stand as a stark contrast to any teaching that encourages engagement with such practices, even if framed as harmless or beneficial. The steadfast emphasis on the sanctity of marriage, as outlined in passages such as Genesis 2:24 and reflected in Jesus' teachings, would also expose any teaching that seeks to redefine or undermine this divine institution. When we engage in this comparative analysis, we are not engaging in a subjective exercise of personal preference. We are adhering to a divine mandate to test all things and hold fast to that which is good (**I Thessalonians 5:21**).

In essence, the Bible is not just a book; it is a divinely inspired blueprint for spiritual truth. When presented with any teaching, prophecy, or spiritual experience, the command to compare it against the Bible is a direct application of the wisdom given to us by God. This comparison serves as our primary tool for discernment, enabling us to distinguish between the genuine and the counterfeit. It requires diligence, humility, and a commitment to God's Word above all else. By consistently holding external teachings up to the unadulterated light of the Bible, we equip ourselves to recognize and resist the spirit of deception, remaining steadfast in the truth that sets us free. This ongoing process of comparison is not merely an intellectual exercise; it is a vital act of spiritual warfare, ensuring that our faith remains anchored in the unshakeable foundation of God's unchanging Word.

La Wanda Blackmon

CHAPTER FIVE:

Strategies for Liberation from Deception

The journey away from the grip of deception is not solely an external battle against false teachings; it is, in fact, a profoundly internal one, requiring a willingness to confront our own spiritual vulnerabilities. At the very heart of this liberation lies the transformative power of repentance and confession. These are not mere religious formalities but foundational acts that dismantle the hold of falsehood and pave the way for genuine spiritual freedom. When we find ourselves entangled in deceptive influences, acknowledging our susceptibility and actively confessing our complicity are the essential first steps toward breaking free and reorienting ourselves toward God's unwavering truth.

Repentance, in its deepest biblical sense, is a profound turning – a radical reorientation of the heart, mind, and will. It signifies a turning *away* from something – in this context, from error, deceit, and anything that deviates from God's truth – and a turning *towards* God and His revealed will. This is not a superficial regret for being deceived, but a deep sorrow over sin and a conscious decision to align oneself with righteousness. The urgency of repentance becomes particularly apparent when we realize how easily we can be swayed by persuasive voices, sophisticated arguments, or even compelling spiritual experiences that lack biblical grounding. The Apostle Paul urged believers in Corinth, "Examine yourselves, whether ye be in the faith; prove your own selves. Know ye not your own selves, how that Jesus Christ is in you, except ye be reprobates?" (**II Corinthians 13:5**). This exhortation highlights a critical responsibility we have to regularly assess our spiritual state, ensuring our foundations are firmly established in truth. When we discover that we have strayed, perhaps by embracing doctrines contrary to Scripture or by participating in practices that dishonor God, repentance is the necessary corrective.

The act of confession is intimately linked with repentance. Confession is the verbal or articulated acknowledgment of our failings and transgressions before God, and sometimes, before others. It is a raw, honest admission of how we have erred, how we have allowed ourselves to be led astray, and where we may have even contributed to the deception. This is not about self-flagellation, but about sincere humility and a recognition of our desperate need for God's mercy and grace. When we confess our susceptibility to deception, we are acknowledging that our discernment faculties can be dulled, our spiritual senses impaired, and our hearts can be captivated by things that are not of God. This admission opens the door for divine intervention.

In the Old Testament, the Israelites' confession of their sins was a recurring and essential element in their covenant relationship with God, often preceding periods of revival and restoration. Similarly, in the New Testament, the early church practiced confession, as seen in passages like **I John 1:9**: "*If we confess our sins, he is faithful and just to forgive us our sins, and to cleanse us from all unrighteousness.*" This verse is powerful because it assures us that confession is met with God's faithfulness to forgive and cleanse, preparing us for a renewed walk in truth.

The process of turning from deception involves a conscious decision to reject the false narratives and embrace the authentic. This turning is fueled by repentance, which acts as a spiritual pivot. It is like a ship changing course to avoid a treacherous reef; the captain, upon realizing the danger, steers the vessel away from destruction and back towards safe waters. When we recognize the deceptive nature of specific teachings or influences, repentance is the act of deliberately steering our spiritual lives away from that danger. This turning requires a courageous re-evaluation of our beliefs and practices. It might mean setting aside cherished ideas that have been proven false, distancing ourselves from associations that perpetuate error, or challenging ingrained patterns of thought that have allowed deception to take root.

Confession, in this context, is the articulation of this turning. It is the spoken or internalized declaration: "I have been deceived. I have believed or followed that which is not of God. I confess this to You, Lord, and I choose to turn away from it." This act of verbalizing our admission solidifies our resolve and makes us accountable, both to God and to ourselves. It is akin to a patient admitting to a doctor that they have been ingesting a harmful substance; only through such an admission can the healing process begin. Likewise, confessing our part in embracing deception allows God to start the work of restoring our spiritual discernment and cleansing our minds from the residue of falsehood. The Bible speaks of the tongue's power, and when wielded in confession, it becomes an instrument of liberation.

Consider the example of individuals who have fallen prey to cultic teachings or manipulative spiritual movements. Often, their liberation begins with a moment of profound realization, a shattering of the carefully constructed illusion. This realization is then followed by a confession of their complicity – acknowledging that they allowed themselves to be drawn in, that they perhaps ignored warning signs, or that they placed their trust unwisely. This confession, coupled with a genuine repentance – a turning away from the false doctrines and practices – is what truly sets them free. Without this internal work, being presented with factual counter-evidence may not be enough. The emotional and psychological grip of deception is powerful, and it is the inward turning of repentance and the honest articulation of confession that breaks that grip.

Furthermore, repentance and confession are not one-time events but ongoing disciplines. The spiritual journey is one of continuous growth and sanctification, and there will undoubtedly be moments where our discernment may falter or where subtle forms of deception attempt to reassert themselves. Therefore, maintaining a posture of humble repentance and readiness to confess is crucial. This means cultivating a sensitivity to the Holy Spirit's promptings, which often highlight areas where we may be drifting or holding onto unbiblical notions. In **I John 1:8,** John wrote, "*If we say that we have no sin, we deceive ourselves, and the truth is not in us*" (KJV, 2023). This applies to all forms of sin, including the sin of allowing deception to take hold. Acknowledging our ongoing need for God's cleansing and correction is a sign of spiritual maturity, not weakness.

The scriptural emphasis on repentance is foundational. Jesus' ministry began with the proclamation, "Repent ye: for the kingdom of heaven is at hand" (**Matthew 4:17**). This was not merely a call to turn from societal sins but a call to turn from any worldview, any reliance on self, any adherence to falsehood that stood between humanity and the reign of God. When we have been deceived, we have, in essence, built our spiritual house on shifting sands, ignoring the solid rock of God's Word. Repentance is the process of demolishing that flawed structure and laying a new foundation of truth. It involves a deep introspection into *why* we were susceptible to it. Was it a lack of biblical knowledge? Was it an unfulfilled longing that we sought to satisfy through deceptive means? Was it a desire for belonging or recognition that made us vulnerable to manipulation? Honest answers to these questions, expressed in confession, are vital for preventing future entrapment.

The confession of our error allows God's healing power to flow into the wounded places of our souls. Deception often leaves behind a residue of confusion, doubt, and even shame. By confessing our part in falling prey to it, we are inviting God to bring His restorative grace to bear upon these areas.

He can heal the fractured understanding, restore confidence in His Word, and renew our spiritual vision. This healing is not merely the absence of deception, but the active presence of God's truth and the vitality it brings to our lives. It is a process of spiritual renewal that equips us to stand firm against future attempts to mislead.

Moreover, the act of confession can often be a catalyst for communal healing and accountability. While the primary confession is to God, there are times when confessing to trusted spiritual leaders or mature believers can be incredibly beneficial. This provides an opportunity for encouragement, prayerful support, and practical guidance as one navigates the path back to biblical truth. It also serves as a testament to the power of God's grace and the reality of His restorative work, which can encourage others who may be struggling with similar issues. However, this aspect of confession must be approached with wisdom, ensuring that it is done in a way that is edifying and not merely for public display.

The liberating power of repentance and confession lies in their ability to break the cycle of deception. When we refuse to acknowledge our role, we remain trapped. We may blame external factors, but until we turn inward and confess our part, the door to genuine freedom remains shut. Repentance is the key that unlocks that door, and confession is the act of turning that key. It is through these acts that we reclaim our spiritual agency, no longer passive victims of falsehood, but participants in God's plan for truth and freedom.

Ultimately, embracing repentance and confession is an act of faith. It is a belief that God is willing and able to forgive, to cleanse, and to restore, even when we have wandered far from His path. It is a trust in His faithfulness, even when our own understanding has been compromised. By humbly acknowledging our errors and turning back to His Word, we position ourselves to experience the full liberating power of His truth. This is not a sign of weakness, but the hallmark of a soul truly committed to walking in the light, unclouded by the shadows of deception. It is the courageous, yet grace-filled, response that re-establishes our footing on the solid ground of God's unshakeable Word. This process is crucial for rebuilding a robust spiritual defense, ensuring that the infiltration of deceptive elements is not only identified but also effectively purged, allowing the pure stream of God's truth to flow unimpeded in our lives. It is the essential cleansing that readies the soil of our hearts for the enduring seeds of divine truth to flourish.

It is essential for us not only to read the Bible but also to memorize key scriptures and passages to use in our spiritual warfare battles that we will face. In addition to memorization, journaling is also beneficial because it reinforces what we have read or heard. When we journal, we take key points from a large text and organize our thoughts about it in writing. These writings help us at later dates when we need to remind ourselves of God's blessings and promises, as we quote them to rebut Satan and his minions.

The foundational strategies for building an unshakeable defense against deception, rooted deeply in the faithful study and memorization of Scripture, have been explored. We have seen how immersing ourselves in the Word acts as a vital bulwark, renewing our minds and providing the doctrinal ammunition necessary to discern truth from falsehood. This intellectual engagement, as crucial as it is, operates in concert with a more profound, spiritual dynamic—the indispensable guidance of the Holy Spirit. Without His active participation, our understanding of God's Word, however diligent, remains incomplete, susceptible to the very deceptions we seek to overcome.

The believer's liberation from deception is not solely an intellectual act; it is more a spiritual work orchestrated by the Holy Spirit. Jesus Himself promised as recorded in **John 16:13**, *"But when he, the Spirit of truth, is come, he will guide you into all truth: for he shall not speak of himself; but whatsoever he shall hear, that shall he speak: and he will shew you things to come"* (KJV, 2023). This pivotal verse underscores the Holy Spirit's essential role as our divine guide, the very revealer of truth. He is not merely an interpreter of the written Word, but the active agent who illuminates its depths, making its truths applicable and convicting to our hearts. To combat deception effectively, we must cultivate an intimate, dependent relationship with this indwelling Counselor, a relationship nurtured through fervent prayer and unwavering obedience.

The Holy Spirit's ministry of guidance is multifaceted. Firstly, He indwells every believer, establishing His residence within our innermost being. This personal presence means that His guidance is not an external, detached commentary, but an intimate, internal compass. He knows the mind of God and is commissioned to communicate that to us. This is why the Apostle Paul in **I Corinthians 2:9-10** could write, *"But as it is written, Eye hath not seen, nor ear heard, neither have entered into the heart of man, the things which God hath prepared for them that love him. However, God hath revealed them unto us by his Spirit: for the Spirit searcheth all things, yea, the deep things of God"* (KJV, 2023).

The "deep things of God," the profound truths that elude natural understanding, are brought to light by the Spirit. This includes understanding the intricacies of God's plan, the spiritual warfare in which we are engaged, and the deceptive tactics employed by the adversary. When we encounter teachings that seem plausible but subtly deviate from biblical doctrine, it is the Spirit within us that provides the inner witness —the gentle yet firm nudge of conviction that something is amiss.

Secondly, the Holy Spirit acts as the supreme interpreter of Scripture. While diligent study of the King James Version, with its rich vocabulary and linguistic nuances, provides the textual foundation, it is the Spirit who breathes life into the written word, making it a living, active force in our lives. He ensures that our understanding aligns with God's intended meaning, preventing the misapplication and distortion that are hallmarks of deceptive teachings. Consider the interaction between Philip and the

Ethiopian eunuch in the Acts of the Apostles. The eunuch was reading from the prophet Isaiah, but he did not understand what he was reading. Philip, empowered by the Spirit, in **Acts 8:35** wrote "*opened his mouth, and began at the same scripture, and preached unto him Jesus*" (KJV, 2023).

The Spirit guided Philip to the eunuch, gave him the understanding to connect Isaiah's prophecy to Christ, and enabled him to communicate the truth effectively. This is the Spirit's ongoing work: connecting the dots of Scripture, revealing the person of Christ in every passage, and making the application of God's truth personal and transformative. He grants us discernment, an ability to weigh teachings against the plumb line of biblical truth, not just intellectually, but with a God-given spiritual intuition.

Cultivating an intimate relationship with the Holy Spirit is therefore paramount in our defense against deception. This intimacy is not fostered solely through intellectual exercises but through consistent prayer and obedient living. Prayer is the conduit through which we communicate our dependence on the Spirit and seek His wisdom. In **Luke 11:13**, Jesus Himself commanded, "*If ye then, being evil, know how to give good gifts unto your children: how much more shall your heavenly Father give the Holy Spirit to them that ask him?*" (KJV, 2023). The asking here is not a perfunctory request, but a sincere petition born of a recognition of our need. When we pray, acknowledging our limitations and seeking the Spirit's illumination, we open ourselves to His powerful ministry. We can pray for discernment, for clarity, for the wisdom to understand God's Word and to recognize error. Such prayers are not merely requests for information; they are acts of surrender, placing our minds and spirits under the guidance of the Spirit.

Obedience is the other critical pillar in our relationship with the Spirit. Jesus stated in **John 14:15-17**, "*If a man loves me, he will keep my commandments. Moreover, I will pray the Father, and he shall give you another Comforter, that he may abide with you forever; even the Spirit of truth; whom the world cannot receive, because it seeth him not, neither knoweth him: but ye know him; for he dwelleth with you, and shall be in you*" (KJV, 2023). The indwelling of the Spirit is linked to our love for Christ expressed through obedience. When we deliberately choose to obey God's commands, we create an environment where the Spirit can freely operate and guide us. Conversely, willful disobedience grieves the Spirit (**Ephesians 4:30**) and can dull our sensitivity to His voice, making us more vulnerable to deception. It is a reciprocal relationship: as we obey, the Spirit's guidance becomes clearer; as the Spirit guides, we are empowered to obey.

The Holy Spirit's conviction is a powerful internal alarm system against deception. He is convicted of sin, but also of error that leads away from truth. **John 16:8** reminds us, "*And when he is come, he will reprove the world of sin, and of righteousness, and of judgment.*" (KJV, 2023). This judgment extends to the deceptive doctrines and practices that lead souls astray. When a teaching clashes with the established truths of Scripture, truths that the Spirit has helped us internalize through prayer and meditation, He will bring a sense of unease. This discerning check prompts further investigation or outright rejection. This is not a matter of intellectual debate but of a deep-seated spiritual certainty. The BIBLE, in its comprehensive unfolding of God's truth, provides the objective standard against which the Spirit works. He uses the very words we have committed to memory and meditated upon to expose falsehood. A teaching that relies on twisting or omitting verses, or on presenting a skewed view of God's character, will often encounter the internal resistance of the Spirit-filled believer.

Consider the insidious nature of some modern spiritual movements that, while appearing Christian, subtly introduce Gnostic elements or embrace universalistic themes. A believer who has diligently studied the BIBLE, particularly passages concerning the unique person and salvific work of Jesus Christ (e.g., **John 14:6, Acts 4:12**), and who actively prays for the Spirit's guidance, will often feel an immediate dissonance when encountering such teachings. The Spirit highlights the exclusivity of Christ, the biblical concept of sin and redemption, and the clear distinctions between the saved and the lost. This internal conviction, powered by the Spirit and informed by Scripture, serves as an immediate filter, preventing the casual acceptance of potentially soul-damaging error. It is the internal compass pointing unerringly towards the truth, calibrated by God's Word and activated by His Spirit.

Furthermore, the Spirit's role in empowering us to resist temptation and to stand firm in the face of spiritual opposition cannot be overstated. Deception is often employed as a weapon by the adversary, designed to weaken our faith and draw us away from God. The Holy Spirit equips us with the spiritual fortitude to withstand these assaults. As Paul writes in **Ephesians 6:10-11**, "*Finally, my brethren, be strong in the Lord, and in the power of his might. Put on the whole armour of God, that ye may be able to stand against the wiles of the devil.*" (KJV, 2023). The "power of his might" is the power of the Holy Spirit. When we are tempted to compromise biblical truth, to accept popular but unbiblical ideas, or to shrink back from proclaiming the unvarnished Gospel, it is the Spirit who strengthens our resolve. He enables us to speak the truth in love, even when it is unpopular, and to maintain our spiritual integrity in the face of pressure.

This is the essence of His guidance: making the truth of God's Word directly applicable to our present circumstances, serving as an immediate counter-argument to any form of falsehood. The journey of liberation from deception is thus a dynamic partnership between the believer and the Holy Spirit. It requires our diligent study and application of God's Word, as well as our conscious cultivation of a Spirit-led life through prayer and obedience. The Spirit acts as our internal teacher, guide, convictor, and empowerer. He ensures that our understanding of Scripture is pure, that our discernment is keen, and that our resolve to stand for truth is unwavering.

To neglect cultivating this relationship with the Holy Spirit is to leave ourselves exposed and vulnerable to the very deceptions we are striving to escape. By leaning into His gentle but firm guidance, we are assured of walking in the light of truth, protected from the shadows of error, and firmly anchored on the solid rock of God's infallible Word. His presence within us is the ultimate assurance of our liberation, the divine guarantee that we can indeed know and walk in all truth. This reliance on the Holy Spirit is not a passive waiting, but an active pursuit, a daily recommitment to allowing His divine wisdom to direct every step of our spiritual journey, ensuring that our minds remain sharp, our hearts are true, and our lives are a testament to the liberating power of God's unchanging truth.

The liberation from deception, while a profoundly personal journey involving the diligent study of Scripture and the indispensable guidance of the Holy Spirit, is not meant to be undertaken in isolation. The divine architecture of the Christian life is inherently communal in nature. God, in His wisdom, did not design believers to be solitary fortresses against the onslaught of falsehood, but rather to be parts of a living, breathing body, interconnected and mutually supportive. This brings us to a critical strategy for fortifying ourselves against deception: cultivating a community of truth and accountability. The strength derived from shared commitment to God's Word and mutual spiritual oversight is an invaluable asset in discerning and rejecting deceptive claims. The biblical mandate for fellowship is clear and pervasive throughout the New Testament. From the earliest days of the church, believers were not merely encouraged but exhorted to gather together in community. **Acts 2:42** paints a vibrant picture of this nascent community: *"And they continued steadfastly in the apostles' doctrine and fellowship, and in the breaking of bread, and in prayers."* (KJV, 2023). This foundational text highlights several key elements that are essential for a community that guards against deception.

Firstly, steadfastness in the "apostles' doctrine" signifies a shared commitment to the foundational truths of the Gospel as taught by Christ's chosen witnesses. This doctrinal unity is the bedrock upon which adequate discernment is built. When a community is aligned in its understanding of core biblical tenets, it possesses a collective yardstick against which any new teaching or assertion can be measured. Deception often thrives in environments where doctrinal foundations are shaky or where there is a lack of common understanding of what constitutes truth.

Secondly, the mention of "fellowship" in **Acts 2:42** refers to more than just social interaction; it signifies a profound, intimate sharing in Christ, characterized by mutual reliance and a shared purpose. This is the kind of fellowship that fosters vulnerability and opens the door for authentic accountability. It is within such a context that individuals feel safe to admit their struggles with understanding a particular teaching or their susceptibility to a persuasive but ultimately unbiblical argument. Without this deep sense of community, those who are being subtly led astray may remain silent, afraid of appearing ignorant or weak, thereby allowing deception to take root unchallenged.

The Apostle Paul, in his epistles, repeatedly emphasizes the importance of mutual edification and care within the body of Christ. In **Hebrews 10:24-25**, the exhortation is stark: "*And let us consider one another to provoke unto love and to good works: Not forsaking the assembling of ourselves together, as the manner of some is; but exhorting one another: and so much the more, as ye see the day approaching.*" (KJV, 2023). The phrase "provoke unto love and to good works" suggests an active, intentional encouragement that moves believers towards Christ-likeness. This includes encouraging one another in the pursuit of truth and in the application of God's Word. When a community is actively engaged in this mutual stimulation, it creates an environment where deceptive ideas, which often lead to ungodly or harmful practices, are quickly identified and challenged. The call not to forsake assembling is a direct antidote to the isolation that deception frequently seeks to impose. Isolation makes individuals more susceptible to manipulation, as they lack the benefit of other perspectives and the collective wisdom of the community.

Furthermore, the concept of accountability is deeply woven into the fabric of biblical community. In **Galatians 6:1**, Paul instructs, "*Brethren, if a man be overtaken in any fault, ye which are spiritual restore such an one in the spirit of meekness; considering thyself, lest thou also be tempted.*" (KJV, 2023). This passage highlights the responsibility that believers have towards one another, particularly in helping to restore those who have stumbled. Such restoration requires discernment, gentleness, and an understanding of one's own potential for error — all elements that are best fostered within a supportive community. If someone is falling prey to deception, it often manifests as a deviation from sound doctrine or an embrace of unbiblical attitudes or actions. A healthy community, equipped with spiritual discernment, can identify these deviations and offer corrective counsel. This accountability is not about judgment or condemnation, but about a loving commitment to helping one another remain on the path of truth.

The protective function of such a community against deception can be illustrated through the various ways deceptive ideologies or false teachings gain traction. Often, they begin with subtle distortions of scripture, appeals to emotion over reason, or the promotion of a "special revelation" that supersedes or contradicts established biblical truth.

In a vibrant community of faith, where believers discuss the teachings of the Bible and hold one another accountable to its precepts, these distortions are far less likely to go unnoticed. A teaching that, for instance, subtly downplays the deity of Christ or promotes a works-based salvation would likely be flagged by members who are grounded in passages like **John**

1:1, John 3:16, or Romans 3:28. The collective understanding and commitment to the unchanging Word of God serve as a robust defense system. Moreover, a community committed to truth provides a crucial layer of support when individuals face doubt or confusion.

The spiritual journey is not always smooth; there will be times when deceptive arguments seem particularly compelling, or when the sheer volume of conflicting information can be overwhelming. In these moments, the encouragement and reasoned counsel of fellow believers are indispensable. Sharing one's struggles with a trusted elder or a fellow mature believer can provide clarity, reaffirm foundational truths, and help to expose the flaws in deceptive reasoning. This is the essence of mutual encouragement—strengthening one another's faith and resolve in the face of challenges. The Lord established the church not just for worship, but for the equipping of the saints (**Ephesians 4:12-13**), and this equipping includes preparing us to stand firm against deceptive teachings.

The establishment and maintenance of such a community require intentional effort and a willingness to embrace the responsibilities that come with Christian fellowship. It begins with a shared commitment to the authority of Scripture. When a congregation or small group prioritizes sound biblical exposition and encourages members to engage deeply with the text, they are laying the groundwork for a community that can effectively discern truth. This involves regular preaching and teaching that faithfully unpacks God's Word, but also fostering an environment where members feel empowered to ask questions, engage in thoughtful discussion, and challenge interpretations that do not align with the broader biblical narrative.

Furthermore, fostering an atmosphere of humble inquiry is vital. No single individual has a monopoly on spiritual understanding. The Holy Spirit illuminates all believers, and by engaging in dialogue, sharing insights gained from personal study and prayer, and respectfully considering differing perspectives within the bounds of biblical orthodoxy, a community can arrive at a richer and more accurate understanding of God's truth. This process can help to expose individual blind spots and prevent the entrenchment of personal interpretations that subtle deceptions may influence. It is about collective wisdom, guided by the Spirit, that surpasses the wisdom of any individual member.

The practice of delivering open and honest feedback with love and grace is another cornerstone of accountability within a truth-oriented community. When a believer begins to exhibit an unusual attachment to a fringe doctrine, expresses a fascination with controversial or unbiblical spiritual practices, or consistently misinterprets key biblical passages in a way that leads to error, others within the community have a spiritual responsibility to address it. This is not about policing consciences, but about safeguarding the spiritual health of the individual and, by extension, the community. The process should ideally involve seasoned, spiritually mature individuals who can approach the person with empathy, grounding their concerns in Scripture and prayer.

Consider the example of a believer who, perhaps influenced by modern esoteric teachings, begins to emphasize personal "spiritual experiences" above the clear teachings of Scripture, or who starts to endorse a form of universalism that contradicts the biblical exclusivity of salvation through Christ. Within a healthy, truth-centered community, this deviation would not likely go unnoticed for long.

Fellow members, grounded in their Bible studies and accustomed to mutual encouragement, might gently inquire about the source of these new ideas, inviting them to share and then offering a biblical perspective. Passages such as **John 14:6**, "*Jesus saith unto him, I am the way, the truth, and the life: no man cometh unto the Father, but by me,*" or **Acts 4:12**, "*Neither is there salvation in any other: for there is none other name under heaven given among men, whereby we must be saved,*" (KJV, 2023), would be readily brought to bear. The community serves as a collective conscience and a doctrinal compass, guiding individuals back to the solid foundation of God's revealed Word.

The protective aspect of this communal approach is multifaceted. Firstly, it provides an early warning system. Deception often seeks to operate in the shadows, preying on individuals who are isolated or lack a robust understanding of biblical truth. A connected community shines a light on these deceptive tactics, making them far more difficult to propagate. Secondly, it offers a reservoir of spiritual strength. When one member is wavering, others can lend their faith and their understanding to support them. This is akin to a military formation where soldiers stand shoulder to shoulder, providing mutual defense.

Thirdly, a community of truth cultivates a culture of discernment. When believers are accustomed to dissecting teachings, comparing them against the Bible, and discussing their spiritual implications, they develop a sharper ability to recognize error. This is not about becoming overly critical or suspicious, but about cultivating a healthy skepticism towards anything that deviates from the clear and consistent message of Scripture. Such a culture is a powerful deterrent against deceptive influences, which often rely on novelty, emotional appeal, or a departure from established biblical frameworks to gain a foothold.

Moreover, the commitment to mutual care within such a community means that when deception does ensnare someone, the community rallies to support their recovery. This involves patient instruction, prayer, and a demonstration of unwavering love, even when the individual has strayed from the path. The goal is not to shame or alienate, but to lovingly bring them back to the truth. This restorative approach, modeled by Christ Himself, is a vital component of a healthy, truth-oriented fellowship. It recognizes that vulnerability to deception is a reality for all believers, and that the body of Christ is designed to provide healing and restoration.

In essence, a community of truth and accountability functions as a robust spiritual ecosystem. It nourishes faith through sound doctrine, strengthens resolve through mutual encouragement, and protects its members through collective discernment and accountability. By actively participating in and contributing to such a community, believers not only safeguard themselves from the pervasive threat of deception but also fulfill a core aspect of their calling as members of Christ's body. It is a living testament to the truth that while the path to liberation from deception is empowered by the Spirit and grounded in the Word, it is most effectively and safely navigated when undertaken in fellowship with others who are equally committed to walking in the light.

The preceding discussion has underscored the vital role of community in the believer's defense against deception. We have seen how fellowship, mutual accountability, and a shared commitment to God's Word form a formidable bulwark against the insidious workings of falsehood. However, the Christian's spiritual arsenal is not solely defensive; it is also powerfully offensive, enabling active engagement against the very forces that seek to mislead. This offensive capability is rooted in a profound and often underutilized truth: the spiritual authority that believers possess through their union with Jesus Christ. This authority is not an inherent quality of the individual believer but a delegated power, bestowed by Christ Himself, empowering us to act in His name against the dominion of deception and its architect, the adversary.

Our Lord Jesus Christ, in His earthly ministry, consistently demonstrated this authority. He cast out demons, healed the sick, and rebuked the forces of darkness, all with an inherent power that revealed His divine commission. He did not merely teach about the kingdom of God; He *established* its presence through His authoritative actions. The Gospel accounts are replete with instances where Christ's word and touch brought liberation. Consider the encounter with the demon-possessed man in the synagogue at Capernaum **(Mark 1:23-26)**. As the unclean spirit cried out, Jesus, with a simple command, "*Hold thy peace, and come out of him,*" (KJV, 2023), brought immediate freedom. This was not a plea or a suggestion; it was an exercise of absolute authority, an unequivocal declaration of Christ's dominion over the spiritual realm.

Crucially, this authority was not confined to Christ alone. Before His ascension, Jesus commissioned His followers, granting them a participatory role in His work. In **Matthew 28:18**, He declared, "*All power is given unto me in heaven and in earth.*" (KJV, 2023). This statement is not merely a declaration of His supreme sovereignty but a preface to the Great Commission, which immediately follows: "*Go ye therefore, and teach all nations, baptizing them in the* name of the Father, and of the Son, and of the Holy Ghost: Teaching them to observe all things whatsoever I have commanded you: and, lo, I am with you always, even unto the end of the world. Amen."* (KJV, 2023). the explicit mention of casting out demons is found in **Mark 16:17**, *"And these signs shall follow them that believe; In my name shall they cast out devils; they shall speak with new tongues; they shall take up serpents; and if they drink any deadly thing, it shall not hurt them; they shall lay hands on the sick, and they shall recover,"* (KJV, 2023), the principle is clear: the authority Christ wielded is made available to believers.

The key to exercising this authority lies in understanding its source and its application. It is exercised *in Christ's name*. This is not a mere incantation or a word to be spoken casually. To invoke "the name of Jesus" is to invoke His person, His power, His authority, and His accomplished work on the cross. It signifies acting as His representative, with His backing and His full endorsement. When we stand against deception, whether it is a subtle doctrinal distortion, a manipulative spiritual influence, or a personal temptation to believe a lie, we do so not by our own strength, but by invoking the authority of Him who has already defeated the prince of this world.

The Apostle Paul, a fervent proponent of this truth, exhorted believers in **Ephesians 6:10-11**, *"Be strong in the Lord, and in the power of his might. Put on the whole armour of God, that ye may be able to stand against the wiles of the devil."* (KJV, 2023), subsequent verses detail the armor, culminating in standing *"therefore, having your loins girt about with truth, and having on the breastplate of righteousness; And your feet shod with the preparation of the gospel of peace; Above all, taking the shield of faith, wherewith ye shall be able to quench all the fiery darts of the wicked. Moreover, take the helmet of salvation, and the sword of the Spirit, which is the word of God."* (KJV, 2023).

This armor equips us for spiritual warfare, but the offensive capability—the ability to actively repel and dismantle deception—is inherent in wielding the sword of the Spirit—the Word of God—in conjunction with faith and the authority of Christ's name.

The exercise of this authority is primarily manifested through prayer and faith. Prayer is our direct line of communication with the divine source of all authority. When we are confronted with deceptive claims or spiritual attacks, we are called to bring these matters before God in prayer, not as helpless victims, but as empowered agents of His kingdom. This is not a prayer of desperation, but a prayer of faith, recognizing that Christ has already won the battle and that we are now enforcing that victory. In **Luke 10:19,** Jesus told His disciples, *"Behold, I give unto you power to tread on serpents and scorpions, and over all the power of the enemy: and nothing shall by any means hurt you."* (KJV, 2023). This is the foundation upon which we stand; we are not merely enduring, but actively overcoming.

Consider the practical application of this principle when facing a deceptive teaching. It might be a teaching that subtly undermines the sufficiency of Scripture, promoting esoteric experiences or humanistic philosophies as equal or superior sources of truth. Instead of passively absorbing such claims or becoming entangled in endless debate, a believer, armed with the authority of Christ's name, can engage in prayer. This prayer would be a declaration of God's truth against the falsehood. It might involve praying, "*Father, in the name of Jesus, I reject this deceptive teaching that exalts human reasoning over Your infallible Word. I declare that Jesus is the truth, and Your Word is the ultimate authority. I ask for Your wisdom and discernment to see this deception for what it is and to stand firm in the truth.*" This is not an arbitrary utterance; it is a spiritual act of alignment with God's will and a forceful proclamation of Christ's victory over deceit.

Faith is the engine that drives the exercise of this authority. It is the unwavering conviction that God's Word is true and that His promises are sure. It is the belief that when we act in accordance with His will and in His name, His power is made manifest. The Apostle John wrote in **I John 4:4**, "*Ye are of God, little children, and have overcome them: because greater is he that is in you, than he that is in the world.*" (KJV, 2023). This inherent superiority of Christ within the believer is what enables us to overcome our weaknesses. Deception thrives on doubt and fear, but faith anchors us in the certainty of Christ's victory and His presence with us.

When a believer understands that they have been clothed with Christ's authority, they can begin to reclaim ground that has been lost to deception proactively. This is not about personal dominion but about asserting the Lordship of Christ over every thought, every sphere of life, and every deceptive influence. It means refusing to allow lies to take root in our minds or to influence our actions. It involves a conscious decision to align our thinking with God's revealed truth, using the authority granted to us to cast down imaginations and every high thing that exalts itself against the knowledge of God (**II Corinthians 10:5**).

The adversary, also referred to as the devil, is described as the "father of lies" (John 8:44). His strategy involves sowing seeds of doubt, twisting the truth, and creating confusion. He is the great deceiver. However, Jesus, in the same discourse, also states, "*And I, if I be lifted up from the earth, will draw all men unto me.*" He is the truth, and wherever His name and His finished work are proclaimed with authority, deception loses its power. Believers are His representatives on earth, and in His name, we have the mandate to expose and dismantle lies.

This exercise of authority is not about aggressive confrontation or a self-aggrandizing display of spiritual power. Instead, it is a calm, confident assertion of Christ's victory and truth, born out of a deep understanding of our identity in Him. It is about speaking the truth in love, using the authority vested in us to bring freedom from falsehood. The Bible's clear, authoritative language often serves to reinforce this clarity and power. For instance, passages like **John 14:6**, *"Jesus saith unto him, I am the way, the truth, and the life: no man cometh unto the Father, but by me,"* (KJV, 2023), are not mere theological statements; they are declarations of absolute truth that carry spiritual authority. When a believer holds to these truths and declares them in Christ's name against deception, they are wielding a spiritual weapon.

The scope of this authority extends to personal thought life as well. Deception often begins with subtle whispers in the mind, suggestions that subtly shift our perspective away from biblical truth. A believer, recognizing these intrusions, can, in Christ's name, reject them. This might look like consciously redirecting a thought process that is veering into speculation or doubt about God's goodness or His Word. For example, if a thought arises suggesting that God's commands are restrictive or that His will is not for one's best interest, the believer can, in the authority of Christ, counter that thought with truth and prayer. "Lord, in Jesus' name, I cast down this thought that contradicts Your perfect love and Your righteous commands. Your ways are good, and Your will is perfect." This internal spiritual warfare is a crucial aspect of living free from deception.

Moreover, this authority empowers believers to stand against deceptive systems and influences in the world. While direct confrontation with every false ideology is not practical or necessary, believers are called to be salt and light, influencing their surroundings with the truth of Christ. This involves speaking truth, living righteously, and, when opportunities arise, discerning and challenging the deceptive foundations of ungodly philosophies or practices. It is about radiating Christ's truth and authority into the darkness, not through coercion, but through the compelling power of the Gospel and the lives of those who are truly liberated from deception.

The consistent and faithful exercise of spiritual authority in Christ's name is a direct means of reclaiming spiritual territory that may have been usurped by deception. When a believer or a community consciously chooses to operate under this authority, they are, in essence, pushing back the darkness and asserting Christ's rightful dominion. This proactive stance is essential for maintaining spiritual freedom. It requires a mature understanding of our position in Christ and a willingness to step into the authority He has graciously bestowed.

This authority is not a license for presumption, nor is it a guarantee that all opposition will cease instantly. The adversary is persistent. However, it is a divine enablement to stand firm, to resist effectively, and to prevail ultimately. It is grounded in the assurance that He who is in us is greater than he who is in the world. Therefore, embracing and actively exercising this spiritual authority is a fundamental biblical strategy for liberation from deception, enabling believers to live in the full inheritance of their freedom in Christ, unhindered by the lies that seek to enslave. It is the active realization of Christ's victory in the believer's life and in the world around them, a testament to His enduring power and truth.

Spiritual Warfare Armor

The Christian life, though outwardly lived in the tangible world we perceive, is fundamentally engaged on a far more profound and pervasive plane—an unseen battlefield. This is not a battlefield of asphalt and concrete, of nations and armies in conventional warfare, but a realm of spiritual realities, a cosmic struggle that shapes the very fabric of our existence. To be a follower of Christ is to be enlisted in this ongoing conflict, a conflict that involves forces beyond our ordinary senses, yet whose impact is undeniably felt in our thoughts, emotions, relationships, and the world around us. Understanding this fundamental truth—that we are engaged in a real, continuous, and consequential spiritual war—is not an optional add-on to the Christian faith; it is the bedrock upon which all other aspects of our spiritual life must be built. Without this foundational understanding, much of what scripture teaches about perseverance, discernment, and God's provision for His people can seem abstract or even unnecessary. However, once we grasp the reality of this unseen arena, the urgency and profound importance of spiritual preparedness, particularly the divine provision of the armor of God, becomes overwhelmingly clear.

The Bible, from its earliest accounts to its final prophetic pronouncements, consistently depicts a universe in which benevolent divine forces and malevolent spiritual entities are in active opposition. This is not a dualistic struggle where both sides are equal, for scripture unequivocally establishes the ultimate sovereignty of God. However, within that framework, there exists a powerful adversarial force, often referred to by various names—Satan, the devil, the tempter, the accuser, the serpent—whose primary objective is to thwart God's purposes and to draw humanity away from Him. This adversary operates through deception, manipulation, and the exploitation of our weaknesses. The Apostle Paul, in his letter to the Ephesians, provides some of the most direct and comprehensive teaching on this subject, famously declaring in **Ephesians 6:12**, "*For our struggle is not against flesh and blood, but against the rulers, against the authorities, against the powers of this dark world and against the spiritual forces of wickedness in the heavenly realms.*" (KJV, 2023). This verse is pivotal. It directly confronts any notion that spiritual warfare is merely a psychological struggle or a metaphorical battle against internal sin. While sin and psychological battles are indeed aspects of the Christian journey, Paul anchors them in a larger, cosmic conflict. He explicitly states that our true opponents are not human beings, not even organized human systems in their ultimate reality, but rather spiritual powers and authorities arrayed in opposition to God.

To grasp the significance of this statement, we must consider the nature of these "spiritual forces of wickedness." These are not mere abstract concepts; they are described as organized entities with hierarchical structures—"rulers," "authorities," "powers." This suggests a deliberate, strategic opposition to God's kingdom. They operate in the "heavenly realms," a term that does not necessarily refer to distant physical locations, but rather to the spiritual dimensions that interpenetrate and influence our earthly existence. Think of it as a parallel reality, a spiritual ecosystem, where unseen beings engage in activities that have tangible effects on our lives and on the world. This is why, for instance, intense spiritual struggles can manifest as overwhelming feelings of despair, persistent temptations, or irrational fears. These are not random occurrences; they can be the direct result of spiritual forces actively attempting to destabilize and defeat the believer.

The biblical narrative provides ample evidence of this spiritual dimension. In the Old Testament, spiritual warfare is depicted in various ways. Consider the encounter between God's people and the surrounding nations, which often had a spiritual dimension, involving opposition from forces that sought to lead Israel astray into idolatry and rebellion against God. The story of Balaam in Numbers, hired to curse Israel, illustrates the attempt to engage spiritual powers against God's people. Even in the battles of ancient Israel, there was an underlying spiritual reality in which obedience to God's commands and reliance on His power were paramount to victory, often more so than military might. The prophets often spoke of spiritual blindness and the influence of demonic forces leading nations astray.

In the New Testament, the reality of spiritual warfare is even more pronounced, with Jesus Himself being the prime example. His ministry was characterized by casting out demons, confronting spiritual blindness, and directly challenging the power of Satan. The temptation of Jesus in the wilderness (**Matthew 4:1-11; Luke 4:1-13**) is a foundational text for understanding spiritual warfare. Satan, the adversary, directly confronted Jesus with temptations designed to make Him compromise His divine mission and turn away from God's will. Jesus' victory was not achieved through brute force, but by wielding the Word of God, demonstrating that spiritual truth and reliance on God are the ultimate weapons against demonic assault. In **Matthew 13:1-23,** His words, "*Away from me, Satan! For it is written...*" (KJV, 2023). Highlight the power of scripture in spiritual combat. His parables, such as the Parable of the Sower (), speak of the "wicked one" coming to snatch away the word sown in people's hearts, illustrating how seeds of truth can be immediately attacked and disrupted by spiritual forces.

Furthermore, the early church faced intense spiritual opposition. The book of Acts is replete with accounts of believers facing persecution, demonic activity, and supernatural opposition. In Acts 19, Paul confronts the sorcerers in Ephesus, demonstrating the clash between the power of God and the forces of darkness. The epistles are replete with exhortations concerning spiritual warfare. Peter, in his first letter **(1 Peter 5:8-9)**, *urges believers to "Be alert and of sober mind. Your enemy, the devil, prowls around like a roaring lion looking for someone to devour. Resist him, standing firm in the faith, because you know that the family of believers throughout the world is undergoing the same kind of sufferings."* (KJV, 2023). This imagery is powerful and evocative. The lion is a symbol of predatory power. The description of Satan "prowling" suggests a constant, relentless search for weakness and vulnerability. The call to "resist him, standing firm in the faith" is a direct command to engage in spiritual warfare with a specific posture of resilience and reliance on God.

The understanding of this unseen battlefield is not meant to foster a spirit of fear or paranoia, but rather a sober awareness and a readiness to act. It is about recognizing that our spiritual journey is not a passive stroll through a pleasant garden but an active engagement in a cosmic conflict. This awareness should not paralyze us but empower us, because it is precisely within this understanding that God's provisions for our defense and victory are revealed. The enemy's objective is to incapacitate us through deception, doubt, and discouragement, making us ineffective for God's purposes. He wants us to believe we are alone, outmatched, or that the struggle is futile. However, scripture assures us that this is a lie. God has not left us defenseless. He has equipped us.

The Apostle Paul, recognizing the severity and reality of this spiritual conflict, penned one of the most comprehensive passages on spiritual warfare in **Ephesians 6:10-18**. This passage, which forms the bedrock of our understanding, is not merely a poetic description of Christian living; it is a strategic briefing for combat. The entire context of Paul's letter to the Ephesians builds towards this ultimate exhortation. He has already spoken about the spiritual blessings believers have in Christ (**Ephesians 1**), the mystery of God's plan revealed through Christ (**Ephesians 2-3**), and the practical implications of living out this new life in unity and love (**Ephesians 4-5**). Now, he turns to the crucial matter of how to live this life effectively in the face of relentless spiritual opposition.

Paul's emphasis is on *strength* and *standing firm*. He begins by commanding believers to "Be strong in the Lord and in his mighty power." This is not a call to self-reliance or to muster our own human strength. It is a directive to draw upon the inexhaustible power of God. The phrase "in the Lord" signifies our union with Christ, from whom all spiritual strength flows. It is in Him that we are made complete and empowered to face any adversity. This is the fundamental source of our ability to engage in spiritual warfare. Our victory is not a testament to our prowess, but to God's power working through us. The "mighty power" refers to the same power that raised Christ from the dead, a power that transcends any earthly force and is more than capable of overcoming the spiritual forces arrayed against us. This power is not a static reserve; it is dynamically available to us through our relationship with God. To be strong "in the Lord" means to be connected to Him, to be dependent on Him, and to be infused with His power through the Holy Spirit. This is the first and most crucial step in spiritual preparedness: recognizing our need for God's strength and actively drawing upon it.

Following this command for strength, Paul immediately presents the solution: "Put on the whole armor of God." This is not a suggestion; it is a divine mandate, an essential directive for survival and victory in the spiritual arena. The imperative mood ("Put on") underscores the necessity of this action. It is not optional; it is a requirement for standing against the enemy. This armor is not something we create or discover; it is a provision from God Himself, designed to protect us against the specific tactics of the adversary.

The imagery of armor is not arbitrary. Paul, drawing on his understanding of Roman military strategy and the equipping of soldiers, employs a vivid metaphor to convey the completeness and effectiveness of God's provision. Roman soldiers were meticulously equipped from head to toe with defensive and offensive gear that allowed them to withstand enemy onslaughts and to engage effectively in battle. Each piece of armor served a specific purpose, and when worn together, they provided comprehensive protection. Similarly, the armor of God is a complete spiritual defense system, designed to shield every vulnerable area of the believer's life. It is vital to understand that this armor is not merely symbolic in a passive sense. It is to be *put on*. This implies an active, intentional choice on our part. It is not like putting on a coat and forgetting about it; it is more akin to gearing up for a serious engagement, where each piece is consciously secured and utilized. This active engagement is what allows the armor to function effectively.

The purpose of this divine provision is clearly stated: "...so that you can take your stand against the devil's schemes." The enemy is not passive; he employs "schemes," which implies cunning, planning, and deception. He does not always attack with overwhelming force, but often with subtle, insidious strategies designed to undermine our faith, sow discord, and lead us astray. The armor of God is specifically designed to counter these very schemes. Each piece serves as a direct antidote to a specific type of spiritual attack. Therefore, understanding each component of the armor is not just an academic exercise; it is a matter of practical spiritual survival and effectiveness. The context of Paul writing to the church in Ephesus is also significant. Ephesus was a major Roman city, a hub of commerce and culture, but also a place where pagan religions and occult practices were prevalent.

The believers in Ephesus were likely exposed to a constant barrage of opposing worldviews and spiritual influences. Paul's message was therefore highly relevant to their immediate circumstances, warning them of the very real spiritual dangers they faced. However, the universality of the principles he lays out means that this teaching is just as relevant to believers today, in whatever cultural or societal context we find ourselves. The nature of the enemy and his tactics may manifest differently, but the underlying spiritual reality and God's provision remain the same.

The ultimate goal articulated in **Ephesians 6:13** is to **"take your stand" or "stand firm."** This phrase is repeated throughout the passage, emphasizing its importance. It signifies resilience, steadfastness, and an unwavering refusal to be moved or defeated by the enemy's assaults. It is about remaining solid in one's faith, doctrine, and personal integrity, regardless of the pressure or opposition faced. Standing firm is not about being aggressive or initiating conflict; it is about maintaining one's ground with unshakeable conviction, rooted in God's strength and His provided defenses. It implies an inner fortitude that enables one to endure hardship, resist temptation, and remain faithful even in the face of adversity.

This enduring posture is the essence of victory in spiritual warfare. It is not necessarily characterized by spectacular displays of power or the annihilation of the enemy, but by the faithful maintenance of one's position in Christ, refusing to yield to deception or despair. It is about preserving the integrity of one's faith and life in the face of relentless pressure. The armor of God is the means by which this steadfastness is achieved. It provides the protection and the stability necessary to stand firm, not in our own might, but in the power and provision of God.

Therefore, grasping the concept of the unseen battlefield is the indispensable first step. It is the lens through which we must view our Christian walk. Without this perspective, the spiritual armor becomes an abstract collection of metaphors, and the commands to be strong and stand firm lose their urgency and context. However, when we understand that we are engaged in a real, ongoing conflict against powerful spiritual adversaries, the necessity of God's complete provision becomes crystal clear. It ignites a desire for spiritual preparedness, a willingness to engage with scripture, and a commitment to drawing upon the divine strength available to us. This foundational understanding equips us not just to survive the spiritual battles of life but to emerge victorious, standing firm in Christ and advancing His kingdom on earth. It shifts our focus from the visible challenges of the world to the underlying spiritual dynamics, enabling us to engage with wisdom, courage, and the assurance of God's unfailing power. This is the starting point for equipping ourselves for the inevitable battles, yet ultimately winnable, through God's provision.

The intricate tapestry of the Christian walk, as we have established, is woven against a backdrop of unseen realities. This is not a mere poetic metaphor; it is the foundational truth that informs our understanding of spiritual warfare. We are not passive observers in a cosmic drama, but active participants engaged in a genuine conflict. To engage effectively, we must first understand our enemy. The Apostle Paul, in his seminal instruction on spiritual warfare found in Ephesians 6:11, urges us to "Put on the whole armor of God so that you can take your stand against the devil's schemes." The emphasis here is on "schemes." This word, from the Greek *'methodeia'* (μεθοδεία), speaks of a systematic approach, a cunning plan, a wily method, or a stratagem. It implies that our adversary, Satan, is not a crude brute force but a strategist who employs calculated and often deceptive tactics. He does not lash out randomly; he plots, schemes, and devises ways to undermine our faith, compromise our integrity, and ultimately defeat us.

To understand these schemes is to begin the process of recognizing and resisting them. The Bible presents us with a comprehensive, albeit often disturbing, portrayal of this adversary. He is described in various ways, each revealing a facet of his character and modus operandi. He is the serpent who tempted Eve in the Garden of Eden, a being of ancient cunning and persuasive deception. He is the accuser of the brethren, perpetually seeking to cast doubt on our standing with God and to highlight our failures (**Revelation 12:10**). He is the tempter, actively luring us into sin through attractive but ultimately destructive propositions (**Matthew 4:1-11**). He is the deceiver, the father of lies, who twists truth and masquerades as an angel of light to gain influence (**John 8:44; 2 Corinthians 11:14**). This multifaceted nature means his schemes are equally varied and can manifest in subtle, insidious ways, making identification all the more critical.

One of the devil's most pervasive schemes is the **scheme of deception and lies**. This is his primary tool, his native tongue. Jesus Himself identified Satan in **John 8:44** as "*a murderer from the beginning, and does not stand in the truth, because there is no truth in him. When he speaks a lie, he speaks from his own resources, for he is a liar and the father of it*" (KJV, 2023). This means that anything contrary to God's truth, anything that distorts God's character, His word, or His plan for humanity, originates from him. His lies are not always blatant falsehoods; more often, they are subtly interwoven with kernels of truth, making them harder to detect. He might twist scripture, take it out of context, or appeal to our emotions and desires to justify actions that God has forbidden.

Consider, for example, the lie that God is too harsh or too restrictive. When we feel constrained by biblical commands about sexuality, finances, or relationships, Satan whispers that God is holding out on us, that He does not want us to experience true joy or freedom. This is a direct echo of his lie to Eve: "For God knows that when you eat from it your eyes will be opened, and you will be like God, knowing good and evil" (Genesis 3:5). The implication was that God's command was out of spite, to keep them from something good. This same lie continues today, masquerading as "enlightenment" or "personal truth" that supersedes divine revelation.

Another insidious aspect of this scheme is the **promotion of doubt**. Satan excels at planting seeds of doubt in our minds about God's goodness, His faithfulness, and the veracity of His Word. He whispers questions like, "Did God really say…?" or "Is God really in control?" or "Does God truly forgive *that*?" He exploits our unanswered questions, our disappointments, and our suffering to foster a sense of alienation from God. If he can make us doubt God's presence or His power, he can paralyze us and render us ineffective. When facing difficult circumstances, it is easy to fall prey to the thought that God has abandoned us or that our prayers are not being heard. This is a classic tactic of Satan, aiming to isolate us and foster despair.

The devil also actively works to **sow discord and division** among believers. Unity is a cornerstone of the church, a powerful testament to God's presence. Satan, therefore, targets this unity with ruthless efficiency. He exploits misunderstandings, amplifies minor offenses, and fuels gossip and slander. He can use our own pride, our differing opinions, or our personal offenses to create rifts within the body of Christ. His goal is to weaken the church by fracturing its fellowship, making it easier to attack and less effective in its mission. A church divided cannot stand, and Satan knows this well. He works through gossip, slander, and the fueling of unforgiveness to create alienation and bitterness, thereby crippling the church's witness and its collective spiritual strength. The subtle way he can turn a minor disagreement into a major feud, or fan the flames of suspicion between individuals or groups within the church, is a testament to his devious nature.

Furthermore, Satan operates through **temptation**, often presenting sin in an appealing light. He does not always present sin as inherently evil. Instead, he disguises it, repackages it, and offers it as something desirable, enjoyable, or even necessary. He preys on our natural desires and weaknesses, twisting them to lead us away from God. He might tempt us with illicit pleasures, with the allure of wealth or power gained through ungodly means, or with the satisfaction of revenge. These temptations are carefully calibrated to our individual vulnerabilities, making them particularly potent.

The temptation to compromise integrity, for instance, is a standard scheme. In the workplace, the pressure to cut corners, to lie on a report, or to engage in unethical practices can be immense. Satan whispers that it is just a small thing, that everyone does it, or that it is necessary for survival or advancement. These are rationalizations designed to mask the spiritual compromise. Similarly, in relationships, the temptation to engage in gossip, speak harshly, or harbor unforgiveness can erode our spiritual foundation. Satan's approach is often to normalize these behaviors, making them seem less significant than they truly are in the spiritual realm.

Another critical scheme is the **assault on our identity in Christ**. If Satan cannot get us to abandon our faith entirely, he will try to make us ineffective by undermining our confidence in who God says we are. He whispers lies about our worthlessness, our failures, and our inability to live a victorious Christian life. He wants us to focus on our sins and shortcomings rather than on Christ's finished work on the cross. He whispers, "You are not good enough," "You will never overcome this addiction," "God is disappointed in you." This tactic is designed to paralyze us with shame and guilt, preventing us from stepping into the fullness of our inheritance in Christ. He seeks to replace the truth of our identity as beloved children of God, redeemed and empowered by His Spirit, with the shame and condemnation that he himself embodies.

Moreover, Satan actively **hinders the spread of the Gospel**. Jesus Himself spoke of the wicked one snatching away the word sown in people's hearts, preventing the seeds of faith from taking root (Matthew 13:19). This can manifest in many ways: through the persecution of believers, through the promotion of secular ideologies that reject biblical truth, or through the sheer apathy and distraction of everyday life that keeps people from ever hearing or considering the Gospel message. He works to obscure the truth and to fill the minds of unbelievers with prejudice and resistance to God's message.

Let us delve deeper into some practical illustrations of these schemes. Consider the **scheme of spiritual lethargy**. This is not a sudden attack but a slow, creeping apathy that dulls our spiritual senses. It is the gradual loss of passion for prayer, the neglect of scripture reading, the decline in fellowship, and the waning of zeal for evangelism. Satan whispers, "You have done enough," or "Take a break, you deserve it," or "These spiritual disciplines are boring and unproductive." He will offer countless distractions – entertainment, hobbies, busyness – that can fill our time and energy, leaving little room for the things of God. This scheme is perilous because it does not appear to be an attack, but a natural winding down, a period of rest. It is a calculated strategy to disconnect us from our source of power—God.

Consider the concept **of misplaced blame**. When things go wrong, Satan can subtly influence us to blame others, or circumstances, or even God Himself, rather than taking personal responsibility. He can magnify the faults of a spouse, a pastor, or a fellow church member, deflecting attention from our own sin or inaction. This scheme prevents us from dealing with our own heart issues and from seeking reconciliation. For example, a believer might blame their pastor for a lack of spiritual growth, rather than examining their own commitment to scripture and prayer. Alternatively, they might blame their spouse for marital difficulties, ignoring their own contributions to the conflict. This tactic serves to foster bitterness and prevent personal accountability, which are essential for spiritual maturity.

The **scheme of emotional manipulation** is also incredibly potent. Satan can exploit our fears, our anxieties, and our insecurities to control our thoughts and actions. He can amplify feelings of inadequacy, worthlessness, or panic, leading us to make decisions based on emotion rather than on faith and truth. The intense fear that grips someone when contemplating a major life decision, or the overwhelming anxiety that paralyzes them in the face of uncertainty, can be a direct assault. He whispers, "You cannot handle this," or "It is going to end badly," or "You are going to fail." These thoughts, if entertained, can lead us to retreat from God's will and to succumb to despair.

Another cunning approach is the **scheme of the "good" alternative**. Satan does not always present outright sin. Sometimes, he offers something that appears good, beneficial, or even spiritual, but that ultimately distracts us from God's best. This could be a ministry opportunity that appears noble but ultimately leads to burnout and neglect of one's family, or a pursuit of knowledge that becomes an idol, or even a legitimate desire for comfort that results in complacency. The key is that it subtly diverts our primary allegiance and energy away from God. He can present a "Christian" political platform that emphasizes human solutions over divine dependence, or a "spiritual" practice that focuses on self-empowerment rather than God's empowerment. These can be incredibly deceptive because they are cloaked in a veneer of righteousness.

We must also be aware of the **scheme of spiritual deception through false teachings and philosophies**. The world is awash in ideas that subtly, or overtly, contradict biblical truth. New Age spirituality, secular humanism, prosperity gospel distortions, and various other ideologies can creep into the church or influence believers outside of it. Satan is the master of twisting truth and blending it with falsehood. He can use appealing personalities, eloquent arguments, or emotionally resonant experiences to present these deceptive systems as viable alternatives to the clear teachings of scripture. The danger lies in accepting these ideas without critical, biblically informed discernment, allowing them to erode our foundational faith. He thrives on introducing doctrines that dilute or distort the person and work of Christ, or that offer salvation or fulfillment apart from His atoning sacrifice.

The **scheme of over-spiritualization or under-spiritualization** is also worth noting. Some believers tend to see every minor inconvenience or personal failing as a direct demonic attack, leading to paranoia and an inability to exercise common sense or personal responsibility. On the other hand, some neglect the spiritual dimension entirely, attributing all struggles to psychological issues or mere circumstance, thereby ignoring the very real spiritual forces at play. Satan delights in pushing believers to these extremes, as both prevent a balanced and effective engagement with spiritual warfare. He wants us to be either so consumed with fear that we are ineffective or so dismissive of his existence that we are entirely caught off guard.

The subtle **scheme of weariness and discouragement** is incredibly effective. Spiritual warfare is a marathon, not a sprint. The constant vigilance, the sustained effort, and the inevitable setbacks can take a toll on one's mental and physical well-being. Satan's goal is to wear us down, to make us feel like giving up, to convince us that the fight is too complicated and that victory is impossible. He whispers, "You have been praying for so long, and nothing has changed," or "You are not making any progress," or "It is just not worth it." This scheme is often accompanied by a sense of isolation, making believers feel as though they are alone in their struggles. He wants us to believe that our efforts are futile, thereby undermining our hope and motivation.

Recognizing these schemes requires a diligent and prayerful approach. It involves a deep immersion in God's Word, which serves as our ultimate source of truth and our guide for discernment. It means cultivating a vibrant prayer life, where we can communicate with God, seek His wisdom, and rely on His strength. It also necessitates a strong connection with the community of faith, where we can receive support, accountability, and the benefit of shared discernment.

When we encounter a thought, a feeling, or a situation that seems designed to pull us away from God, to sow discord, or to promote falsehood, we must pause and engage our spiritual discernment. We must ask: Is this thought aligned with God's Word? Is this feeling rooted in faith or fear? Does this situation invite me to compromise my integrity or my commitment to Christ? Is this a temptation disguised as something good? By consistently asking these questions and seeking God's perspective, we begin to identify the enemy's subtle tactics.

The armor of God, which we will explore in detail, is specifically designed to counter these schemes. The belt of truth counters deception. The breastplate of righteousness guards against accusations and sin. The shoes of the gospel of peace ground us amidst turmoil. The shield of faith extinguishes the fiery darts of doubt and fear. The helmet of salvation protects our minds and assures us of our identity. The sword of the Spirit, the Word of God, is our offensive weapon against lies and deception. Each piece is a direct antidote to a specific aspect of the devil's strategies.

Understanding the schemes of the devil is not about fostering a mindset of constant paranoia, but a posture of sober awareness and preparedness. It is about recognizing that the spiritual battles we face are real and that our enemy is cunning and persistent. However, this understanding should not lead to fear, but to reliance on the God who has already secured our victory through Christ. By identifying the enemy's plans, we are better equipped to stand firm, to resist his onslaughts, and to live out the victorious life that God intends for us, not by our own strength, but by the power of His might working through us. The battle is real, the enemy is strategic, but our God is sovereign, and His provision is complete.

The Apostle Paul, in the heart of his letter to the Ephesians, delivers a powerful and enduring call to action. It is a clarion call that resonates through the centuries, urging every follower of Christ to embrace a posture of spiritual resilience and unwavering fortitude. This imperative is encapsulated in the verses that form the very bedrock of our understanding of spiritual engagement: "Finally, be strong in the Lord and in the power of His might. Put on the whole armor of God, so that you may be able to stand firm against the schemes of the devil" (Ephesians 6:10-11). This is not merely a piece of spiritual advice; it is a divine mandate, a foundational command from God Himself, delivered through His chosen apostle, that forms the essential starting point for any serious consideration of spiritual warfare. To be strong in the Lord is not an optional extra for the Christian life; it is a non-negotiable directive, the very prerequisite for navigating the spiritual landscape effectively.

The phrasing, "Finally," signals a culmination, a bringing together of the theological truths previously expounded to this burgeoning church in Ephesus. Paul has, in the preceding chapters, laid out the magnificent tapestry of God's plan of salvation, the unfathomable depth of His grace, the mystery of the church as the body of Christ, and the transformative power of the indwelling Holy Spirit. Having established this rich theological framework, he now pivots to the practical outworking of this faith in the face of an active spiritual opposition. The exhortation to strength and the subsequent call to don the armor are not isolated pronouncements but the logical conclusion of everything that has come before. They are the equipping for the journey, the preparation for the ongoing reality of spiritual conflict that every believer, in every age, will inevitably encounter.

The imperative "be strong" (Greek: *'endynamoō'*, ἐνδυναμόω) carries a profound weight. It is not a passive state of being, but an active command to be empowered and made strong. It speaks of drawing upon an external source of power, a power that is not inherent within us but is graciously provided by God. This is crucial because human strength, willpower, and natural resolve are utterly insufficient for the spiritual battles we face. The enemy we contend with is not of flesh and blood but a spiritual entity of immense power and cunning, a being who has waged war against God and humanity since the fall. Therefore, to "be strong" is to tap into the inexhaustible reservoir of divine power actively. It is to cease relying on our own limited capabilities and to draw upon the might of God deliberately.

This divine empowerment is directly linked to "the power of His might." The repetition of "power" (Greek: *'dynamis'*, δύναμις) emphasizes the sheer magnitude of the strength available to believers. It is not a modest measure of power, but the very omnipotence of God made accessible to us through our union with Christ. This is the power that raised Jesus from the dead, the power that holds the universe in His hand, the power that conquers sin and death. To be strong in the Lord is to embrace this truth, to understand that our spiritual warfare is not fought in our own strength, but in the overwhelming power of our Almighty God. This assurance, this knowledge that the same power that dwells in Christ now dwells in us, is the true source of our resilience and victory.

The context in which Paul writes to the Ephesians is vital for grasping the urgency and universality of this command. Ephesus was a significant city in the Roman province of Asia Minor, a bustling hub of commerce and culture, but also a center of pagan worship and occult practices. The Temple of Artemis, one of the Seven Wonders of the Ancient World, was located there, a place deeply steeped in idolatry and demonic influence. Paul had spent a considerable amount of time ministering in Ephesus, a period marked by both remarkable success in establishing the church and intense opposition from those invested in the prevailing spiritual darkness (**Acts 19**). He knew firsthand the spiritual forces at play in a city so deeply ensnared by idolatry and false religion.

Therefore, his words to the Ephesians were not abstract theological musings, but practical, battle-ready instructions for believers living in a spiritually charged environment. They were surrounded by the visible manifestations of spiritual opposition – sorcery, demon possession, and idolatrous rituals. Paul's instruction to "be strong" and "put on the armor" was a direct response to the tangible realities they faced daily. His teachings extended far beyond the specific historical context of first-century Ephesus. The principles Paul articulates are timeless and universally applicable to every believer in Christ, regardless of their geographical location or the particular cultural milieu in which they find themselves.

The schemes of the devil, as Paul introduces them in verse 11, are not random acts of chaos but calculated strategies. The word "schemes" (*'methodeia'*, μεθοδεία) Implies a methodical, cunning, and often deceptive approach. It suggests a wily stratagem, a carefully planned operation designed to undermine, deceive, and ultimately defeat its objectives. This understanding is crucial if we are going to recognize Satan's attacks and, through our discernment, prevent being ensnared by them.

The command to "stand firm" (Greek: *'stēnai'*, στῆναι) is the direct objective of putting on the armor. It signifies not just remaining in place, but holding one's ground, resisting the enemy's advance, and refusing to be moved. This is not a call to an offensive charge, but a defensive stance, a resolute refusal to yield. It acknowledges that the spiritual battle is often characterized by pressure, as attempts are made to dislodge us from our position of faith and obedience. The armor is not designed for aggressive warfare in itself, but rather to enable us to withstand the enemy's onslaughts and maintain our spiritual integrity.

The entire passage, from verse 10 to verse 20, functions as a cohesive unit, a divinely provided manual for spiritual resilience. **Verse 10,** *"Finally, be strong in the Lord and in the power of His might,"* establishes the necessary foundation. It is the internal disposition, the reliance on God's power. **Verse**

11, *"Put on the whole armor of God, so that you may be able to stand firm against the schemes of the devil,"* provides the external equipping and the immediate purpose. This subsection focuses specifically on this foundational imperative and the overarching purpose it serves, setting the stage for a deeper exploration of each component of the armor in the subsequent sections.

The imperative to "be strong in the Lord" is a recognition of our inherent weakness. Humanity, since the Fall, is predisposed to sin and vulnerable to spiritual attack. Our natural state is one of spiritual bankruptcy, incapable of standing against the forces of darkness on our own. Thus, the strength Paul calls us to is not a self-generated strength but a divinely imparted strength. It is the strength that flows from our union with Christ, who has already triumphed over sin and death. This is the essence of Christian empowerment. We are not called to be tough, but to be divinely empowered. Our resilience is not a product of grit and determination alone, but of actively drawing from God's inexhaustible supply of power.

Consider the analogy of a soldier entering a battlefield without proper armor, weapons, and training; their chances of survival, let alone victory, are minimal. The Christian life is presented as a spiritual campaign. The enemy is real, his tactics are cunning, and the stakes are eternal. God, in His infinite wisdom and love, has provided the necessary equipment and the essential power source for His soldiers. The command to be strong in the Lord is the directive to plug into this power source, to activate the divine resources available to every believer through the Holy Spirit.

The Ephesians lived in a society where spiritual power was understood, albeit in a distorted form. They were accustomed to the idea of spiritual forces influencing human lives, often through sorcery, incantations, and idol worship. Paul's message was not alien to their conceptual framework, but he reoriented their understanding of spiritual power. He presented the true source of power, not in demonic manipulation but in the sovereign God of the universe. He taught them that true spiritual strength came not from appeasing pagan deities or engaging in occult practices, but from a direct relationship with the living God through Jesus Christ.

The command to "be strong in the Lord" is not a one-time event but an ongoing orientation of the will. It requires a conscious and continuous reliance on God. It means consciously choosing to draw upon His strength in every situation, particularly in moments of trial, temptation, or spiritual opposition. This active dependence is what distinguishes the Christian approach to spiritual warfare. It is not about self-reliance but about God-reliance. It is about understanding that our victory is not contingent on our ability, but on God's ability working through us.

The "power of His might" further emphasizes that the strength available is not a generic spiritual energy, but the specific, potent power that belongs to God. This is the same power that brought creation into existence, the power that sustains the universe, and the power that conquered death at the resurrection of Christ. When Paul speaks of this power, he is pointing to the active, dynamic force of God that is available to believers through the indwelling Holy Spirit. It is the power that enables us to live holy lives, to resist temptation, to serve God effectively, and to stand firm against the adversary. This is not a passive endowment but a dynamic force that is accessed through faith and obedience.

The immediate consequence of this divine empowerment, as Paul states, is the ability "to stand firm against the schemes of the devil." The concept of standing firm is central to the metaphor of spiritual warfare. It implies a stable, unyielding position. It suggests resilience in the face of pressure, the ability to withstand attacks without crumbling. The devil's schemes are designed to destabilize, to unnerve, and to dislodge believers from their spiritual foundations. They aim to sow confusion, doubt, and fear, thereby weakening our resolve and compromising our effectiveness.

The armor of God, which is the means by which we stand firm, is not a collection of passive pieces of equipment but divinely provided resources that enable us to resist the enemy actively. Each piece of armor corresponds to a specific aspect of God's provision and our response of faith, designed to counter the devil's various stratagems. This is why Paul emphasizes the *whole* armor of God. To neglect any part is to leave oneself vulnerable to the enemy's targeted attacks. It is essential to be equipped in every aspect of our spiritual being to counter the multifaceted nature of spiritual opposition effectively.

The universality of this instruction cannot be overstated. Paul was writing to a specific church in a specific historical context, but the spiritual realities he addressed are universal in nature. Every generation of believers faces the same adversary, employing similar tactics, albeit with variations adapted to the cultural context. Whether the challenges come in the form of overt persecution, subtle deception, societal pressures, or internal spiritual battles, the command to be strong in the Lord and to be equipped with the armor of God remains the timeless directive for victorious living.

To understand this mandate is to grasp that spiritual warfare is not an optional pursuit for the hyper-spiritual or the exceptionally zealous. It is a fundamental aspect of the Christian journey for every single believer. God does not call us to engage in spiritual combat without providing the necessary strength and the means to defend ourselves. He equips those whom He calls. Our part is to respond in obedience, to draw upon His strength actively, and to put on the whole armor He has provided. This fundamental understanding forms the bedrock upon which all further engagement with the reality of spiritual warfare must be built. It is the essential starting point, the divine mandate that underscores the seriousness and the capability of the Christian walk in the face of an unseen, yet very real, adversary. The call to be strong in the Lord is, therefore, a call to embrace our dependence on Him, to recognize His unfailing power, and to actively engage in the spiritual battles He has called us to, fully equipped and fully confident in His ultimate victory.

The Apostle Paul, in the heart of his letter to the Ephesians, delivers a powerful and enduring call to action. It is a clarion call that resonates through the centuries, urging every follower of Christ to embrace a posture of spiritual resilience and unwavering fortitude. This imperative is encapsulated in the verses that form the very bedrock of our understanding of spiritual engagement: "Finally, be strong in the Lord and in the power of His might. Put on the whole armor of God, so that you may be able to stand firm against the schemes of the devil" (Ephesians 6:10-11). This is not merely a piece of spiritual advice; it is a divine mandate, a foundational command from God Himself, delivered through His chosen apostle, that forms the essential starting point for any serious consideration of spiritual warfare. To be strong in the Lord is not an optional extra for the Christian life; it is a non-negotiable directive, the very prerequisite for navigating the spiritual landscape effectively.

The phrasing, "Finally," signals a culmination, a bringing together of the theological truths previously expounded to this burgeoning church in Ephesus. Paul has, in the preceding chapters, laid out the magnificent tapestry of God's plan of salvation, the unfathomable depth of His grace, the mystery of the church as the body of Christ, and the transformative power of the indwelling Holy Spirit. Having established this rich theological framework, he now pivots to the practical outworking of this faith in the face of an active spiritual opposition. The exhortation to strength and the subsequent call to don the armor are not isolated pronouncements but the logical conclusion of everything that has come before. They are the equipping for the journey, the preparation for the ongoing reality of spiritual conflict that every believer, in every age, will inevitably encounter.

The imperative "be strong" (Greek: *'endynamoō'*, ἐνδυναμόω) carries a profound weight. It is not a passive state of being, but an active command to be empowered and made strong. It speaks of drawing upon an external source of power, a power that is not inherent within us but is graciously provided by God. This is crucial because human strength, willpower, and natural resolve are utterly insufficient for the spiritual battles we face. The enemy we contend with is not of flesh and blood but a spiritual entity of immense power and cunning, a being who has waged war against God and humanity since the fall. Therefore, to "be strong" is to tap into the inexhaustible reservoir of divine power actively. It is to cease relying on our own limited capabilities and to draw upon the might of God deliberately.

This divine empowerment is directly linked to "the power of His might." The repetition of "power" (Greek: *'dynamis'*, δύναμις) emphasizes the sheer magnitude of the strength available to believers. It is not a modest measure of power, but the very omnipotence of God made accessible to us through our union with Christ. This is the power that raised Jesus from the dead, the power that holds the universe in His hand, the power that conquers sin and death. To be strong in the Lord is to embrace this truth, to understand that our spiritual warfare is not fought in our own strength, but in the overwhelming power of our Almighty God. This assurance, this knowledge that the same power that dwells in Christ now dwells in us, is the trustworthy source of our resilience and victory.

The context in which Paul writes to the Ephesians is vital for grasping the urgency and universality of this command. Ephesus was a significant city in the Roman province of Asia Minor, a bustling hub of commerce and culture, but also a center of pagan worship and occult practices. The Temple of Artemis, one of the Seven Wonders of the Ancient World, was located there, a place deeply steeped in idolatry and demonic influence. Paul had spent a considerable amount of time ministering in Ephesus, a period marked by both remarkable success in establishing the church and intense opposition from those invested in the prevailing spiritual darkness **(Acts 19)**. He knew firsthand the spiritual forces at play in a city so deeply ensnared by idolatry and false religion. Therefore, his words to the Ephesians were not abstract theological musings, but practical, battle-ready instructions for believers living in a spiritually charged environment. They were surrounded by the visible manifestations of spiritual opposition – sorcery, demon possession, and idolatrous rituals. Paul's instruction to "be strong" and "put on the armor" was a direct response to the tangible realities they faced daily. However, the profundity of his teaching extends far beyond the specific historical context of first-century Ephesus. The principles Paul articulates are timeless and applicable to every believer in Christ, regardless of their geographical location or era in which they live.

The schemes of the devil, as Paul introduces them in verse 11, are not random acts of chaos but calculated strategies. The word "schemes" (*'methodeia'*, μεθοδεία) implies a methodical, cunning, and often deceptive approach. It suggests a wily stratagem, a carefully planned operation designed to undermine, deceive, and ultimately defeat its objectives. This understanding is crucial because it elevates our perception of the enemy beyond mere superficial challenges or personal failings. It recognizes an active, intelligent, and malevolent force that is constantly devising ways to ensnare us.

The command to "stand firm" (Greek: *'stēnai'*, στῆναι) is the direct objective of putting on the armor. It signifies not just remaining in place, but holding one's ground, resisting the enemy's advance, and refusing to be moved. This is not a call to an offensive charge, but a defensive stance, a resolute refusal to yield. It acknowledges that the spiritual battle is often characterized by pressure, as attempts are made to dislodge us from our position of faith and obedience. The armor is not designed for aggressive warfare in itself, but rather to enable us to withstand the enemy's onslaughts and maintain our spiritual integrity.

The entire passage, from verse 10 to verse 20, functions as a cohesive unit, a divinely provided manual for spiritual resilience. Verse 10, "Finally, be strong in the Lord and in the power of His might," establishes the necessary foundation. It is the internal disposition, the reliance on God's power. Verse 11, "Put on the whole armor of God, so that you may be able to stand firm against the schemes of the devil," provides the external equipping and the immediate purpose. This subsection focuses specifically on this foundational imperative and the overarching purpose it serves, setting the stage for a deeper exploration of each component of the armor.

The imperative to "be strong in the Lord" is a recognition of our inherent weakness. Humanity, since the Fall, is predisposed to sin and vulnerable to spiritual attack. Our natural state is one of spiritual bankruptcy, incapable of standing against the forces of darkness on our own. Thus, the strength Paul calls us to is not a self-generated strength but a divinely imparted strength. It is the strength that flows from our union with Christ, who has already triumphed over sin and death. This is the essence of Christian empowerment. We are not called to be tough, but to be divinely empowered. Our resilience is not a product of grit and determination alone, but of actively drawing from God's inexhaustible supply of power.

Consider the analogy of a soldier entering a battlefield. Without proper armor, weapons, and training, their chances of survival, let alone victory, are minimal. Similarly, the Christian life is presented as a spiritual campaign. The enemy is real, his tactics are cunning, and the stakes are eternal. Therefore, God, in His infinite wisdom and love, has provided the necessary equipment and the essential power source for His soldiers. The command to be strong in the Lord is a directive to tap into this power source and activate the divine resources available to every believer.

The Ephesians lived in a society where spiritual power was understood, albeit in a distorted form. They were accustomed to the idea of spiritual forces influencing human lives, often through sorcery, incantations, and idol worship. Paul's message was not alien to their conceptual framework, but he reoriented their understanding of spiritual power. He presented the true source of power, not in demonic manipulation but in the sovereign God of the universe. He taught them that true spiritual strength came not from appeasing pagan deities or engaging in occult practices, but from a direct relationship with the living God through Jesus Christ.

The command to "be strong in the Lord" is not a one-time event but an ongoing orientation of the will. It requires a conscious and continuous reliance on God. It means consciously choosing to draw upon His strength in every situation, particularly in moments of trial, temptation, or spiritual opposition. This active dependence is what distinguishes the Christian approach to spiritual warfare. It is not about self-reliance but about God-reliance. It is about understanding that our victory is not contingent on our ability, but on God's ability working through us.

The "power of His might" further emphasizes that the strength available is not a generic spiritual energy, but the specific, potent power that belongs to God. This is the same power that brought creation into existence, the power that sustains the universe, and the power that conquered death at the resurrection of Christ. When Paul speaks of this power, he is pointing to the active, dynamic force of God that is available to believers through the indwelling Holy Spirit. It is the power that enables us to live holy lives, to resist temptation, to serve God effectively, and to stand firm against the adversary. This is not a passive endowment but a dynamic force that is accessed through faith and obedience.

The immediate consequence of this divine empowerment, as Paul states, is the ability "to stand firm against the schemes of the devil." The concept of standing firm is central to the metaphor of spiritual warfare. It implies a stable, unyielding position. It suggests resilience in the face of pressure, the ability to withstand attacks without crumbling. The devil's schemes are designed to destabilize, to unnerve, and to dislodge believers from their spiritual foundations. They aim to sow confusion, doubt, and fear, thereby weakening our resolve and compromising our effectiveness.

The armor of God, which is the means by which we stand firm, is not a collection of passive pieces of equipment but divinely provided resources that enable us to resist the enemy actively. Each piece of armor corresponds to a specific aspect of God's provision and our response of faith, designed to counter the devil's various stratagems. This is why Paul emphasizes the *whole* armor of God. To neglect any part is to leave oneself vulnerable to the enemy's targeted attacks. It is essential to be equipped in every aspect of our spiritual being to counter the multifaceted nature of spiritual opposition effectively.

The universality of this instruction cannot be overstated. Paul was writing to a specific church in a specific historical context, but the spiritual realities he addressed are universal in nature. Every generation of believers faces the same adversary, employing similar tactics, albeit with variations adapted to the cultural context. Whether the challenges come in the form of overt persecution, subtle deception, societal pressures, or internal spiritual battles, the command to be strong in the Lord and to be equipped with the armor of God remains the timeless directive for victorious living.

To understand this mandate is to grasp that spiritual warfare is not an optional pursuit for the hyper-spiritual or the exceptionally zealous. It is a fundamental aspect of the Christian journey for every single believer. God does not call us to engage in spiritual combat without providing the necessary strength and the means to defend ourselves. He equips those whom He calls. Our part is to respond in obedience, to draw upon His strength actively, and to put on the whole armor He has provided. This fundamental understanding forms the bedrock upon which all further engagement with the reality of spiritual warfare must be built. It is the essential starting point, the divine mandate that underscores the seriousness and the capability of the Christian walk in the face of an unseen, yet very real, adversary. The call to be strong in the Lord is, therefore, a call to embrace our dependence on Him, to recognize His unfailing power, and to actively engage in the spiritual battles He has called us to, fully equipped and fully confident in His ultimate victory.

The question that naturally arises from Paul's profound instruction is: Why is this armor necessary? The answer lies not in some abstract theological necessity but in the very nature of our spiritual existence and the relentless opposition we face. God, in His boundless love and foresight, has not left us to navigate the perilous terrain of spiritual warfare without comprehensive provision. The armor of God is not a human invention, a strategic adaptation from earthly military science, but a direct, divine provision—a complete spiritual defense system meticulously designed by the Creator Himself. It is a testament to God's proactive care for His people, ensuring that we are not only empowered but also thoroughly protected against the insidious assaults of the adversary.

Each component of this spiritual panoply is more than just a metaphorical shield or sword; it represents a facet of Christ's redemptive work and the ongoing empowerment of the Holy Spirit within the believer. These are not abstract concepts, but living realities - divine resources that provide tangible protection and enable steadfastness. When we consider the historical context of Paul's writing, the image of the Roman soldier, equipped with his meticulously crafted armor, would have been a familiar and potent symbol. Roman legionaries were renowned for their discipline and their formidable protective gear, which enabled them to withstand enemy onslaughts and maintain formation under extreme pressure. Paul masterfully appropriates this imagery, not to suggest that our spiritual defense is merely an imitation of human military technology, but to illustrate the completeness, effectiveness, and divine origin of the provisions God has made for us.

The effectiveness of the Roman soldier's armor lay in its comprehensiveness. A well-equipped soldier was protected from head to toe, each piece designed to counter specific threats. A missing greave, a dented helmet, or a poorly fitted breastplate could be the very point of vulnerability that an enemy would exploit. Similarly, Paul's emphasis on the w*hole* armor of God highlights that our spiritual defense is only as strong as its weakest link. God's provision is holistic, covering every aspect of our spiritual being. There is no lacuna in His protection, no unprotected flank, provided we avail ourselves of all that He has made available. This completeness is crucial because the enemy's schemes are diverse and aim to exploit any area of weakness or point of vulnerability in our spiritual lives. The persistent and malevolent nature of the spiritual enemy underscores the necessity of this divine provision. The devil, often referred to as Satan, is not a mere abstract force or a personification of evil. He is a fallen angelic being, a personal entity possessing intelligence, will, and immense power, actively engaged in a cosmic rebellion against God. His singular aim is to thwart God's purposes and to lead humanity away from Him. Since the fall of Adam and Eve, Satan has relentlessly sought to deceive, corrupt, and destroy. His strategies are ancient yet ever-evolving, constantly adapting to the cultural and psychological landscape of each era. He masquerades as an angel of light, employing deception and subtlety to achieve his destructive ends. He attacks not our physical bodies directly, but our minds, our wills, and our hearts—the very core of our spiritual identity and our relationship with God.

The armor of God is not an optional accessory for the Christian journey; it is an essential equipping for survival and victory. It is God's answer to the enemy's arsenal of lies, temptations, accusations, and spiritual assaults. Each piece of armor is a manifestation of God's grace and power, specifically designed to neutralize the enemy's tactics and secure our spiritual well-being. This is why Paul presents it as something to be *put on*. It requires our active participation and our conscious decision to embrace and utilize the spiritual resources that God has so generously provided. It is an expression of our faith and obedience, acknowledging our dependence on God for protection and strength in the face of overwhelming spiritual opposition. The provision of the armor is intrinsically linked to the person and work of Jesus Christ. Indeed, each piece of armor finds its ultimate reality and effectiveness in Him. He is the embodiment of truth, righteousness, peace, faith, salvation, and the Word of God. As we don the spiritual armor, we are, in essence, putting on Christ Himself, allowing His finished work and His indwelling Spirit to equip and protect us. This is the profound depth of God's provision: He does not just give us tools; He gives us Himself, enabling us to stand not in our own power, but in the victory He has already secured.

This divine provision is also a demonstration of God's deep love and concern for His children. He knows our vulnerabilities, our propensity to fall, and the intensity of the spiritual battles we face. He does not wish for any to perish, but for all to come to repentance and to live in the fullness of His grace and power. The armor of God is a tangible expression of this desire, a paternal provision for the protection and flourishing of His spiritual offspring. It assures us that we are never alone in the battle, that the One who is infinitely greater than our adversary stands with us, has equipped us, and guarantees our ultimate triumph. This understanding of the armor as divine provision, rather than human invention, shifts the focus from our own efforts to God's unfailing faithfulness and power, transforming our approach to spiritual warfare from one of anxious self-reliance to one of confident dependence on our sovereign Lord. It is His provision, His power, and His plan that enable us to stand firm.

The directive to "stand firm" is not a passive invitation to merely exist in a state of spiritual neutrality, but an active, dynamic posture of unwavering resolve. It is the culmination of being strong in the Lord and being equipped with the whole armor of God. To stand firm means to refuse to be dislodged from one's spiritual foundations, to hold one's ground against the relentless pressures and assaults of the adversarial forces. This is not a call to an offensive charge, aiming to conquer territory, but a strategic imperative is to maintain one's position, resist the enemy's advance, and preserve spiritual integrity. The Christian life, viewed through the lens of spiritual warfare, is a campaign fought on multiple fronts, and the ability to stand firm is the bedrock of sustained engagement and ultimate victory.

This steadfastness is deeply rooted in faith and an unwavering commitment to truth. The enemy, as identified by Paul, operates through "schemes," which implies cunning, deception, and methodical planning. These schemes are designed to sow doubt, fear, and confusion, to erode our confidence in God's Word and His promises, and to lead us away from the path of righteousness. To stand firm, therefore, is to anchor ourselves in the unshakeable truths of the Gospel, to remain steadfast in our doctrinal understanding, and to live lives that are consistent with our faith. It means resisting the temptation to compromise biblical principles for the sake of convenience or popular opinion. It requires a resolute adherence to the teachings of Scripture, allowing them to be the plumb line for our beliefs and practices, even when such adherence invites opposition or discomfort.

The resilience implied in "standing firm" is not a matter of human willpower alone. While determination is a component, the trustworthy source of our ability to withstand is divine empowerment. It is the strength imparted by the Lord, flowing through the Holy Spirit, that enables us to resist the pressures of the world, the temptations of the flesh, and the insidious attacks of the devil. This resilience is cultivated through consistent spiritual disciplines: prayer, the study of Scripture, fellowship with other believers, and active obedience to God's commands. These practices, when undertaken in dependence on God, build spiritual fortitude, creating an inner core of strength that can withstand the external onslaught. When we face adversity, discouragement, or feelings of being overwhelmed, it is this God-given resilience that prevents us from giving up.

Consider the implications of remaining unyielding in faith and doctrine. The spiritual adversary seeks to introduce subtle distortions, to twist the truth, and to promote counterfeit versions of reality. This can manifest in various ways: through persuasive arguments that subtly undermine biblical authority, through the allure of alternative philosophies that contradict God's revealed will, or through the erosion of sound theological teaching within the church itself. To stand firm in doctrine means to diligently guard the truth, to test all teachings against the clear standard of Scripture, and to refuse to be swayed by novel interpretations that deviate from the foundational truths of the Christian faith. It is a commitment to the "once for all delivered to the saints" faith **(Jude 1:3)**, safeguarding its purity and integrity.

Standing firm extends to our practice. Our lives should be a tangible expression of our faith. This means living in a manner that honors God, demonstrates love for one another, and reflects the character of Christ in all our interactions. The enemy often targets our behavior, seeking to find inconsistencies, hypocrisy, or areas of unrepentant sin that can be used as footholds for his attacks. To stand firm in practice is to maintain a life of integrity, to live consistently with our profession of faith, and to actively pursue holiness. It means confessing our sins when we fall, seeking forgiveness, and allowing the transforming power of the Holy Spirit to mold us into the image of Christ. This consistent walk of obedience is a powerful testament to God's power and a bulwark against the enemy's accusations.

The concept of standing firm also encompasses a refusal to be moved by the enemy's tactics of intimidation or discouragement. The adversary often seeks to paralyze believers through fear, doubt, or a sense of hopelessness. He whispers lies that we are insufficient, that our efforts are futile, or that God's promises are unreliable. To stand firm is to reject these demoralizing narratives and to reaffirm our confidence in God's sovereignty, His goodness, and His ultimate victory. This requires cultivating a perspective that transcends our immediate circumstances and remains fixed on eternal realities. When difficulties arise, when opposition mounts, or when our faith is tested, it is the ability to hold fast to God's promises and to trust in His unfailing power that allows us to remain steadfast.

The victory in spiritual warfare, as understood through the metaphor of standing firm, is not necessarily characterized by aggressive offensives or the complete annihilation of the enemy's forces in a temporal sense. Instead, it is a victory of endurance, of faithfulness, and of maintaining one's spiritual integrity. It is the triumph of holding one's ground, of refusing to yield to the enemy's pressures, and of continuing to live out one's faith with unwavering resolve. This perspective is crucial, as it shifts the focus from an exhausting pursuit of immediate, visible conquest to a godlier emphasis on faithfulness and perseverance. God's ultimate victory is assured, but our participation in that victory involves a daily commitment to stand firm.

The enemy's schemes are often subtle and designed to wear down the believer over time. He employs a strategy of attrition, seeking to slowly erode our faith, our joy, and our effectiveness. This is why endurance is so vital. It is the ability to continue in faith and obedience, even when faced with prolonged trials, persistent temptations, or discouraging circumstances. This endurance is not born of stubbornness or self-reliance, but of a deep-seated trust in God's provision and plans. It is fueled by the knowledge that He who began a good work in us will bring it to completion (**Philippians 1:6**). The metaphor of standing firm also underscores the importance of community. While each believer is called to be strong, we are also part of a larger spiritual army. The armor of God is designed for individual equipping, but its effectiveness is amplified when worn by a united body of believers. Standing firm together means supporting one another, encouraging those who are wavering, and praying for those who are under particular attack. The church, as the body of Christ, is meant to be a place of mutual strengthening and fortification. When one member suffers, all suffer with it; when one member is honored, all rejoice with it (**I Corinthians 12:26**). This communal aspect of standing firm is a powerful deterrent to the enemy, who seeks to isolate and divide believers.

    The cost of not standing firm can be severe, both personally and corporately. Compromise, surrender, or a wavering commitment can lead to spiritual decline, a loss of effectiveness, and a diminished witness for Christ. The enemy is eager to exploit any weakness, any crack in our defenses, to gain a foothold in our lives or in the life of the church. This underscores the urgency and the profound importance of Paul's exhortation. It is a call to vigilance, to intentionality, and to a resolute commitment to the spiritual disciplines that fortify us. The assurance that we *can* stand firm rests entirely on God's power and His provision. He has not called us to an impossible task. The armor He provides is complete, and the strength He offers is inexhaustible. Our role is to embrace this provision, to actively put on the armor daily, and to draw upon His power in every circumstance consciously. This is the essence of spiritual preparedness: not a state of passive waiting, but an active engagement with God's resources, resulting in a steadfast and unyielding stance against the adversary. It is a commitment to remain rooted in Christ, unswayed by the winds of opposition, and unwavering in our devotion, knowing that our ultimate victory is secured in Him. This unwavering posture is not about being immovable in our own strength, but about being rooted in the unshakeable power of God, allowing His might to be our foundation and His truth to be our shield.

CHAPTER SIX:
The Gift of Discernment— Necessary for the Last Days

The spiritual battleground upon which believers find themselves engaged is not a static one; instead, it shifts and intensifies, particularly as we approach the culmination of God's redemptive plan. To truly grasp the necessity of the gift of discernment, we must situate ourselves within the prophetic framework of what the Scriptures describe as the "last days." This phrase, often used in both Old and New Testament prophecy, does not refer to a single, instantaneous event but rather to a prolonged period leading up to Christ's ultimate return and the establishment of His eternal kingdom. It is a period characterized by distinct spiritual markers, chief among them being an escalating wave of deception and apostasy. Understanding this eschatological context is not merely an academic exercise; it is foundational to recognizing the urgency and critical importance of spiritual discernment for every believer living in this present era, as it prepares us for the unique spiritual realities that lie ahead.

The Old Testament prophets frequently spoke of a future time of great tribulation and spiritual testing. **Isaiah 29:9-10** laments a people who are spiritually dulled: "*Stay yourselves, and wonder; cry ye out, and cry: they are drunken, but not with wine; they stagger, but not with strong drink. For the Lord hath poured out upon you the spirit of deep sleep, and hath closed your eyes: the prophets and your rulers, the seers hath he covered.*" (KJV, 2023).

This imagery of spiritual blindness and intoxication speaks to a state where truth is obscured, and genuine spiritual perception is lost. This state is directly linked to a departure from God's ways, a theme that permeates prophetic pronouncements. The prophet Jeremiah, echoing this concern, foresaw a time when people would "err in spirit" and those who were "rushed on" would not understand (**Jeremiah 49:26**). This prophetic vision of widespread error and misunderstanding is a stark precursor to the intense spiritual warfare waged through deception.

The concept of the "last days" finds significant elaboration in the New Testament, particularly in the teachings of Jesus and the apostles. When Jesus spoke of His second coming and the signs that would precede it, He explicitly warned His disciples about the prevalence of deception. In **Matthew 24:4-5**, He stated, "*Take heed that no man deceive you. For many shall come in my name, saying, I am Christ; and shall deceive many.*" (KJV, 2023).

This initial warning is not a minor footnote but a central theme in His Olivet Discourse. The impersonation of Christ, or the claiming of His authority for false purposes, is identified as a primary tool of deception. Furthermore, Jesus warned of "false Christs" and "false prophets" who would arise and perform great signs and wonders to lead astray, if possible, even the elect (**Matthew 24:24**). This prophecy underscores that deception in the last days will not be subtle or easily detectable; it will be sophisticated, attractive, and overwhelming, cloaked in religious or spiritual guise.

The Apostle Paul, in his epistles, provides further clarity and urgency regarding the characteristics of the last days. To Timothy, he writes a poignant passage in **II Timothy 3:1-5**, which serves as a powerful diagnostic of the spiritual climate of this era: "*This know also, that in the last days perilous times shall come. For men shall be lovers of themselves, covetous, boasters, proud, blasphemers, disobedient to parents, unthankful, unholy, Without natural affection, trucebreakers, false accusers, incontinent, fierce, despisers of good things, Traitors, heady, highminded, lovers of pleasure more than lovers of God; Having a form of godliness, but denying the power thereof: from such turn away.*" (KJV, 2023).

This comprehensive list describes not only outward societal decay but also a profound internal spiritual corruption within the religious community itself. The critical phrase, "having a form of godliness, but denying the power thereof," is particularly relevant to discernment. It points to a counterfeit spirituality, one that mimics religious practice and language but lacks the transformative substance and divine authority that comes from a genuine relationship with God. This is precisely the kind of deception that discernment is designed to expose.

Paul's warning in **II Thessalonians 2:3-4** is equally critical for understanding the prophetic context. He speaks of a "falling away" that must come first, preceding the "man of lawlessness" (interpreted as the Antichrist). He then elaborates, "*Let no man deceive you by any means: for that day shall not come, except there be a falling away first, and that man of sin be revealed.*" (KJV, 2023).

The "falling away," or apostasy, is not merely a secularization of society but a departure from the core tenets of the faith from within the professing church. This apostasy is fueled and facilitated by deception. The adversary's strategy is to blind minds and distort truth, leading people away from the pure gospel. This is why the gift of discernment becomes an indispensable tool for navigating these turbulent spiritual waters, enabling believers to identify and resist the subtle yet pervasive influences that lead to doctrinal error and spiritual compromise.

The Apostle Peter also addresses the reality of false teachers and deceptive doctrines in the last days. In **II Peter 2:1-3**, he issues a severe warning: "*But there were false prophets also among the people, even as there shall be false teachers among you, who privily shall bring in damnable heresies, even denying the Lord that bought them, and bringing upon themselves swift destruction. Moreover, many shall follow their pernicious ways; by reason of whom the way of truth shall be evil spoken of. Moreover, through covetousness shall they with feigned words make merchandise of you: to whom the sentence long ago is not idle, and their damnation slumbereth not.*" (KJV, 2023).

This passage highlights several key characteristics of last-day deception: its insidious nature ("privily"), its denial of Christ's redemptive work, its ability to attract followers, its association with greed ("covetousness"), and its use of manipulative language ("feigned words"). These are precisely the kinds of spiritual dynamics that the gift of discernment is equipped to identify and counteract. The "way of truth" being spoken of negatively is a direct consequence of the proliferation of these deceptive teachings.

The biblical portrayal of the last days, therefore, is not one of passive observation but of active spiritual engagement. It is a period marked by intensified spiritual warfare, with deception as a primary weapon of the adversary. The prophecies from both the Old and New Testaments converge on this point: the closer we get to the consummation of God's plan, the more pervasive and sophisticated the spiritual deception will become.

This escalating challenge makes the cultivation and exercise of the gift of discernment not a peripheral spiritual discipline but an essential component of the believer's walk and witness. It is the spiritual compass that allows us to navigate the increasingly treacherous terrain of spiritual claims, distinguishing the voice of the Good Shepherd from the many counterfeits that seek to lead the flock astray.

Without this vital gift, believers are vulnerable to the very forces that Jesus and the apostles so earnestly warned against, risking being swept away by currents of error that undermine the foundations of faith and lead to spiritual shipwreck. The prophetic context, therefore, serves as a solemn call to vigilance and a profound impetus to actively seek and utilize the God-given capacity for spiritual discernment.

The intensifying spiritual climate of the "last days" is not a matter of conjecture but an explicit prophetic declaration that demands a robust response from the faithful. Scripture repeatedly portrays this era as one marked by a heightened spiritual battle, with deception serving as one of the enemy's most potent weapons. Understanding this prophetic context is crucial, as it highlights the vital importance of the gift of discernment in the lives of every believer. It moves discernment from a passive appreciation of truth to an active, necessary defense against the escalating onslaught of falsehood that characterizes this age.

The Old Testament prophets, in their stark pronouncements, laid the groundwork for this understanding. **Isaiah 29:9-10** paints a grim picture of spiritual immaturity and delusion: "*Stay yourselves, and wonder; cry ye out, and cry: they are drunken, but not with wine; they stagger, but not with strong drink. For the Lord hath poured out upon you the spirit of deep sleep, and hath closed your eyes: the prophets and your rulers, the seers hath he covered.*" (KJV, 2023).

This is not merely a description of societal moral decay but a profound spiritual blindness that affects even those in positions of spiritual leadership. The imagery of being "drunk" and "asleep" signifies a state of spiritual unawareness, a failure to perceive truth, and an inability to distinguish reality from delusion. This condition is directly linked to a departure from God's ways and a susceptibility to error.

This theme resonates throughout prophetic literature and finds its ultimate amplification in the New Testament's depiction of the last days. Jeremiah, too, warned of a time when people would "err in spirit" and "those who were rushed on would not understand" (**Jeremiah 49:26**). This prophetic foresight highlights the pervasive nature of misunderstanding and error that would come to characterize specific periods, particularly those leading up to God's judgments and the establishment of His kingdom.

The New Testament significantly elaborates on this prophetic outlook, situating the concept of the "last days" as a distinct epoch leading up to Christ's second coming. Jesus Himself, in His Olivet Discourse recorded in **Matthew 24:4-5**, issued a direct warning concerning the prevalence of deception. He cautioned, "*Take heed that no man deceive you. For many shall come in my name, saying, I am Christ; and shall deceive many*" (KJV, 2023).

This was not an offhand remark but a foundational element of His eschatological teaching. The identification of "false Christs" and "false prophets" performing signs and wonders to mislead, if possible, even the elect (**Matthew 24:24**), reveals that deception in this final era would be sophisticated, alluring, and potentially overwhelming. It would not be confined to the periphery but would infiltrate the very core of religious life, masquerading as divine truth. The capacity to discern the genuine from the counterfeit becomes, therefore, an essential survival skill for the believer in this age of spiritual sophistication.

The Apostle Paul's epistles offer further critical insights into the characteristics of the last days, painting a detailed picture of the spiritual and moral landscape. In his letter to Timothy, **II Timothy 3:1-5**, he writes a chillingly accurate prophecy: "*But know this, that in the last days perilous times shall come. For men shall be lovers of themselves, covetous, boasters, proud, blasphemers,* *disobedient to parents, unthankful, unholy, without natural affection, trucebreakers, false accusers, incontinent, fierce, despisers of good things, traitors, heady, highminded, lovers of pleasure more than lovers of God, having a form of godliness, but denying the power thereof: from such turn away*" (KJV. 2023)

These scriptures detail not only outward societal corruption but also a deep-seated spiritual decay within the professing church. The phrase "*having a form of godliness, but denying the power thereof*" is particularly significant for our discussion on discernment. It points to a hollow religiosity, a religious façade that mimics true devotion but lacks the authentic transformative power of God. This counterfeit spirituality is precisely the kind of spiritual fog that discernment is designed to penetrate, enabling believers to see beyond the outward appearance to the actual spiritual reality.

Paul warns in **II Thessalonians 2:3-4**: "*Let no one deceive you by any means; for that Day will not come unless the falling away comes first, and the man of lawlessness is revealed.*" (KJV, 2023). The term "*falling away*" (apostasia) refers not simply to societal secularization but to a defection from the core truths of the Christian faith from within. This apostasy is linked to deception.

The adversary's strategy is to cloud minds, distort truth, and divert people from the pure gospel. This makes the gift of discernment an indispensable tool, enabling believers to identify and resist the subtle yet pervasive influences that lead to doctrinal error, spiritual compromise, and ultimately, a turning away from Christ. The deceptive currents are strong, and discernment is the anchor that holds the believer firm.

The Apostle Peter, in his second epistle, provides a direct and consequential warning about the proliferation of false teachers and deceptive doctrines that will characterize the last days. In **II Peter 2:1-3**, he declares, "*But there were also false prophets among the people, just as there will be false teachers among you. They will secretly introduce destructive heresies, even denying the sovereign Lord who bought them—bringing swift destruction upon themselves. Many will follow their depraved conduct and, as a result, the way of truth will be maligned. In their greed, these teachers will exploit you with fabricated stories. Their condemnation has long been hanging over them. Their destruction has not been sleeping.*" (KJV, 2023).

This passage illuminates several key characteristics of last-day deception: its stealthy and insidious nature ("secretly introduce"), its denial of Christ's saving work, its appeal to followers who adopt "depraved conduct," its exploitation of believers through manipulative language and fabricated stories ("fabricated stories" and "greed"), and the ultimate consequence of truth being "maligned." These are precisely the spiritual dynamics that the gift of discernment is equipped to identify, analyze, and counteract. The pervasive influence of these false teachings can lead to the distortion and discrediting of the very "way of truth."

The collective prophetic voice of Scripture thus paints a clear picture of the "last days" as a period of intensified spiritual conflict, with deception as a primary tool of the adversary. The escalating challenges require a corresponding escalation in the believer's spiritual preparedness.

The gift of discernment is not merely an optional spiritual enhancement; it is a necessary equipping for survival and steadfastness in an era of profound spiritual turbulence. It is the means by which believers can navigate the increasingly complex landscape of spiritual claims, differentiating the authentic voice of God from the myriad counterfeits that seek to lead astray. Without this vital capacity, believers are vulnerable to the very forces that Jesus and the apostles warned against, risking being swept into the currents of error that can erode faith, compromise doctrine, and lead to spiritual ruin. The prophetic context, therefore, serves as an urgent call to vigilance and a profound mandate to actively seek, cultivate, and exercise the God-given capacity for spiritual discernment. It is the spiritual radar that allows us to detect incoming threats and the spiritual discernment that enables us to avoid their deadly impact.

The preceding discussion has firmly established the prophetic backdrop of the "last days" as a period defined by intensifying spiritual warfare and a pervasive, sophisticated wave of deception. This eschatological understanding is not merely an intellectual exercise; it serves as the indispensable foundation for appreciating the vital necessity of the spiritual gift of discernment. Without this divinely bestowed capacity, believers are ill-equipped to navigate the treacherous spiritual currents that characterize this present age and are prophesied to grow even stronger.

The gift of discernment, as enumerated by the Apostle Paul in his foundational discourse on spiritual gifts in **I Corinthians 12**, is presented not as an optional spiritual enhancement but as a crucial equipping for the faithful. This particular gift is described with a specific Greek term, *diakrisis pneumaton*, which literally translates to "discernment of spirits." This immediately signals that its operation is beyond mere human intellect or psychological analysis; it is a supernatural ability imparted by the Holy Spirit.

The Apostle Paul, in **I Corinthians 12:10**, lists "*the distinguishing of spirits*" as one of the manifestations of the Spirit. The phrase 'Diakrisis pneumaton' is not limited to discerning demonic spirits in the narrow sense, although that is undoubtedly a significant aspect. Instead, it encompasses a broader spiritual capacity to differentiate between various spiritual realities. This includes discerning the genuine from the counterfeit in terms of spiritual manifestations, prophetic utterances, teachings, motivations, and even the spiritual character of individuals.

It is the God-given ability to perceive the trustworthy spiritual source and nature of what is being presented, whether it originates from the Holy Spirit, from fallen spiritual beings, or from the unredeemed human spirit. In an era where the adversary is adept at masquerading as an angel of light (**II Corinthians 11:14**), such a gift is not a luxury but a lifeline.

This gift operates on a level that transcends logical deduction or empirical evidence. While sound reasoning and biblical knowledge are essential complements, discernment itself is an intuitive, inner conviction often accompanied by a distinctive "knowing" that arises from the Holy Spirit's illumination. It is a spiritual radar that can detect subtle shifts in spiritual atmosphere, identify dissonance between outward claims and inner reality, and recognize the underlying spiritual agenda at play.

For instance, a prophecy might be delivered with apparent conviction and even produce some temporary positive results. Still, a discerning believer might sense an underlying pride, a subtle manipulation, or a deviation from the core tenets of Scripture. This is not about judging individuals harshly, but about accurately assessing the spiritual authenticity and source of a message or manifestation.

Consider the early church; in **I Thessalonians 5:21**, Paul instructed them to *"Test everything; hold fast to what is good"* (KJV, 2023). This imperative to "test" is rooted in the concept of discernment. It implies an active, critical engagement with spiritual claims, not a passive acceptance. Where spiritual gifts were in operation and potentially sensational manifestations could occur, the ability to discern the source and validity of these occurrences was crucial for maintaining doctrinal purity and preventing the infiltration of false teachings. The Thessalonian believers were encouraged to be discerning, to weigh what they heard and experienced against the established truth of the Gospel and the guidance of the Holy Spirit.

Furthermore, the gift of discerning spirits is crucial for identifying the subtle yet potent influence of false teachings that often masquerade as genuine spirituality. Jesus Himself warned in **Matthew 7:15**, *"Beware of false prophets, who come to you in sheep's clothing, but inwardly they are ravenous wolves."* (KJV, 2023). These "wolves" are not always easily identifiable. They may use religious language, quote Scripture (often out of context), claim divine inspiration, and even perform acts that appear miraculous.

The sheep, lacking discernment, can easily be led astray, not by overt heresy, but by a gradual erosion of biblical truth, a subtle distortion of God's character, or a misplaced emphasis that ultimately undermines the core message of salvation through Christ. The gift of discernment allows a believer to "see" the wolf beneath the sheep's skin, to recognize the underlying agenda that seeks to devour the flock rather than nurture it.

The operation of this gift is also vital in discerning the spiritual state and intentions of individuals within the body of Christ. While we are called to love and extend grace, the New Testament also acknowledges that some may seek to infiltrate the church with ulterior motives, or whose spiritual fruit does not align with their professed faith. Jesus said in **Matthew 7:16**, *"By their fruits you will recognize them"* (KJV, 2023).

Discernment is the supernatural insight that helps us understand what those "fruits" truly signify. It can help identify spiritual pride masquerading as confidence, manipulation disguised as care, or an agenda of self-aggrandizement hidden behind seemingly altruistic endeavors. This is not about exposing every minor failing, but about recognizing patterns of behavior and speech that are indicative of a spirit not aligned with Christ.

The Apostle Paul's own ministry exemplifies the profound importance of this gift. In **Acts 13:9-10**, when Saul (later Paul) and Barnabas were ministering in Antioch, Elymas the sorcerer opposed them. Luke records that "*But Saul, who was also called Paul, filled with the Holy Spirit, looked intently at him and said, 'O full of all deceit and all cunning, you son of the devil, you enemy of all righteousness, will you not stop twisting the straight ways of the Lord?*'" (KJV, 2023). This immediate and accurate identification of Elymas as "full of all deceit," a "son of the devil," and an "enemy of all righteousness" was a powerful manifestation of the discerning of spirits. Paul was able to perceive the true spiritual nature of Elymas, cutting through his sorcery and opposition to the Lord's work. This ability to pierce through spiritual deception and identify the trustworthy source of opposition is a hallmark of the gift of discernment.

In the context of the last days, this gift becomes even more critical. As prophecy foretells a great falling away and an increase in deception, the spiritual landscape will become increasingly complex and perilous. False prophets, false teachers, and counterfeit spiritual movements will proliferate, often bearing the veneer of genuine Christianity. The adversary's objective is to deceive the masses, and particularly to deceive believers if possible. The gift of discernment acts as a spiritual filter, enabling believers to process the deluge of spiritual information and experiences that will characterize this era, separating the wheat from the chaff, the genuine from the counterfeit.

Consider the possibility of encountering teachings that seem biblically sound on the surface but subtly shift the emphasis away from the centrality of Christ's atoning sacrifice, or that promote a prosperity gospel that downplays the reality of suffering and the cross, or that incorporate mystical experiences that lack the grounding of Scripture. These are the kinds of nuanced deceptions that require more than just a good biblical education; they demand the supernatural insight of the discerning of spirits. It is this gift that enables a believer to discern when a teaching, however appealing, is leading them astray from the true North of the Gospel. It is the inner alarm bell that rings when spiritual waters become polluted.

The exercise of discernment is not about fostering suspicion or judgmentalism within the church. Instead, it is about promoting spiritual health, doctrinal purity, and the safeguarding of the flock. A discerning believer, guided by the Holy Spirit, can help others avoid falling prey to deception, can identify potential pitfalls in teaching or practice, and can contribute to the overall spiritual stability and maturity of the community. It is a ministry of truth, a protective grace that fortifies the body of Christ against the pervasive forces of error.

The gift of discerning spirits is, therefore, one of the most practical and necessary spiritual endowments for the believer living in these challenging times. It is a supernatural capacity granted by the Holy Spirit to distinguish between the divine, the human, and the demonic. It equips us to evaluate spiritual claims critically, identify false teachings, discern the true nature of spiritual manifestations and individuals, and ultimately, to remain steadfast in truth amidst the escalating currents of deception. Without this discerning capacity, we are vulnerable, open to manipulation, and at risk of being led astray by the very forces that Scripture warns us to be vigilant against. It is a gift that empowers us to walk in the truth and to help others, a vital safeguard in the ongoing spiritual battle for the hearts and minds of believers. It is the very lens through which the spiritual realities of the last days can be accurately perceived and responded to in faith and truth.

The journey of cultivating the spiritual gift of discernment, as we have established, is not merely an intellectual pursuit but a profound reliance on the Holy Spirit's illumination. However, like any divine endowment, its effective operation can be significantly hindered by internal dispositions—attitudes of the heart and mind that subtly yet powerfully obstruct its flow. Among the most pervasive and insidious of these hindrances are apathy and pride. These **twin adversaries** can render even the most devout believer susceptible to the deceptions that are prophesied to intensify in the latter days. Recognizing and actively combating these internal barriers is not a secondary aspect of spiritual growth; it is foundational to wielding the gift of discernment with the efficacy God intends.

The first of these adversaries is Apathy. In the context of spiritual discernment, **Apathy** manifests as a form of spiritual laziness or a profound disinterest in the rigorous engagement required to accurately assess spiritual truths. It is a passive resignation, an unwillingness to invest the time and effort necessary to truly understand God's Word, to test the spirits, and to critically examine the doctrines and manifestations that bombard us daily. This is not necessarily a rejection of faith, but rather a comfortable complacency that shies away from the challenging work of spiritual warfare. When a believer allows apathy to take root, they essentially surrender their spiritual vigilance. The rich tapestry of Scripture, which serves as the ultimate plumb line for truth, becomes a neglected resource. Instead of diligently studying to show oneself approved, rightly handling the word of truth (**II Timothy 2:15**), the apathetic believer opts for the path of least resistance, accepting information at face value, particularly if it is presented with charisma or within familiar circles. This **spiritual lethargy (apathy)** makes one particularly vulnerable. The adversary is not passive; he is actively seeking whom he may devour (**I Peter 5:8**). If a believer is disengaged, unstudious, and unconcerned with the nuances of biblical doctrine, they become an easy target. Deceptive teachings, which often prey on a lack of foundational knowledge, can insidiously creep into their belief system.

Imagine a ship drifting without a captain or a crew actively manning the helm. It is at the mercy of the currents and tides, susceptible to being dashed against hidden rocks. Similarly, a believer surrendered to apathy risks being swept away by currents of false doctrine, emotional manipulation, or subtle distortions of the Gospel. The warnings of Jesus and the apostles about false prophets and teachers who would arise in the last days become distant thunder, unheeded because the effort to understand their gravity and implications is deemed too burdensome.

The antidote to spiritual apathy lies in cultivating a fervent desire for truth, fueled by a deep love for God and a commitment to His Word. This is not a passive state but an active pursuit. It involves prioritizing the study of Scripture, not just as a religious duty, but as a lifeline of divine truth. It means engaging with biblical commentaries, theological resources, and sound Christian fellowship that encourages rigorous examination and discussion. It requires a conscious decision to invest time and energy into understanding the foundational doctrines of Christianity, the historical context of biblical writings, and the discerning principles laid out by the apostles. When a believer commits to this active pursuit, they are building a robust internal defense against deception. Their minds become sharpened, their understanding deepened, and their ability to discern the genuine from the counterfeit is significantly enhanced. It is through this diligent engagement that the Holy Spirit can most effectively illuminate the truth and expose error.

The second formidable enemy of discernment is pride. Pride is a greater foe than apathy. It masquerades as confidence, conviction, and spiritual maturity. Prideful reliance on one's own intellect, insights, or experiences can create a formidable barrier to the humble submission required for true discernment. The proud individual believes they have arrived, that their understanding is sufficient, and that they no longer need the diligent study or the humble reliance on the Holy Spirit that characterized their early faith journey. They may dismiss the counsel of others, particularly if it challenges their established views, and become resistant to admitting they might be mistaken. This self-sufficiency is the opposite of the dependence on God that Jesus Himself extolled (**Matthew 18:3-4**).

Prideful discernment often manifests in a premature judgment of others, a tendency to label people or movements as "off" without a solid biblical basis, or conversely, an uncritical acceptance of teachings that align with their pre-existing biases. The discerning of spirits is not about developing a superior spiritual intellect that can outwit others or identify every perceived flaw. It is, as we have seen, a supernatural ability bestowed by the Spirit, accessed through humility and dependence. When pride infects this process, it corrupts it. Instead of seeking the Holy Spirit's guidance, the proud individual trusts their own instincts or intellectual prowess, which makes them susceptible to demonic influence, causing them to dismiss a genuine prophetic word because it was not delivered in a manner or by the person they prefer. They will sometimes embrace a teaching that appeals to their intellectual vanity, even if it subtly contradicts Scripture.

The Scriptures offer numerous warnings against pride. **Proverbs 16:18** states, "*Pride goes before destruction, and a haughty spirit before a fall.*" (KJV, 2023). This principle is particularly relevant to the realm of spiritual discernment. A haughty spirit is ill-equipped to perceive the subtle stratagems of the enemy. It is too convinced of its own righteousness and too quick to dismiss potential warnings. When confronted with a teaching that sounds plausible but has a subtly unbiblical undertone, the proud individual may rationalize away the discrepancy, believing their own interpretation is more accurate or sophisticated. They may reject the gentle, persistent promptings of the Holy Spirit because they do not align with their pre-conceived notions or their intellectual framework.

The danger here is profound. The enemy is exceptionally adept at exploiting pride. He can feed a person's ego, inflate their sense of importance, and convince them that they are uniquely enlightened or resistant to deception. This creates a dangerous isolation. The proud individual becomes less likely to seek counsel, less open to correction, and increasingly entrenched in their own potentially flawed perspective. They may even begin to view those who express concern or offer a different interpretation as unspiritual or lacking insight. This is the ultimate perversion of discernment: using a supposed spiritual gift to assert intellectual or spiritual superiority, rather than to protect oneself and the community from error.

Overcoming pride in the pursuit of discernment requires a radical commitment to humility. This means recognizing that our intellect, our experiences, and even our spiritual gifts are not inherent possessions but temporary trusts from God. It involves actively practicing self-examination, constantly asking the Holy Spirit to reveal any arrogance or self-reliance in our thinking. It means valuing the Word of God above our own opinions and being willing to be corrected by Scripture, even if it means admitting we were wrong. A humble believer is teachable. They are eager to listen to the perspectives of others within the body of Christ, to weigh their counsel, and to test their own understanding against the collective wisdom and scriptural grounding of the community.

Furthermore, true humility fosters a dependence on the Holy Spirit that is essential for accurate discernment. Instead of relying on intellectual prowess, the humble believer looks to the Spirit for illumination and guidance. They understand that their own understanding is limited and that true spiritual insight comes from God. This reliance creates an openness to receive truth from unexpected sources, to recognize the Spirit's voice even when it is quiet, and to discern the subtle nuances of spiritual realities. It is a posture of surrender, a willingness to be led by the Spirit, rather than to lead the Spirit with our own preconceived notions.

A practical application of combating apathy and pride involves creating disciplines that foster both. For apathy, this means establishing regular times for focused Scripture study, perhaps joining a small group for in-depth Bible discussion, or committing to prayerfully considering current events and spiritual trends through a biblical lens. It is about making discernment an active part of one's spiritual routine, not an occasional afterthought. For pride, it involves cultivating a habit of seeking counsel from trusted, mature believers, particularly when encountering new or challenging teachings. It means embracing accountability and being willing to have one's interpretations and convictions tested. It also means remembering Paul's exhortation in **Philippians 2:3**: "*Do nothing from selfish ambition or conceit, but in humility count others more significant than yourselves.*" (KJV, 2023). This mindset, applied to spiritual matters, creates an environment where discernment can flourish, unhindered by the corrosive effects of apathy and pride.

In essence, the path to effective spiritual discernment in the last days is a path of active engagement and humble dependence. It requires a conscious rejection of spiritual laziness and a diligent pursuit of God's truth through His Word. It demands a ruthless eradication of pride, replacing self-reliance with an unwavering trust in the Holy Spirit's guidance. When believers embrace these disciplines, they become formidable opponents of deception, equipped by God to navigate the increasingly complex spiritual landscape with clarity, truth, and unwavering faith, thereby fulfilling their role as faithful stewards of the Gospel in these critical times. The cultivation of discernment is not merely about possessing a spiritual gift; it is about cultivating the character and the disciplines that allow that gift to operate effectively in the face of overwhelming opposition and deception.

The cultivation of the spiritual gift of discernment, as we have underscored, is not a passive reception of divine insight but an active engagement of the believer's spirit, mind, and heart, under the anointing of the Holy Spirit. Having addressed the critical internal disciplines of combating apathy and pride, we now turn our attention to the tangible outworking of this gift in the arena of corporate worship and doctrinal adherence. The latter days are characterized by an intensification of spiritual activity, both genuine and counterfeit, making the ability to discern the spirits and their manifestations absolutely crucial for the health and integrity of the Church. This practical application requires us to be ever vigilant, employing the tools and discernment the Spirit provides, not for self-aggrandizement, but for the safeguarding of truth and the edification of the body of Christ.

Corporate worship is the focal point of Christian community, a sacred assembly where believers gather to exalt God, receive His Word, and fellowship with one another. However, it is also a prime environment where the enemy seeks to sow confusion, introduce error, and lead astray the unwary. Therefore, exercising discernment in worship means more than simply enjoying the music or feeling moved by a sermon. It involves a critical, Spirit-led evaluation of the entire experience, from the doctrinal underpinnings of the songs sung to the theological accuracy of the preached Word, and even the spiritual atmosphere that pervades the service.

When engaging in corporate worship, the believer endowed with discernment must become a discerning listener and an observant participant. This begins with the selection of songs and hymns. While emotional uplift and communal expression are valuable aspects of worship, the lyrical content must be rigorously examined against the unshakeable foundation of Scripture. Are the words sung truly exalting the God of the Bible, or do they subtly promote a diluted gospel, a prosperity-focused theology, or a subjective, experience-driven spirituality that bypasses biblical truth?

The gift of discernment <u>will prompt questions</u>: Does this song accurately reflect the nature of God, the work of Christ, and the role of the Holy Spirit as revealed in the Bible? Does it promote biblical teachings on sin, repentance, salvation, and holiness?

A lack of discernment <u>might lead one to sing along uncritically</u>, swept up in the collective emotion. At the same time, the discerning believer listens with an ear attuned to theological soundness, gently questioning any lyrics that deviate from biblical orthodoxy. This is not about creating a sterile, joyless worship environment, but about ensuring that our praise is directed towards God and that our worship is rooted in truth, not merely sentiment.

The preached Word is another critical area for the application of discernment. While many faithful pastors and teachers faithfully exposit Scripture, the last days are foretold to see an increase in those who preach "itching ears" (**II Timothy 4:3**), proclaiming messages that are pleasing but not necessarily true. The discerning believer is not merely a passive recipient of the sermon but an active partner with the Holy Spirit in evaluating its content. This involves comparing every teaching, every anecdote, and every interpretation back to the plumb line of the Bible. Does the sermon align with the overall narrative and theological framework of Scripture? Does it accurately handle the text of the Bible, or does it twist verses out of context to support a pre-determined agenda? Are the applications drawn from the text biblically sound and consistent with the character of God?

The gift of discernment encourages us to ask probing questions, not in a spirit of arrogance or criticism, but in a sincere desire for truth. If a preacher emphasizes a particular spiritual experience or a new revelation, the discerning believer will ask, "Is this experience biblical?" Does it lead one closer to Christ and His Word, or does it elevate the experience above Scripture? If a teaching seems novel or controversial, the discerning believer will seek confirmation from Scripture, perhaps consulting commentaries from trusted theologians or discussing the matter with mature, biblically grounded Christians. The Holy Spirit often imparts a sense of unease or a gentle prompting when something is amiss, a spiritual "red flag" that should not be ignored. This prompting is not meant to create suspicion towards all teaching, but to foster a healthy intellectual and spiritual skepticism that drives us to verify truth.

Discernment extends to evaluating spiritual experiences within a worship service. This could include manifestations of spiritual gifts, prophetic utterances, or perceived spiritual encounters. Paul exhorted believers to "test everything; hold fast to what is good" (**I Thessalonians 5:21, NIV, 2023**). The gift of discernment is the primary tool for this testing. When witnessing or experiencing a purported spiritual manifestation, the discerning believer will ask, "Does this honor Christ?" Does it align with the character and Word of God? Does it produce the fruit of the Spirit (love, joy, peace, patience, kindness, goodness, faithfulness, gentleness, self-control– **Galatians 5:22-23**)? Or does it promote division, self-exaltation, emotionalism devoid of biblical truth, or a disregard for God's Word?

For instance, a supposed prophetic word might be delivered with great fervor and conviction, but if it contradicts clear biblical teaching, leads to confusion, or encourages unbiblical behavior, the discerning believer will recognize it as not from the Holy Spirit. Similarly, intense emotional outbursts or claims of miraculous healing, while potentially genuine, must be assessed by their fruit and their adherence to biblical principles. The enemy is adept at mimicking spiritual phenomena, employing emotional manipulation, and even performing deceptive wonders. Therefore, discernment is our defense, ensuring that our spiritual encounters are authentic and glorifying to God.

The spiritual atmosphere of a service is another aspect that the gift of discernment can perceive. Is the prevailing atmosphere one of genuine reverence and awe for God, or is it characterized by a restless, superficial excitement, or perhaps a sense of spiritual oppression or confusion? The Holy Spirit brings peace, conviction, and clarity. Deception or demonic influence may manifest as a chaotic, anxious, or even fear-based atmosphere. The discerning believer, sensitive to the Spirit, can often sense these underlying currents, prompting a prayer for spiritual clarity and protection for themselves and for the congregation.

Applying discernment in these practical ways is not a call to become overly critical or to judge individuals harshly. Instead, it is a call to responsible stewardship of the truth entrusted to us. It is about exercising the spiritual faculty God has given us to navigate the spiritual landscape faithfully. This requires diligence, a humble heart, and a deep reliance on the Holy Spirit's guidance. It means being willing to take the time to study, to question, and to confirm while not being easily swayed by charisma, emotion, or the perceived spiritual maturity of a speaker, but by the truth of God's Word.

The ultimate goal of applying discernment in worship and doctrine is to protect oneself and the community of faith from error, to ensure that our worship is pure and acceptable to God, and to deepen our understanding and application of His Word. As the world becomes increasingly saturated with competing spiritual claims and deceptive ideologies, the ability to discern the truth of the Gospel and to recognize spiritual counterfeits will become an even more vital aspect of our Christian walk. It is a gift that, when faithfully exercised, serves to strengthen the Church and to keep us firmly anchored in the truth of Jesus Christ, the Truth Incarnate. It is an ongoing process of learning, of testing, and of clinging to what is true, guided by the unwavering light of the Holy Spirit and the immutable Word of God.

The currents of the modern era, characterized by what many have termed a "post-truth" environment, present a formidable challenge to the faithful Christian walk. In such a landscape, objective reality is frequently subjected to skepticism, and subjective experience or popular opinion often eclipses verifiable facts. This pervasive relativism, where truth is perceived as fluid and personal rather than fixed and absolute, directly assaults the foundations of our faith, which are built upon the immutable Word of God and the person of Jesus Christ, who Himself declared in **John 14:6**, "*I am the way, the truth, and the life*" (KJV, 2023).

It is precisely within this disorienting milieu that the spiritual gift of discernment, as bestowed by the Holy Spirit, assumes even greater importance and significance. The ability to distinguish between truth and falsehood, between the divine and the deceptive, is no longer merely an advantage; it is an essential survival skill for navigating the spiritual and intellectual terrain of our times.

To operate effectively in a post-truth world, the believer must first and foremost anchor their understanding of reality in the unshakeable bedrock of Scripture. The Bible stands as a testament to divine revelation, a comprehensive and authoritative account of God's nature, His dealings with humanity, and His eternal plan. While the surrounding culture may champion subjective feelings, sensational narratives, or the echo chambers of social media as arbiters of truth, the discerning Christian understands that these are ephemeral and unreliable guides.

The Holy Spirit, our divine Teacher, illuminates the Word, making it accessible and applicable to our lives. Therefore, discerning truth amidst deception begins with a steadfast commitment to saturating oneself in biblical truth. This involves diligent study, prayerful meditation, and a consistent habit of cross-referencing all claims—whether from secular media, popular culture, or even well-meaning religious figures—against the clear teachings of the Bible. When faced with a narrative that seems plausible or emotionally compelling but contradicts biblical principles, the gift of discernment acts as an internal alarm, prompting further investigation and a reliance on the established Word rather than fleeting impressions.

The erosion of objective truth in society has led to an environment where misinformation and disinformation proliferate at an unprecedented speed and reach. The internet and social media platforms, while offering many benefits, have also become fertile ground for the rapid propagation of falsehoods, conspiracy theories, and outright lies. These can range from politically charged propaganda to subtly disguised theological distortions. In this context, the discerning believer is called to exercise a critical, yet Spirit-led, approach to information consumption.

This is not about cynicism or a refusal to engage with the world, but about a responsible stewardship of one's mind and spirit. The Holy Spirit grants wisdom to filter the deluge of information, to identify patterns of deception, and to discern the underlying motives behind various messages. For instance, when encountering a viral news story or a persuasive online argument, the discerning individual will ask not only, "Is this factually correct?" but also, "What is the source of this information? What agenda might it serve? Does it align with the character and revealed will of God?" The gift of discernment, in this regard, provides a crucial lens through which to view the digital landscape, enabling the believer to avoid being swept away by currents of untruth or manipulated by malicious actors.

Furthermore, the post-truth era often promotes a form of intellectual and spiritual pluralism that equates all beliefs as equally valid. In this view, religious truth is reduced to personal preference, and the uniqueness of Christ as the exclusive path to salvation is often dismissed or even vilified. The gift of discernment is indispensable in resisting this seductive ideology. It enables the believer to hold firm to the non-negotiable truths of the Gospel, understanding that while we are called to love and respect all people, we cannot compromise the foundational doctrines of our faith. The Holy Spirit helps us to articulate and defend the truth with grace and firmness, recognizing that true discernment involves not only identifying error but also boldly affirming truth. This means that when presented with teachings that, for example, suggest salvation through means other than faith in Christ, or that redefine core biblical concepts like sin, repentance, or the nature of God, the discerning Christian will recognize these as deviations from divine revelation. The gift prompts us to seek out biblical corroboration, to engage with mature believers for counsel, and to gently but firmly reject any assertion that undermines the authority of Scripture.

The challenge is magnified when these relativistic tendencies seep into the church itself. In a culture that increasingly values emotional resonance over doctrinal accuracy, there can be a temptation to embrace teachings or practices that are popular or feel good, even if they lack biblical grounding. The post-truth mentality can manifest as a preference for anecdotal evidence over systematic theology, or a focus on subjective spiritual experiences that are not testable against the Word of God.

Discernment, therefore, is vital for maintaining the purity of doctrine and the integrity of worship within the Christian community. It guards against the infiltration of syncretism, where elements of the world's philosophies or spiritualities are blended with Christian belief, thereby diluting the Gospel. The Holy Spirit empowers the discerning believer to recognize when a sermon, a worship song, or a ministry initiative, while perhaps well-intentioned, is subtly drifting away from biblical moorings. This might involve observing an overemphasis on humanistic psychology, a downplaying of sin and the need for repentance, or the promotion of a prosperity gospel that misrepresents God's character and promises.

The ability to discern truth in this climate requires a proactive rather than reactive stance. It means actively cultivating spiritual sensitivity. This involves disciplines such as consistent prayer for wisdom and understanding, engaging in disciplined Bible study, seeking out sound theological resources and mentors, and cultivating a humble spirit. Pride can be a significant impediment to discernment, leading individuals to believe they already possess all the truth and are immune to deception. The post-truth environment can exacerbate this, creating an illusion of informed skepticism that masks an underlying spiritual arrogance. The gift of discernment, however, is intrinsically linked to humility—a recognition of our dependence on God's Spirit for actual knowledge. It fosters a teachable spirit, one that is eager to learn, willing to be corrected, and committed to aligning one's beliefs and actions with God's revealed will.

Consider, for instance, the proliferation of "spiritual but not religious" movements or the growing acceptance of Eastern mystical practices among individuals who identify as Christian. These trends often bypass the explicit declarations of Scripture, prioritizing personal spiritual exploration and frequently adopting a universalist or pantheistic worldview. The discerning believer recognizes these as significant departures from biblical truth. The Holy Spirit will likely impress upon such a believer a sense of cognitive dissonance when encountering these ideas, a feeling that something is fundamentally out of alignment with the God revealed in the Bible. This prompting is not about immediate condemnation, but about an inner call to test these new teachings against the unchanging Word of God. It is about asking: Does this perspective honor Christ as the unique Son of God? Does it uphold the biblical understanding of sin and redemption? Does it lead to a deeper, more obedient relationship with the Triune God, or does it promote a vague, self-directed spirituality?

Moreover, the post-truth era often leverages emotional appeals and psychological manipulation to promote its narratives. In a world that is increasingly desensitized and seeking authentic connection, people can be susceptible to teachings that resonate emotionally, even if they lack substance or truth. The gift of discernment is a powerful antidote to this. It allows the believer to distinguish between genuine spiritual conviction and emotional manipulation.

For example, a speaker might use powerful storytelling, evocative music, and charismatic delivery to create an overwhelming emotional experience, leading listeners to accept their message without critical examination. The discerning individual, however, will look beyond the emotional veneer to the underlying message and its biblical fidelity. They will ask: Does this emotional response stem from a genuine encounter with God's truth, or is it a manufactured experience designed to bypass rational thought and biblical scrutiny?

The call to discernment in the post-truth era is therefore a call to intellectual and spiritual robustness, rooted in a deep and abiding relationship with God and His Word. It is a mandate to resist the cultural drift towards relativism and to stand firm in the objective truth of the Gospel. It requires us to be discerning consumers of information, critical evaluators of teaching, and courageous defenders of biblical doctrine.

The Holy Spirit empowers us to navigate this complex landscape, not with suspicion or fear, but with confident assurance that in Christ, we have access to unchanging truth. This gift ensures that our faith remains anchored, our worship pure, and our witness unwavering, even in the most disorienting of times. It is a vital equipping for the believer, enabling them to live faithfully and to testify boldly to the truth in an age that increasingly questions its very existence. The unwavering compass of divine revelation, illuminated by the Spirit, is our surest guide through the fog of deception, leading us ever onward in the pursuit of truth.

CHAPTER SEVEN:
The Spiritual Fortification Defense

The bedrock of a faith committed to the immutable truth of God's Word is the unwavering assurance that this Word (the Bible) has been, and continues to be, divinely preserved. This doctrine of preservation is not merely a comforting thought; it is a theological necessity, a pillar upon which the entire edifice of biblical authority rests.

Without it, our trust in Scripture would be as fragile as the papyrus and parchment upon which it was originally penned, susceptible to the ravages of time, the errors of scribes, and the deliberate corruptions of men. The Bible occupies a unique and cherished place in this discussion, widely regarded by many scholars and believers as a direct beneficiary and faithful conduit of this divine preservation.

In most of the books I write, I try to incorporate other sources to support my claims. I could give you tons of quotes from the American Psychiatric Association and renowned psychiatrists who tell of the horrors, manipulations, and chronic illnesses that occur as a result of deception, both as the deceiver and the person who is the prey of the deceiver/manipulator. However, I do not want to bore you with those details.

So, at this point, we are going to agree to a consensus on these points:

1) Deception and manipulation have adverse effects on the deceiver and the recipient
2) The Bible is the word of God as it was given through the inspiration of the Holy Ghost to anointed men (prophets) of God.

3) We agree that the word of God gives the best solutions to the problem of deception.
4) We accept the fact that deception is an illness as the American Psychiatric Association designates based on its symptoms (Bipolar, schizophrenia, aggressive manipulator, con-artist, etc.)

Spiritual Armor of the Christian Warrior

> **Ephesians 6:10-18**—*Finally, my brethren, be strong in the Lord, and in the power of his might. Put on the whole armour of God, that ye may be able to stand against the wiles of the devil. For we wrestle not against flesh and blood, but against principalities, against powers, against the rulers of the darkness of this world, against spiritual wickedness in high places. Wherefore take unto you the whole armour of God, that ye may be able to withstand in the evil day, and having done all, to stand. Stand therefore, having your loins girt about with* **truth**, *and having on the* **breastplate** *of righteousness; And your feet shod with the preparation of the* **gospel of peace**; *Above all, taking the shield of faith, wherewith ye shall be able to quench all the fiery darts of the wicked. Moreover, take the helmet of salvation, and the sword of the Spirit, which is the word of God:*
> **Praying** *always with all prayer and supplication in the Spirit, and watching thereunto with all perseverance and supplication for all saints;* (KJV, 2023).

Belt of Truth:

The Roman Soldiers who were responsible for Paul each day had on their required uniforms and armor. This armor was a constant visual in Paul's daily life. Therefore, for him to use this as an example for us to follow as spiritual warriors looks pretty logical. These soldiers used a belt to hold their swords close to their bodies, but secure enough that if they freed up their hands, allowing them more mobility. The belt, when applied correctly, protects the sword against the body without restricting the soldier's movements. It also supported the breast plate, which was essential for protecting the heart and lungs.

This belt was made of leather for those who could afford it. Others used a thick, durable, tweed-style material that was sturdy and would not break from the weight of the sword. This belt was wrapped around the soldier's tunic in an unusual manner, at the high hip area. It was worn similarly to the tool belts that carpenters and construction workers wear on job sites. The sword was the soldier's tool, like the hammer is the carpenter's tool.

The sword was as essential to the soldier's uniform as a gun is to a law enforcement officer's uniform today. We, as Christian warriors, must know that Satan is the father of all lies. He is the master deceiver. He wants more than anything else to catch us at a moment without our armor on. Without the belt of truth that holds our sword—without our minds filled with the word of God and our hearts committed to Jesus—Satan has a spiritual kill shot that he will use to manipulate how we think, change our perspective, and cause us to compromise.

Tolerance and compromise are the 21st-century forms that Satan uses to attack us mentally and emotionally. When we fall prey to Satan's attack, we will not be initially tempted to sin. He initially uses complacency and tolerance. When he has been successful in that arena, he then moves to tolerance, and eventually he reaches the point where he deceives us so thoroughly that we will convince ourselves that sin is no longer a sin.

If we do not have on the whole armor of God daily, Satan can attack our minds with reminders of our past mistakes and sins. When he constantly reminds us of things we have done that were wrong, it makes us feel unworthy. When this occurs, it is easier for Satan to get us to be complacent.

The only way we can stand for truth is through Jesus. In **John 14:6**, He said, "*I am the way, the truth, and the life.*" (KJV, 2023). We must first understand who we are in Christ Jesus, then plant the word of God in our hearts and minds. When we read and pray daily, we put on the whole armor of God. This gives us power through the Holy Ghost.

Another scripture to stand on is: **Hebrews 4:12**, "*For the word of God is alive and active. Sharper than any double-edged sword, it penetrates even to dividing soul and spirit, joints and marrow; it judges the thoughts and attitudes of the heart.*" (NIV).

In other words, we have to plant the word of God into our hearts and minds, then we, through FAITH, stand on those words. When we quote the scriptures to Satan, he WILL flee. **John 8:32** says, *"Then you will know the truth, and the truth will set you free"* (KJV, 2023).

Breast Plate of Righteousness:

The breastplate of righteousness is the second piece of armor that is mentioned in the book of Ephesians. The breastplate that Roman soldiers wore was made of metal, and the arrows could not penetrate it. If a soldier were to have a fatal chest wound, the arrow or sword had to hit one of the areas that the breast plate did not cover.

If a soldier was in close hand-to-hand combat, his opponent could use a smaller sword (the size of a kitchen knife) and stab the soldier below the breast plate and shove upward, or stab him with a downward thrust at the top of the plate, hitting either a main neck artery or piercing the upper lobe of the lungs. From a spiritual perspective, this is a reason why we should avoid close association with evil. I am not talking about not witnessing or trying to get people to come to God. I am talking about letting into your homes and your inner circle people who you know want to discredit or destroy your reputation.

For example, if you knew that person was a sex trafficking kidnapper, would you invite them to your house for dinner every Saturday evening? No, you would not want that individual to know your routine or be around your children. If they developed a relationship with your children, it would be easier for them to lure your kids into their car at a later date. The same holds with our spiritual lives. If we know that someone wants to take away our most precious possession outside of salvation (our reputation and our ministry), then why do we have that person in our inner circle of friends? That person is just as significant a threat to you as a sex trafficker would be to your children.

However, Satan knows that if he can get individuals around you who are demonized (not possessed, but influenced by the works of the flesh), those individuals can initiate a spiritually lethal chest wound.

You will notice that the first thing that Paul told the Ephesians to do was to put on the belt of truth. If I had been writing this, the nurse in me would have wanted to start with the Helmet of Salvation because I am accustomed to doing "head-to-toe" assessments of my patients. In the past, when I have preached on this, regardless of the order in these verses, I always started with the helmet, because first we must be saved. There is nothing wrong with that thought process; however, when I began studying to write this book, something stood out to me from these verses that I had never noticed before. The belt of truth is first for a good reason.

Truth must be within us, and we must strive for truth and only truth around us. Truth must be present for us to be saved. Truth must be present first so that we can protect our vital organs (spiritually), including the heart, lungs, brain, and gut. If we do not have a spirit of truth, we will not be able to put on the rest of the armor of God. If we have deceit in us, deception is what will come to us and be the "spiritual soldier" that will issue a fatal close-up chest or gut wound.

What I am trying to say is that I realized this week in my personal studies and devotions that I can put on the armor Paul talks about, but if I leave off the belt of truth, none of the other parts of the armor will be of any benefit to me. The belt of truth is the key. It is the initial or first piece of armor I must apply. Truth and Salvation go hand-in-hand. Look at what Paul wrote to the Thessalonians.

> **II Thessalonians 2:3-14**—*Let no man deceive you by any means: for that day shall not come, except there come a falling away first, and that man of sin be revealed, the son of perdition; Who opposeth and exalteth himself above all that is called God, or that is worshipped; so that he as God sitteth in the temple of God, shewing himself that he is God. Remember ye not, that, when I was yet with you, I told you these things? Moreover, now ye know what withholdeth that he might be revealed in his time. For the mystery of iniquity doth already work: only he who now letteth will let, until he be taken out of the way. And then shall that Wicked be revealed, whom the Lord shall consume with the spirit of his mouth, and shall destroy with the brightness of his coming: Even him, whose coming is after the working of Satan with all power and signs and lying wonders, and with all deceivableness of unrighteousness in them that perish; because they received not the love of the truth, that they might be saved. Moreover, for this cause God shall send them strong delusion, that they should believe a lie: That they all might be damned who believed not the truth, but had pleasure in unrighteousness. However, we are bound to give thanks always to God for you, brethren beloved of the Lord, because God hath from the beginning chosen you to salvation through sanctification of the Spirit and belief of the truth:* (KJV, 2023).

What I am trying to explain here is that the breastplate of righteousness is essential for protecting our vital organs (spiritually, our heart, especially), but we cannot protect our hearts without the truth. Everything we do in our Judeo-Christian Walk has to be based on truth—no deception, no lying, no malice (no evil toward others).

If we have the truth of God's word in our minds and hearts, and we have bound all evil in our lives, including letting go of revenge, hate, and malice, then our hearts and minds are ready to go to battle against the evil principalities of darkness that will come against us wanting us to fail. If we have put on this belt of truth, then we are ready to put on the breastplate of righteousness. These two pieces of armor are not only essential to our basic needs, but they also lay the foundation for spiritual growth.

The spiritual purpose of this breastplate of righteousness is to cover our sins with the blood of Jesus Christ, making us righteous so we can stand before God and he can look at us. Without the blood, God cannot look on us. (**Habakkuk 1:13**). This does not mean that he turns his back on us, but it means that if we are going to be in the presence of God when we get to heaven, our sins must be covered with the blood of Jesus Christ. This breastplate of righteousness enables God to look upon us and help us fight our spiritual battles against Satan. (**II Corinthians 5:21**).

Satan does not like righteousness just as much as God does not like sin. So, our breastplate of righteousness shines so bright that it blinds Satan in the battle. If we have truth and righteousness, then we need the third piece of armor to block the fiery darts the throws at our minds. You need to understand that this piece of spiritual armor is not a recommendation. It is an essential tool. In the last days, many will be deceived.

As we prepare for the third piece of armor, the Helmet of Salvation, we will have all of the vital organs covered, our sins under the blood, and truth—nothing but truth living in us.

The scriptures that support this conclusion

<u>Matthew 24:24</u>—*For false Christs and false prophets will arise and will show great signs and wonders, so as to mislead, if possible, even the elect.*

<u>I Timothy 4:1</u>—*But the Spirit explicitly says that in later times some will fall away from the faith, paying attention to deceitful spirits and doctrines of demons,*

> **II Timothy 4:3-4**—*For the time will come when they will not endure sound doctrine; but wanting to have their ears tickled, they will accumulate for themselves teachers in accordance to their own desires, and will turn away their ears from the truth and will turn aside to myths.*
>
> **II Thessalonians 2:3**—*Let no one in any way deceive you, for it will not come unless the apostasy comes first, and the man of lawlessness is revealed, the son of destruction,*

As you can see, with us just on the second piece of armor, the gift of discernment is going to be the most important gift we need to be seeking God for in these last days! In other words, if we have the breastplate of righteousness on, we will live our daily lives with honesty and integrity. Our moral and ethical behavior or conduct will include purity. On paper, this may sound so simple. However, without the help of the Holy Spirit, this would not be possible. We are humans, and our nature is to sin and please ourselves. This mindset is the first thing we have to change in order to receive the gifts from God.

The spiritual armor described by the Apostle Paul in **Ephesians 6** is not merely symbolic; it is a divinely provided arsenal for the believer's engagement in spiritual warfare. Each piece represents a tangible aspect of God's provision that empowers us to stand firm against the devil's schemes. Having considered the belt of truth and the breastplate of righteousness, we now turn our attention to a critical component that directly protects our most vulnerable asset: our mind. This is the helmet of salvation. Paul instructs us to take up this **helmet,** and its significance lies not just in the salvific work of Christ, but in the ongoing assurance and mental fortification it affords the believer. It is the protective covering for our thoughts, our beliefs, and our understanding of God's truth.

The Helmet of Salvation:

The concept of salvation encompasses far more than a singular event of conversion; it is a continuous process that begins with our justification through faith in Christ, continues through our sanctification by the Holy Spirit, and will culminate in our glorification. The helmet of salvation, therefore, speaks to the comprehensive work of God in saving us, and crucially, in securing our minds with the assurance of this salvation. This assurance is not a presumptuous confidence based on our own feelings or performance, but a deep-seated conviction born from the objective truth of God's Word and the internal witness of the Holy Spirit. It is the knowledge, rooted in faith, that our sins are forgiven, that we are reconciled to God through Christ, and that we possess eternal life. This truth acts as an impenetrable shield against the enemy's accusations and doubts, which are often aimed directly at undermining our confidence in God's saving grace.

The enemy, particularly Satan, is relentless in his attempts to sow seeds of doubt and confusion in the minds of believers. He is the master of deception, constantly seeking to whisper lies that contradict God's truth and distort our perception of reality. These lies can manifest in various forms: questioning God's goodness, suggesting that our past sins are unforgivable, implying that we are not truly loved or accepted by God, or fostering anxieties about the future that rob us of present peace. The helmet of salvation is specifically designed to counter these insidious attacks. It is the assurance that, despite our failings and the enemy's accusations, we are indeed saved. This assurance is a powerful deterrent to discouragement and despair. When the enemy attempts to overwhelm us with guilt or shame, the helmet of salvation reminds us that Christ's sacrifice is sufficient, that our standing before God is secure, we are His children, eternally loved and redeemed.

Consider the subtle ways the enemy infiltrates our thinking. He does not always resort to outright blasphemy; more often, he employs suggestion, insinuation, and exaggeration. He might whisper doubts about our spiritual maturity, suggesting that because we still struggle with certain sins, our initial conversion was not genuine. Alternatively, he might amplify our failures, making them appear insurmountable obstacles to God's continued favor.

The helmet of salvation (the assurance of our salvation) directly confronts these insidious whispers. It is the unwavering declaration, "I am saved," not based on a perfect performance, but on Christ's perfect work. This assurance becomes a mental fortress, deflecting the arrows of accusation and doubt. When the enemy shouts, "You are too sinful to be forgiven," the believer, wearing the helmet of salvation, can calmly reply, "But Christ died for my sins, and in Him, I am forgiven and complete."

The renewal of the mind is a crucial aspect of this spiritual fortification. It involves actively engaging with biblical truths that affirm our salvation and challenge the enemy's lies. This means consciously choosing to meditate on God's promises, to recall the finished work of Christ on the cross, and to rely on the Holy Spirit's indwelling presence as the seal of our adoption. The Bible provides a rich treasury of such affirmations. Passages like **Romans 8:1**, "*There is therefore now no condemnation to them which are in Christ Jesus, who walk not after the flesh, but after the Spirit,*" are vital for securing the mind. This verse, with its definitive "no condemnation," is a powerful counter-argument to any accusation that suggests we are still under divine judgment due to our weaknesses. The Bible's precise wording anchors us in the reality of our freedom from condemnation, a truth that, when internalized, becomes a defense against the enemy's onslaughts of guilt.

The assurance of salvation guards us against the deception of worldly philosophies and ideologies that seek to redefine sin and righteousness, or diminish the necessity of Christ's sacrifice. In an age saturated with relativism and a pervasive distrust of absolute truth, the clear, unvarnished message of salvation found in the KJV can seem counter-cultural. However, it is precisely this clarity that makes it such a potent safeguard for the mind. When confronted with teachings that promote self-salvation through good works or that deny the efficacy of Christ's blood, the believer who has internalized the truth of their salvation through the Bible stands firm. They recognize these alternative narratives not as valid options, but as dangerous deviations from the singular truth of God's grace. The helmet of salvation is the mental conviction that our acceptance with God is solely through Christ, a conviction that makes us impervious to the allure of these deceptive systems.

The practical application of taking up the helmet of salvation involves cultivating a disciplined mind. This means being vigilant about what we allow to enter our thoughts. In today's media-saturated world, we are constantly bombarded with information, opinions, and images that can subtly erode our spiritual convictions. The enemy can use these channels to sow seeds of doubt, promote ungodly values, or stir up sinful desires. Therefore, we must intentionally filter what we consume, prioritizing spiritual nourishment over the constant influx of secular or corrupting content. This involves setting boundaries on our media consumption, seeking out edifying fellowship, and intentionally immersing ourselves in God's Word. The KJV, in its completeness and fidelity, offers a pure stream of divine truth, capable of cleansing and fortifying the mind.

The renewal of the mind is also a process of actively replacing negative or deceitful thoughts with God's truth. When a thought of doubt or fear arises, the believer is called to cast it down and bring it into captivity to the obedience of Christ, as Paul instructs in **II Corinthians 10:5**. This is not about suppressing thoughts, but about actively countering them with the truth of our salvation.

For instance, if we are tempted to believe that God is distant or displeased with us because of a recent failure, we must consciously recall and affirm biblical truths about God's unfailing love and the permanence of His grace. Passages like **I John 4:18**, "*There is no fear in love; but perfect love casteth out fear: because fear hath torment,*" are essential (KJV, 2023). The Bible's rendering of "perfect love casteth out fear" is compelling, offering a definitive statement of the power of God's love to expel debilitating anxieties.

The assurance of salvation also provides a stable perspective from which to evaluate the trials and difficulties of life. When faced with adversity, it is easy for the mind to become overwhelmed by despair or to question God's presence and plan. However, the helmet of salvation reminds us that even in our trials, we are still God's children, secure in His eternal love. The trials themselves are often part of the sanctification process, refining our faith and drawing us closer to God. The consistent portrayal of God's sovereignty and His redemptive purposes in all circumstances provides the believer with an anchor in the midst of the storm. For example, the unwavering assertion in **Romans 8:28**, *"And we know that all things work together for good to them that love God, to them who are called according to his purpose,"* (KJV, 2023), is a profound statement of divine providence that can fortify the mind against despair during difficult times. This assurance is a vital part of the helmet, protecting our perspective from the distortions of suffering.

Moreover, the helmet of salvation is inextricably linked to the hope we have in Christ. Our salvation is not merely about our past sins being forgiven; it is also about our future glory. The anticipation of Christ's return and the eternal life that awaits us serves as a powerful motivator and a source of strength. This hope, when firmly grasped, inoculates the mind against the temptations of worldly pleasure and the discouragement of present suffering. The anticipation of resurrection and eternal fellowship with God, as described in passages like **I Thessalonians 4:17**, *"Then we which are alive and remain shall be caught up together with them in the clouds, to meet the Lord in the air: and so shall we ever be with the Lord,"* (KJV, 2023), provides a future focus that can shield the mind from the allure of temporal gratifications and the sting of present troubles.

The practical application of taking up the helmet of salvation involves cultivating a disciplined mind. This means being vigilant about what we allow to enter our thoughts. In today's media-saturated world, we are constantly bombarded with information, opinions, and images that can subtly erode our spiritual convictions. The enemy can use these channels to sow seeds of doubt, promote ungodly values, or stir up sinful desires. Therefore, we must intentionally filter what we consume, prioritizing spiritual nourishment over the constant influx of secular or corrupting content. This involves setting boundaries on our media consumption, seeking out edifying fellowship, and intentionally immersing ourselves in God's Word.

The renewal of the mind is also a process of actively replacing negative or deceitful thoughts with God's truth. When a thought of doubt or fear arises, the believer is called to cast it down and bring it into captivity to the obedience of Christ, as Paul instructs in **II Corinthians 10:5**. This is not about suppressing thoughts, but about actively countering them with truth.

For instance, if we are tempted to believe that God is distant or displeased with us because of a recent failure, we must consciously recall and affirm biblical truths about God's unfailing love and the permanence of His grace. Passages like **I John 4:18**, "*There is no fear in love; but perfect love casteth out fear: because fear hath torment,*" are essential (KJV, 2023). The Bible's rendering of "perfect love casteth out fear" is compelling, offering a definitive statement of the power of God's love to expel debilitating anxieties.

The assurance of salvation also provides a stable perspective from which to evaluate the trials and difficulties of life. When faced with adversity, it is easy for the mind to become overwhelmed by despair or to question God's presence and plan. However, the helmet of salvation reminds us that even in our trials, we are still God's children, secure in His eternal love. The trials themselves are often part of the sanctification process, refining our faith and drawing us closer to God. The consistent portrayal of God's sovereignty and His redemptive purposes in all circumstances provides the believer with an anchor in the midst of the storm. For example, the unwavering assertion in **Romans 8:28**, "*And we know that all things work together for good to them that love God, to them who are called according to his purpose,*" (KJV, 2023), is a profound statement of divine providence that can fortify the mind against despair during difficult times. This assurance is a vital part of the helmet, protecting our perspective from the distortions of suffering.

Moreover, the helmet of salvation is inextricably linked to the hope we have in Christ. Our salvation is not merely about our past sins being forgiven; it is also about our future glory. The anticipation of Christ's return and the eternal life that awaits us serves as a powerful motivator and a source of strength. This hope, when firmly grasped, inoculates the mind against the temptations of worldly pleasure and the discouragement of present suffering. The anticipation of resurrection and eternal fellowship with God, as described in passages like **I Thessalonians 4:17**, "*Then we which are alive and remain shall be caught up together with them in the clouds, to meet the Lord in the air: and so shall we ever be with the Lord,*" (KJV, 2023), provides a future focus that can shield the mind from the allure of temporal gratifications and the sting of present troubles.

Shield of Faith:

The spiritual armor described by the Apostle Paul in **Ephesians 6** is not merely symbolic; it is a divinely provided arsenal for the believer's engagement in spiritual warfare. Each piece represents a tangible aspect of God's provision that empowers us to stand firm against the devil's schemes. The next piece Paul instructs us on is the shield of faith. Paul teaches us to take up this shield, and its significance lies not just in its defensive capabilities but in its proactive power to extinguish the enemy's assaults. It is the broad, unwavering trust in God and His promises that acts as a formidable barrier, quenching the fiery darts of doubt, accusation, and deception that the adversary relentlessly launches against us.

The "fiery darts" are not a metaphor for minor annoyances; they represent the most potent and damaging weapons in Satan's arsenal. These are not mere suggestions but targeted attacks designed to ignite confusion, despair, and outright disbelief. They can manifest as crippling fear, paralyzing doubt about God's character or His plan for our lives, accusations of past or present sin that seek to undermine our standing in Christ, or even subtle distortions of God's Word that lead us astray. These darts are "fiery" because they are meant to burn, to consume our confidence, to scorch our resolve, and to leave us emotionally and spiritually wounded. When these darts find their mark, they can ignite a blaze of spiritual crisis, leaving us vulnerable and ineffective in our walk with God and our witness to the world.

The shield of faith is our defense against these infernal projectiles. It is not a passive piece of equipment; it is an active, dynamic instrument of our spiritual warfare. Faith, as defined in Scripture, is "*the substance of things hoped for, the evidence of things not seen*" (**Hebrews 11:1**). It is our confident reliance on God's character, His promises, and His power, even when our senses or circumstances might suggest otherwise. This faith is not a blind leap into the unknown, but a reasoned trust grounded in the revealed truth of God's Word, providing an inexhaustible wellspring of truth upon which our faith can draw, ensuring that our shield is both broad and impenetrable.

To understand the efficacy of the shield of faith, we must recognize that faith itself is a gift from God, activated by His Spirit and strengthened through consistent engagement with His Word. It is not something we conjure up on our own, but a response to God's revelation and a product of His grace working within us. As the Apostle Paul states in **Ephesians 2:8-9**, "*For by grace are ye saved through faith; and that not of yourselves: it is the gift of God: Not of works, lest any man should boast.*" (KJV, 2023). Faith is the bedrock of our relationship with God, is the very foundation upon which our shield of faith is constructed. It is the initial, profound trust in Christ's atoning work that allows us to stand before God as righteous, and it is this same trust that empowers us to face the daily onslaughts of the enemy.

The primary function of the shield of faith is to *quench* these fiery darts. The word "quench" implies extinguishing, putting out, or rendering ineffective. When a fiery dart strikes the shield of faith, it is met with an immovable resolve rooted in God's truth. For instance, when the enemy launches a dart of accusation, whispering, "You are too sinful to be forgiven; God could never use you," the believer, holding up the shield of faith, can respond with the truth of God's Word. In **I John 1:9**, it *declares, "If we confess our sins, he is faithful and just to forgive us our sins, and to cleanse us from all unrighteousness."* (KJV, 2023). This promise, when believed, acts as a shield against the fiery dart of guilt and condemnation. Our faith in God, coupled with His promise of cleansing, renders the accusation powerless.

Consider the subtle yet devastating nature of doubt. The enemy often employs doubt as a tactic, attempting to erode our confidence in God's love, His power, or His plan. He might plant seeds of doubt during times of suffering, questioning God's goodness or His ability to intervene. "If God truly loved you, He would not allow this trial," the whisper might suggest. In such moments, the shield of faith is our immediate and effective defense. By recalling and believing God's promises of His unwavering presence and His redemptive purposes, even in hardship, we can quench these fiery darts of doubt. Passages like **Romans 8:28**, which are so clearly stated, "And we know that all things work together for good to them that love God, to them who are called according to his purpose" (KJV, 2023), are vital. This truth, when embraced by faith, transforms the perception of suffering from a sign of God's absence to a testament of His sovereign work. Our faith in His overarching plan, even when unseen, extinguishes the fiery dart of doubt that suggests He has abandoned us.

The cultivation of this robust shield of faith is not an automatic process. It requires intentional effort and a deliberate engagement with God's Word and His Spirit. We must actively choose to believe God's promises, recall His past faithfulness, and lean into His strength when our own strength fails. This is why the Apostle Paul's exhortation to "take up" the shield of faith is so significant. It implies a conscious, volitional act. We are not passively protected; we are actively engaging in our defense. This active faith is nurtured through prayer, through fellowship with other believers, and, crucially, through diligent study of Scripture.

The Bible is a comprehensive witness to God's character and His dealings with humanity, provides the essential ammunition for strengthening our faith. Each story of God's deliverance, each prophetic promise, and each explicit declaration of His love builds the substance of our shield.

The effectiveness of the shield of faith is also magnified when it is understood as a collective defense, a community of believers holding up their shields together. While each believer is called to personal faith, the body of Christ is designed to support and strengthen one another. When one member is under a particularly fierce attack, others can intercede, offering prayer and encouragement that bolsters their faith. This communal aspect of faith is vital. The KJV's emphasis on the church as the body of Christ, a fellowship united in Him, underscores this interconnectedness. In **I Corinthians 12:26**, it states, "*And whether one member suffer, all the members suffer with it; or one member be honoured, all the members rejoice with it.*" (KJV, 2023). This shared experience of spiritual warfare strengthens the collective shield of faith, making the entire community more resilient against the enemy's onslaughts.

The shield of faith is not a static object; it is dynamic and responsive. It grows stronger with use and with consistent nourishment. When we face a fiery dart and actively employ our faith in God's Word, that faith is strengthened. Each successful defense builds confidence and resilience for future attacks. Conversely, suppose we neglect to exercise our faith. In that case, if we allow doubt to fester or discouragement to take root, our shield can become weakened, leaving us more susceptible to the enemy's assaults. This highlights the importance of a consistent spiritual discipline. The Bible recounts accounts of individuals who, by faith, overcame immense obstacles — Abraham's willingness to offer Isaac and David's confrontation with Goliath — providing powerful examples and encouragement to maintain a robust faith. These narratives are not mere historical accounts; they are living testimonies to the power of faith and the reliability of God.

One of the most insidious ways the enemy attacks is by distorting God's Word or twisting its meaning. These are perhaps the most dangerous "fiery darts" because they come cloaked in religious language, making them difficult to discern. Satan himself is depicted as a deceiver, capable of presenting himself as an angel of light (**II Corinthians 11:14**). When he launches these deceptive darts, our shield of faith must be anchored in the unwavering truth of Scripture.

For instance, the enemy might use verses out of context to promote a message of cheap grace, suggesting that our actions have no bearing on our spiritual life, or conversely, he might use verses about obedience to foster a spirit of legalism, implying that our salvation depends on our own performance. The Bible's consistent and coherent theological framework provides the antidote to such distortions. By immersing ourselves in its faithful rendering of God's complete counsel, we equip ourselves to recognize and extinguish these deceptive darts. Our faith in the totality of God's revealed truth becomes our defense.

The strength of our shield of faith is also intrinsically linked to our understanding of God's sovereignty. When we truly grasp that God is in control of all things, including the most challenging circumstances, our faith remains unshaken. The enemy often exploits our confusion or lack of understanding about God's permissive will, suggesting that He has lost control or is unable to intervene. God's sovereignty is proclaimed in passages like **Isaiah 46:9-10**, which declares, "*For I am God, and there is none like me, Declaring the end from the beginning, and from ancient times the things that are not yet done: Saying, my counsel shall stand, and I will do all my pleasure,*" (KJV, 2023) are powerful affirmations. When we hold onto this truth by faith, the fiery darts of anxiety and helplessness are rendered ineffective. Our faith is in a God who is not only powerful but also sovereignly in control, working all things according to His perfect plan.

The shield of faith is not only defensive but also offensive in its impact. As it extinguishes the enemy's fiery darts, it also creates an environment of spiritual stability and boldness. When our faith is strong, we are less likely to be paralyzed by fear or defeated by discouragement. Instead, we are empowered to move forward in obedience, to take bold steps of faith, and to advance the kingdom of God. The KJV's rich tapestry of faith-filled lives—from the prophets who stood against kings to the apostles who preached the Gospel in the face of persecution—serves as a constant reminder that faith is not meant to be passive but active and courageous. By relying on the unchanging God revealed in the Bible, our shield of faith becomes a platform from which we can launch our own offensive, sharing the good news of salvation with unwavering conviction.

To cultivate this essential shield of faith, we must engage in practices that strengthen our faith and reliance on God. This includes consistent prayer, not just asking for things, but communing with God and acknowledging our dependence on Him. It also involves actively recalling God's past faithfulness in our lives. When the enemy attempts to create despair, remember how God has brought us through previous trials, how He has provided in times of need, and how He has been faithful to His Word.

The Bible, with its historical accounts and testimonies, provides a vast reservoir of examples of God's faithfulness, serving as a constant reminder of who He is and what He is capable of doing. Meditating on these truths, internalizing them, and allowing them to shape our belief system is the very essence of building a robust shield of faith.

Furthermore, we must be diligent in separating ourselves from influences that can weaken our faith. This includes the ungodly philosophies and ideologies that saturate our culture, as well as the constant barrage of negative or fearful news. While we are called to be in the world, we are not to be *of* the world, and this separation extends to the information and influences we allow into our minds and hearts. The Bible, with its pure and unadulterated message of truth, acts as a spiritual filter. By immersing ourselves in its teachings, we are better equipped to discern truth from error and to resist the subtle corruptions that can erode our faith, thereby fortifying our shield against the insidious attacks of worldly thinking.

The Apostle Paul's instruction to "take up the shield of faith" is a call to active, intentional discipleship. It is a command to consistently and confidently trust in God, His Word, and His promises, especially when faced with the fiery darts of the adversary. This faith is the bedrock of our spiritual defense, extinguishing the flames of doubt, accusation, and deception. By drawing strength from the unwavering truth of Scripture and by actively cultivating a confident reliance on God's character and His sovereign plan, we can ensure that our shield of faith is broad enough to cover every vulnerability and strong enough to block every fiery dart aimed at our hearts and minds. This proactive faith not only protects us but also empowers us to stand firm and advance in the spiritual warfare that is essential to our growth.

We have discussed the helmet of Salvation and the shield of Faith in our spiritual armor arsenal as described by the Apostle Paul in **Ephesians 6.** Now, let us talk about the next tool—the Sword of the Spirit.

The Sword of the Spirit:

The sword of the Spirit is uniquely described as being the *Word of God*. This is a crucial distinction. While the other pieces of armor represent aspects of our spiritual identity and God's provision for us, the sword is directly tied to the communication of God Himself. It is the living, active, and powerful message that proceeds from His mouth. As **Hebrews 4:12**, so clearly articulated in the King James Version, states, "*For the word of God is quick, and powerful, and sharper than any two-edged sword, piercing even to the dividing asunder of soul and spirit, and of the joints and marrow, and is a discerner of the thoughts and intents of the heart.*" (KJV, 2023). This verse emphasizes that God's Word is not merely a collection of ancient writings; it is a divine instrument imbued with the very life and power of God, capable of penetrating the deepest recesses of human experience and discerning the true intentions behind our actions and thoughts.

The effectiveness of the sword of the Spirit is most powerfully illustrated in the temptation of our Lord Jesus Christ in the wilderness, as recorded in **Matthew chapter 4 and Luke chapter 4**. After forty days and forty nights of fasting, Jesus was physically weakened, making Him vulnerable to attack. It was in this state of physical depletion that Satan himself approached, seeking to exploit His hunger and His divine identity. The Tempter's strategy was not one of brute force, but of subtle deception and manipulative argumentation, precisely the tactics we face in our own spiritual battles.

The first temptation, presented in **Matthew 4:2-3**, reads: "*And when he had fasted forty days and forty nights, he was afterward an hungered. And when the tempter came to him he said, If thou be the Son of God, command that these stones be made bread.*" (KJV, 2023). Here, Satan is not questioning Jesus' hunger; he is questioning His *identity* and His *reliance* on God's provision. The implication is clear: "If you truly are the Son of God, you would not be suffering like this. You have the power to fix your situation yourself. This is a classic tactic to sow doubt and encourage self-reliance over faith in the divine.

Jesus' response, as found in **Matthew 4:4**, is a model for our own defense: "*It is written, Man shall not live by bread alone, but by every word that proceedeth out of the mouth of God.*" He does not engage in a philosophical debate or offer a logical counter-argument based on His own perceived rights. Instead, He wields the Sword of the Spirit. He quotes from Deuteronomy

8:3, a passage that reminds Israel of God's faithfulness in leading them through the wilderness and providing for them, teaching them that their true sustenance comes from God's Word. Jesus' use of Scripture demonstrates several critical principles for effective spiritual warfare.

Firstly, He knows the Word. The ability to recall and apply Scripture in the moment of attack is paramount. This is not something that can be achieved through a cursory reading. It requires diligent study, memorization, and meditation. When we internalize the verses of the Bible, they become readily available weapons, sharper than any earthly blade, to cut through the enemy's sophistry.

Secondly, Jesus applies the Word. He does not just recall a verse; He uses it to address the specific temptation. His response directly counters the Tempter's suggestion by asserting the higher spiritual nourishment that comes from obedience to God's Word, even in the face of physical need. This teaches us that our spiritual lives are not sustained solely by material possessions or even basic necessities, but by our active relationship with God and our commitment to His revealed will.

The second temptation, detailed in **Matthew 4:5-6**, involves Satan taking Jesus to the pinnacle of the temple in Jerusalem and saying, "*If thou be the Son of God, cast thyself down: for it is written, He shall give his angels charge concerning thee: and in their hands they shall bear thee up, lest at any time thou dash thy foot against a stone.*" (KJV, 2023). Again, Satan quotes Scripture, twisting it to serve his own deceptive purposes. He uses a psalm that speaks of God's protection over His faithful servants, but he misapplies it to encourage a reckless act of presumption. The implication is, "If you are truly God's Son, prove it by a miraculous leap. God is obligated to save you because it is written."

Jesus' counter-attack, in **Matthew 4:7**, is another masterful display of wielding the Sword of the Spirit: "*It is written again, Thou shalt not tempt the Lord thy God.*" (KJV, 2023). He again draws from Deuteronomy, this time from chapter 6, verse 16, where Moses recounts the Israelites' rebellion at Massah, where they tested God by demanding water. Jesus highlights the danger of using God's Word to manipulate God or to presume upon His grace. This is a vital lesson for us: we must not use Scripture to justify sin, to test God's limits, or to demand that He act according to our desires rather than His perfect will. Our faith must be rooted in submission to God, not in an attempt to control Him.

The third and final temptation, recorded in **Matthew 4:8-9**, sees Satan taking Jesus to a very high mountain and showing Him all the kingdoms of the world and their glory, saying, "*All these things will I give thee, if thou wilt fall down and worship me.*" (KJV, 2023). This is the ultimate temptation, an offer of earthly power and dominion in exchange for the ultimate act of treason against God—worshiping the devil. It is a temptation to compromise, to seek worldly solutions through ungodly means, and to reject God's divine plan for rulership.

Jesus' response, in **Matthew 4:10**, is unequivocal and final: "*Get thee hence, Satan: for it is written, Thou shalt worship the Lord thy God, and him only shalt thou serve.*" (KJV, 2023). This time, Jesus draws from Deuteronomy 6:13 and 10:20, directly commanding the devil to depart and reaffirming the foundational principle of monotheism and exclusive devotion to God. This is the ultimate assertion of divine authority, the definitive severing of the enemy's influence. By declaring the truth of God's sole right to worship, Jesus disarms the Tempter's offer of false power.

These three encounters in the wilderness are not merely historical accounts; they are a living blueprint for how we are to engage in spiritual warfare using the Word of God. The Tempter's strategy remains unchanged. He still seeks to distort our identity, to make us doubt God's provision, to encourage presumption, and to tempt us with worldly power and compromise. He continues to use manipulative language and subtle twists of truth, often cloaked in religious garb.

To wield the sword of the Spirit effectively, we must cultivate a deep and intimate knowledge of God's Word. This means more than just owning a Bible or occasionally reading a devotional. It requires a commitment to in-depth study, memorization, and meditation. We must immerse ourselves in its pages, allowing the Spirit of God to illuminate its truths and to engrave them upon our hearts.

Memorization is not an academic exercise; it is a strategic necessity. When under spiritual attack, we may not have the luxury of consulting a concordance or a theological commentary. We need the Word of God readily accessible within us. Think of it like a soldier carrying his rifle into battle. He does not leave it behind; he carries it, knows how to use it, and has ammunition loaded and ready. The Scripture verses we memorize and internalize become our ammunition. When the fiery darts of doubt, fear, or accusation fly, we can draw forth the appropriate spiritual ammunition—a promise of God's faithfulness, a declaration of His love, a reminder of His victory—to quench the attack.

Consider the practice of memorizing key passages. For instance, knowing **Romans 8:28**, "*And we know that all things work together for good to them that love God, to them who are called according to his purpose,*" can effectively counter despair and discouragement during difficult times. Memorizing passages about God's forgiveness, such as **I John 1:9**, "*If we confess our sins, he is faithful and just to forgive us our sins, and to cleanse us from all unrighteousness,*" can defeat the darts of guilt and condemnation. Verses that speak of God's strength, like **Isaiah 41:10**, "*Fear thou not; for I am with thee: be not dismayed; for I am thy God: I will strengthen thee; yea, I will help thee; yea, I will uphold thee with the right hand of my righteousness,*" are invaluable in overcoming fear.

Furthermore, effective wielding of the sword of the Spirit involves not only knowing and applying Scripture but also *discerning* its true meaning. Satan is a master of distortion, often taking verses out of context, twisting their meaning, or combining them with human philosophies to create deception. This is why a solid understanding of the KJV's consistent theological message is so vital. It provides the necessary context and interpretive framework to recognize and reject these perversions of truth. We must guard against a superficial or selective reading of Scripture. True discernment comes from a comprehensive engagement with God's entire Word, allowing the clearer passages to illuminate the more difficult ones, and letting the overarching narrative of redemption guide our understanding.

The "word of God" is not just the written text; it is also the incarnate Word, Jesus Christ Himself. When we wield Scripture, we are essentially pointing to Christ, reminding the enemy of His victory on the cross and His ultimate authority. The KJV's robust Christology and its clear presentation of Jesus as the Son of God, the Savior of the world, serve as a potent weapon against any ideology that seeks to diminish His deity or His salvific work.

The offensive capability of the Sword of the Spirit extends beyond personal defense. It is the primary tool we have for proclaiming the Gospel of Jesus Christ, which is itself the power of God unto salvation **(Romans 1:16)**. When we share the good news, we are wielding the Word of God, bringing light into darkness, hope into despair, and life into death. The KJV, in its faithful rendering of the Gospel message, empowers believers to articulate this truth with clarity and conviction, disarming the arguments of unbelief and inviting others into the kingdom of God.

In summary, the Sword of the Spirit, the Word of God, is an indispensable weapon in the believer's spiritual arsenal. It is the offensive arm that allows us not only to defend ourselves against the enemy's attacks but also to engage in spiritual warfare actively, advancing the cause of Christ. By diligently studying, memorizing, and applying Scripture, we equip ourselves to counter deception, resist temptation, and assert God's absolute authority. Jesus' example in the wilderness provides a powerful paradigm: know the Word, apply the Word, and stand firm in the truth, for it is through the Word that God's power is unleashed, and the enemy's schemes are rendered powerless. This is the dynamic, life-giving power of God's Word actively engaged in the life of a believer.

Fervent Prayer/Intercessory Prayer:

Prayer, often referred to as the believer's direct line to the Almighty, is far more than a passive request; it is an active, potent weapon in the arsenal of spiritual warfare. When the fiery darts of deception, confusion, and doubt are hurled against us or those we care about, prayer is our primary offensive and defensive maneuver. It is the conduit through which God's power is channeled, His wisdom is sought, and His authority is invoked against the machinations of the enemy. The Apostle Paul's exhortation in **Ephesians 6:18**, *"Praying always with all prayer and supplication in the Spirit, and watching thereunto with all perseverance and supplication for all saints,"* underscores the indispensable nature of prayer in maintaining our spiritual fortifications and engaging effectively in the unseen battles that surround us.

We must understand that prayer is not simply a religious exercise but a strategic engagement. It is the means by which we align ourselves with God's will, seek His direction, and activate His power in earthly circumstances. The enemy, Satan, thrives on chaos, confusion, and the isolation of believers. Prayer combats these very things by bringing order, clarity, and unity. When we pray, we are not whispering into a void; we are engaging in a dynamic dialogue with the Creator of the universe, who has promised to hear and answer those who call upon Him according to His will, as revealed in His Holy Word. The King James Version of the Bible consistently emphasizes the power and efficacy of prayer, providing numerous accounts of how earnest supplication has brought about divine intervention and victory.

One of the most powerful dimensions of prayer in spiritual warfare is intercession. This is the act of standing in the gap for others, praying on their behalf for protection, guidance, and deliverance from spiritual attack. The enemy relentlessly seeks to ensnare individuals, to sow discord within families and churches, and to derail the plans of God's people. Through intercessory prayer, we become active participants in God's redemptive work, extending His kingdom's influence and fortifying the spiritual defenses of our brethren. When we intercede, we act as spiritual soldiers on behalf of others, using the weapon of prayer to shield them from harm and guide them toward truth. The faithful intercessor, armed with the promises of God's Word and a heart aligned with His purposes, can be a formidable force against the kingdom of darkness.

Consider the profound impact of praying for discernment. The enemy's primary tactic is deception, weaving webs of lies that appear plausible, even righteous, to the untrained spiritual eye. The Apostle John instructs us in **I John 4:1**, *"Beloved, believe not every spirit, but try the spirits whether they are of God: because many false prophets are gone out into the world."* This mandate to "try the spirits" is directly facilitated by prayer. When we pray for wisdom and discernment, we are asking God to grant us the ability to distinguish between His voice and the voice of the deceiver, between His truth and the enemy's distortions. The Bible, with its clear theological distinctions and its unwavering commitment to biblical accuracy, provides the very framework through which discernment is honed. By immersing ourselves in its teachings and seeking the Spirit's illumination, we develop an internal compass calibrated to the frequency of divine truth, enabling us to detect and reject spiritual falsehoods.

The effectiveness of praying for discernment is evident in various contexts. In personal life, when faced with significant decisions, career changes, or relationship choices, the enemy may present options that seem advantageous but are, in reality, spiritual traps. A prayer for discernment, coupled with diligent study of Scripture, allows us to filter these options through the lens of God's revealed will. Similarly, in the broader context of the church, discerning false doctrines or manipulative leadership requires a spirit of prayerful inquiry. When teachings deviate from the clear and consistent message of the KJV, a discerning believer, fortified by prayer, will recognize the dissonance and stand firm in the truth.

Furthermore, prayer is an act of asserting divine authority over deceptive forces. The enemy operates through spiritual influences, attempting to control thoughts, emotions, and circumstances. Prayer, when offered in faith and in alignment with God's Word, is the means by which we invoke God's supreme authority over these forces. Jesus demonstrated this principle when He commanded demons to depart. He did not negotiate with them; He spoke with divine authority, rooted in His identity and His Father's will. Our prayers, empowered by the same Spirit that raised Christ from the dead, carry this same authoritative weight. We can pray prayers of command, binding the influence of deceptive spirits, breaking the power of lies, and releasing individuals from spiritual bondage.

The Bible provides ample examples of this authoritative prayer. When Jesus taught His disciples the Lord's Prayer (**Matthew 6:9-13**), He included the petition, "*Thy kingdom come. Thy will be done in earth, as it is in heaven.*" (KJV, 2023). This petition is an assertion of God's sovereign will and a prayer for its establishment on earth, directly countering the enemy's attempts to usurp God's rule. Moreover, the apostle Paul, in **II Corinthians 10:4-5**, describes the spiritual weapons we possess: "*For the weapons of our warfare are not carnal, but mighty through God to the pulling down of strong holds; Casting down imaginations, and every high thing that exalteth itself against the knowledge of God, and bringing into captivity every thought to the obedience of Christ.*" (KJV, 2023). This passage clearly indicates that our warfare is spiritual, and our weapons, particularly prayer, are designed to dismantle the enemy's fortresses of deception and align every thought with Christ.

The consistent and fervent application of prayer in spiritual warfare is paramount. The enemy is persistent; his attacks are often relentless. Therefore, our prayer life must be characterized by perseverance. This means not giving up when the answer is not immediately apparent, not succumbing to discouragement when the spiritual battle seems intense. The Bible's emphasis on enduring faith and steadfastness in prayer encourages believers to remain vigilant and committed, knowing that God's timing and

His methods are perfect. Our prayers, offered in faith and sustained by the Holy Spirit, are the bedrock of our spiritual defense, creating a bulwark against the enemy's onslaught.

Praying for things contrary to God's nature or His stated promises will not yield the desired results. The Spirit of God guides our prayers, prompting us to pray in accordance with God's purposes. This is the essence of praying "in the Spirit." When our prayers are rooted in Scripture and empowered by the Holy Spirit, they become unstoppable forces for good, thwarting the enemy's plans and securing victory in the spiritual realm.

The practice of praying with supplication and thanksgiving is also integral to spiritual fortification. Supplication involves earnest entreaty, a heartfelt bringing of our needs and concerns before God. Thanksgiving, on the other hand, is an acknowledgment of God's faithfulness and His past provision. Both are essential. Thanksgiving can shift our perspective from the immediate pressures of the spiritual battle to the overarching victory that Christ has already secured. It builds our faith and reinforces our confidence in God's power to deliver. As we offer up our supplications, remembering God's past faithfulness, we fortify our resolve and prepare ourselves to receive His intervention. The Bible, with its abundant expressions of praise and gratitude, inspires a thankful heart, fueling more effective prayer.

The spiritual battle is not a passive observation; it is an active engagement where every believer is called to participate. Prayer is the primary instrument of this engagement, a weapon that requires consistent maintenance and skillful use. By embracing the multifaceted nature of prayer—as intercession for others, a pursuit of wisdom and discernment, and an assertion of divine authority—we can effectively counter the enemy's deceptive tactics. Fervent, persistent prayer, steeped in the timeless truths of the Bible and guided by the Holy Spirit, is the ultimate fortification for our spiritual defenses, ensuring our steadfastness and paving the way for assured victory in the unseen realm. It is through this vital spiritual discipline that we move beyond merely enduring the attacks to actively disarming the enemy and advancing the kingdom of God.

To further emphasize the strategic importance of prayer, let us consider its role in dismantling specific forms of deception. The enemy often employs lies that target our identity in Christ, whispering doubts about our worthiness, our acceptance, or our authority as children of God. In such moments, prayer becomes a powerful refutation. We can pray prayers of affirmation, reciting and meditating upon the truths of Scripture that declare our identity as beloved children of God, redeemed by the blood of Jesus. Verses like **Romans 8:15**, "*For ye have not received the spirit of bondage again to fear; but ye have received the Spirit of adoption, whereby we cry, Abba, Father,*" are potent weapons against the spirit of fear and insecurity that the enemy seeks to instill. By praying these truths, we actively counter the enemy's lies, reaffirming our position and strengthening our inner fortifications.

Another area where deception frequently infiltrates is in the realm of emotions and relationships. The enemy can sow seeds of bitterness, unforgiveness, jealousy, or discontent, creating division and hindering spiritual growth. Intercessory prayer for those who have wronged us, or for ourselves to be freed from these negative influences, is a profound act of spiritual warfare. Praying for forgiveness, as modeled by Christ Himself, disarms the enemy's attempts to create lasting rifts. The King James Version's emphasis on love, forgiveness, and reconciliation provides the divine framework for these prayers, enabling believers to actively work towards spiritual health and unity, even in the face of deep hurt. When we pray for the healing of broken relationships or the release from emotional turmoil, we are actively engaging the power of God to restore and to redeem, pushing back the darkness of division and animosity that the enemy seeks to cultivate.

The persistent, often subtle, nature of spiritual attack necessitates a corresponding persistence in prayer. The enemy does not relent in his efforts to mislead and to destabilize. Therefore, our prayer life must be characterized by consistent and unwavering devotion. This means integrating prayer not just into moments of crisis but as a foundational element of our daily spiritual discipline. It is through this ongoing communion with God that our spiritual defenses are continuously reinforced, making us less susceptible to the enemy's attempts to breach our fortifications.

Furthermore, the effectiveness of prayer is amplified when it is offered with genuine humility and a teachable spirit. The enemy thrives on pride, attempting to foster an attitude of self-sufficiency that isolates us from divine guidance. However, when we approach God in prayer with a humble heart, acknowledging our dependence on Him and our need for His wisdom, we open ourselves to His powerful intervention. The Bible consistently exalts humility and warns against pride, guiding believers to approach God with reverence and an eagerness to learn. This posture of humility makes our prayers more receptive to the Spirit's leading, ensuring that we are praying according to God's will and not our own limited understanding. This alignment is crucial for attaining genuine spiritual strength.

The proactive nature of prayer in spiritual warfare cannot be overstated. It is not merely a reaction to an attack; it is a continuous building of spiritual strength and resilience. By engaging in regular prayer, we continually fortify our defenses, making ourselves less vulnerable to the enemy's onslaughts. This discipline prepares us to face the challenges that lie ahead, equipping us with the spiritual armor and the divine power necessary to stand firm.

The spiritual battle is not a singular event, nor is it a conflict that, once engaged, is quickly resolved. The adversary, often referred to in

Scripture as the "accuser of the brethren," is relentless. His strategies are multifaceted, designed to wear down the believer, sow seeds of doubt, and ultimately lead astray from the truth. Therefore, after establishing our initial fortifications through prayer, fasting, and the diligent study of God's Word, the crucial task remains: maintaining and strengthening those defenses through a steadfast commitment to vigilance and spiritual prudence. This is not a passive state of being, but an active, ongoing posture of spiritual awareness and wise decision-making.

Furthermore, the assurance of salvation guards us against the deception of worldly philosophies and ideologies that seek to redefine sin and righteousness, or diminish the necessity of Christ's sacrifice. In an age saturated with relativism and a pervasive distrust of absolute truth, the clear, unvarnished message of salvation found in the KJV can seem counter-cultural. However, it is precisely this clarity that makes it such a potent safeguard for the mind. When confronted with teachings that promote self-salvation through good works or that deny the efficacy of Christ's blood, the believer who has internalized the truth of their salvation through the Bible stands firm. They recognize these alternative narratives not as valid options, but as dangerous deviations from the singular truth of God's grace. The helmet of salvation is the mental conviction that our acceptance with God is solely through Christ, a conviction that makes us impervious to the allure of these deceptive systems.

Vigilance—Not Complacency:

Vigilance in the spiritual arena is akin to the watchfulness of a sentry on duty. It requires a constant, sober awareness of our surroundings, not in a fearful or paranoid manner, but with a clear-eyed understanding of the spiritual realities at play. The Apostle Peter exhorts believers in **I Peter 5:8**, "*Be sober, be vigilant; because your adversary the devil, as a roaring lion, walketh about, seeking whom he may devour*" (KJV, 2023). This imagery is powerful. A lion does not roar to announce its surrender; it roars to intimidate, to sow terror, and to create an opening for attack. Similarly, the enemy's methods are often designed to create an atmosphere of fear or confusion, making us less attentive to the subtle ways he seeks to gain a foothold.

To be vigilant means to cultivate a discerning spirit, one that can recognize the enemy's tactics before they fully manifest. This involves paying close attention to the subtle shifts in our spiritual atmosphere, to the whispers of doubt that seek to undermine our faith, or to the seductive allure of worldly philosophies that appear harmless but subtly contradict biblical truth. It means being acutely aware of our own spiritual condition, acknowledging any areas of weakness or vulnerability that the enemy might exploit. This self-awareness, born from honest introspection and guided by the Holy Spirit, is a cornerstone of spiritual defense. By regularly immersing ourselves in the Bible's teachings, we develop an internal compass that is calibrated to divine truth, enabling us to detect deviations from God's path with greater accuracy.

Complacency is the spiritual enemy of vigilance. It is the dangerous belief that once defenses are in place, the battle is won, or at least paused indefinitely. The reality, however, is that the enemy is always probing, always seeking new angles of attack. Complacency lulls us into a false sense of security, lowering our guard and making us susceptible to deception. This can manifest in various ways: becoming lax in our prayer life, allowing our biblical study to become perfunctory, or neglecting the fellowship and accountability found within the body of Christ. The enemy rejoices when believers become comfortable, for comfort can often be a precursor to spiritual decline. He desires us to become so accustomed to the status quo that we fail to recognize when the enemy is subtly altering the spiritual landscape around us.

Prudence, on the other hand, is the active exercise of wisdom and sound judgment in our spiritual lives. It involves making informed decisions based on a deep understanding of God's Word and a sensitivity to the Holy Spirit's guidance. This is not about humanistic self-reliance, but about leaning on divine wisdom to navigate the complexities of spiritual warfare. Prudence means carefully considering the spiritual implications of our choices, our associations, and the information we consume. It involves asking critical questions: Does this align with biblical truth? Does this strengthen or weaken my faith? Does this draw me closer to God or pull me away?

Anticipating and neutralizing emerging threats is a key aspect of this vigilant and prudent approach. This requires not only reacting to immediate dangers but also discerning potential future challenges. It means understanding the enemy's patterns and motivations, and proactively strengthening our defenses in anticipation of his next move. This might involve studying prophetic portions of Scripture to understand God's long-term plan, thereby recognizing how current events might fit into the broader narrative of spiritual conflict. It also involves being sensitive to shifts in cultural or theological trends that might pose a threat to biblical orthodoxy.

For example, the enemy might introduce a subtle redefinition of core biblical concepts, cloaked in appealing language that appeals to our emotions or intellect. Vigilance is required to recognize that these seemingly innocuous shifts can erode foundational truths. Prudence then guides us in how to respond, whether through further study, engaging in thoughtful dialogue, or clearly articulating and defending the biblical position. The King James Version, by presenting the doctrines of Scripture with clarity and precision, serves as an indispensable tool in this process, allowing us to measure any new teaching against the unchanging standard of God's Word.

Consider the proliferation of teachings that subtly undermine the authority of scripture or that promote a syncretistic approach to faith, blending biblical truth with other spiritual or philosophical systems. A vigilant believer will recognize the danger inherent in such trends, understanding that the enemy's goal is to dilute and ultimately neutralize the transformative power of the Gospel. Prudence will then dictate a course of action that involves deepening one's own commitment to the unadulterated truth of God's Word, and perhaps even speaking out with grace and truth against such distortions. Furthermore, vigilance and prudence are essential in safeguarding our spiritual integrity. This involves not only protecting ourselves from external attacks but also cultivating inner purity and dedication to God. It means actively guarding our hearts and minds against corrupting influences, whether they come through media, social circles, or internal temptations. The Apostle Paul's admonition to us in **Ephesians 6:13** is to "*put on the whole armour of God*" (KJV, 2023). This is a call to continuous engagement, not a one-time donning of spiritual protection. Each piece of the armor requires conscious effort to maintain and to wield effectively.

Prudence guides us in understanding what constitutes a "corrupting influence." It might be the allure of excessive materialism that distracts from spiritual pursuits, the embrace of ideologies that contradict God's moral order, or the cultivation of unhealthy habits that weaken our physical or spiritual resolve. The King James Version, in its consistent emphasis on righteousness, holiness, and self-control, provides the clear moral framework for making prudent choices that safeguard our spiritual integrity. It encourages us to flee from youthful lusts and to pursue purity of heart and life. This ongoing commitment to vigilance and prudence ensures that our spiritual defenses remain robust and our commitment to biblical truth unwavering. It means that we are not taken by surprise by the enemy's schemes. Instead, we are prepared, grounded in the truth, and empowered by the Spirit to stand firm. This proactive stance not only protects us but also enables us to become effective instruments in God's hands, able to discern truth, resist deception, and advance His kingdom, even in the face of opposition. The spiritual life is a marathon, not a sprint, and the disciplines of vigilance and prudence are the essential disciplines that sustain us throughout the race, ensuring that our spiritual fortifications are not only built but also perpetually maintained and strengthened.

Satan is an enemy that thrives on chaos, confusion, and the isolation of believers. Prayer combats these very things by bringing order, clarity, and unity. When we pray, we are not whispering into a void; we are engaging in a dynamic dialogue with the Creator of the universe, who has promised to hear and answer those who call upon Him as revealed in His Holy Word.

One of the most powerful dimensions of prayer in spiritual warfare is intercession. This is the act of standing in the gap for others, praying on their behalf for protection, guidance, and deliverance from spiritual attack. The enemy relentlessly seeks to ensnare individuals, to sow discord within families and churches, and to derail the plans of God's people. Through intercessory prayer, we become active participants in God's redemptive work, extending His kingdom's influence and fortifying the spiritual defenses of our brethren. When we intercede, we act as spiritual soldiers on behalf of others, using the weapon of prayer to shield them from harm and guide them toward truth. The faithful intercessor, armed with God's Word and a heart aligned with His purposes, is a formidable force against the kingdom of darkness.

The practical application of taking up the helmet of salvation involves cultivating a disciplined mind. This means being vigilant about what we allow to enter our thoughts. In today's media-saturated world, we are constantly bombarded with information, opinions, and images that can subtly erode our spiritual convictions. The enemy can use these channels to sow seeds of doubt, promote ungodly values, or stir up sinful desires. Therefore, we must intentionally filter what we consume, prioritizing spiritual nourishment over the constant influx of secular or corrupting content. This involves setting boundaries on our media consumption, seeking out edifying fellowship, and intentionally immersing ourselves in God's Word.

The renewal of the mind is also a process of actively replacing negative or deceitful thoughts with God's truth. When a thought of doubt or fear arises, the believer is called to cast it down and bring it into captivity to the obedience of Christ, as Paul instructs in **II Corinthians 10:5**. This is not about suppressing thoughts, but about actively countering them with the truth of our salvation. For instance, if we are tempted to believe that God is distant or displeased with us because of a recent failure, we must consciously recall and affirm biblical truths about God's unfailing love and the permanence of His grace. Passages like **I John 4:18**, *"There is no fear in love; but perfect love casteth out fear: because fear hath torment,"* are essential (KJV, 2023). The Bible's rendering of "perfect love casteth out fear" is compelling, offering a definitive statement of the power of God's love to expel debilitating anxieties.

The assurance of salvation also provides a stable perspective from which to evaluate the trials and difficulties of life. When faced with adversity, it is easy for the mind to become overwhelmed by despair or to question God's presence and plan. However, the helmet of salvation reminds us that even in our trials, we are still God's children, secure in His eternal love. The trials themselves are often part of the sanctification process, refining our faith and drawing us closer to God. The consistent portrayal of God's sovereignty and His redemptive purposes in all circumstances provides the believer with an anchor in the midst of the storm. For example, the unwavering assertion in **Romans 8:28**, *"And we know that all things work together for good to them that love God, to them who are called according to his purpose,"* (KJV, 2023), is a profound statement of divine providence that can fortify the mind against despair during difficult times. This assurance is a vital part of the helmet, protecting our perspective from the distortions of suffering.

Moreover, the helmet of salvation is inextricably linked to the hope we have in Christ. Our salvation is not merely about our past sins being forgiven; it is also about our future glory. The anticipation of Christ's return and the eternal life that awaits us serves as a powerful motivator and a source of strength. This hope, when firmly grasped, inoculates the mind against the temptations of worldly pleasure and the discouragement of present suffering. The anticipation of resurrection and eternal fellowship with God, as described in passages like **I Thessalonians 4:17**, "*Then we which are alive and remain shall be caught up together with them in the clouds, to meet the Lord in the air: and so shall we ever be with the Lord,*" (KJV, 2023), provides a future focus that can shield the mind from the allure of temporal gratifications and the sting of present troubles.

Consider the proliferation of teachings that subtly undermine the authority of Scripture or that promote a syncretistic approach to faith, blending biblical truth with other spiritual or philosophical systems. A vigilant believer will recognize the danger inherent in such trends, understanding that the enemy's goal is to dilute and ultimately neutralize the transformative power of the Gospel. Prudence will then dictate a course of action that involves deepening one's own commitment to the unadulterated truth of God's Word, and speaking out with grace and truth against such distortions.

Furthermore, vigilance and prudence are essential in safeguarding our spiritual integrity. This involves not only protecting ourselves from external attacks but also cultivating inner purity and dedication to God. It means actively guarding our hearts and minds against corrupting influences, whether they come through media, social circles, or internal temptations. The Apostle Paul's admonition in **Ephesians 6:13** to "*put on the whole armour of God*" (KJV, 2023) is a call to continuous engagement, not a one-time donning of spiritual protection. Each piece of the armor requires conscious effort to maintain and to wield effectively.

Prudence guides us in understanding what constitutes a "corrupting influence." It might be the allure of excessive materialism that distracts from spiritual pursuits, the embrace of ideologies that contradict God's moral order, or the cultivation of unhealthy habits that weaken our physical or spiritual resolve. The Bible, with its consistent emphasis on righteousness, holiness, and self-control, provides a clear moral framework for making prudent choices that safeguard our spiritual integrity. It encourages us to flee from youthful lusts and to pursue purity of heart and life.

This ongoing commitment to vigilance and prudence ensures that our spiritual defenses remain robust and our commitment to biblical truth unwavering. It means that we are not taken by surprise by the enemy's schemes. Instead, we are prepared, grounded in the truth, and empowered by the Spirit to stand firm. This proactive stance not only protects us but also enables us to become effective instruments in God's hands, able to discern truth, resist deception, and advance His kingdom.

The spiritual life is a marathon, not a sprint, and the disciplines of vigilance and prudence are the essential disciplines that sustain us throughout the race, ensuring that our spiritual fortifications are not only built but also perpetually maintained and strengthened. The enduring power of the Bible is a source of absolute truth and divine wisdom, providing the ultimate resource for cultivating these vital spiritual attributes, ensuring that our faith remains uncompromised and our spiritual resilience unshakeable. It is through this steadfast dedication to watchfulness and wise discernment that we truly build an unbreachable defense against the wiles of the adversary. Having considered the belt of truth, the breastplate of righteousness, and the helmet of salvation, we now turn our attention to a critical component that directly protects our most vulnerable asset: our mind, but not solely our mind.

This is not merely symbolic; it is a divinely provided arsenal for the believer's engagement in spiritual warfare. Each piece represents a tangible aspect of God's provision that empowers us to stand firm against the devil's schemes. Having considered the belt of truth, the breastplate of righteousness, the helmet of salvation, and the shield of faith, we now turn our attention to the only offensive weapon in our spiritual arsenal: the sword of the Spirit, which is the Word of God. This is not simply a defensive posture we adopt, but an active means by which we engage the enemy and advance the kingdom of God. It is through the skillful wielding of Scripture that we can effectively counter the lies of the adversary, dismantle his deceptive strategies, and assert the absolute authority of our Creator.

La Wanda Blackmon

CHAPTER EIGHT:
Restoring Truth & Mending What is Broken

The insidious nature of deception, once unleashed, casts a long and destructive shadow, impacting the very fabric of our lives, both personally and communally. It is a poison that, when ingested, slowly but surely corrupts the wellsprings of our spiritual and relational health. The immediate sting of being deceived can be sharp, a sudden realization that the ground beneath our feet is not as firm as we believed. However, the lingering consequences often prove far more damaging, eroding foundations that may have taken years to establish.

On an individual level, the personal consequences of deception can be profound, leading to a deep-seated spiritual confusion. When a person is misled, particularly by someone they trusted, or by teachings that subtly deviate from the clear pronouncements of Scripture, their spiritual compass can become disoriented. A fog of ambiguity and doubt can obscure the clarity that comes from an unwavering commitment to biblical truth. This confusion is not merely intellectual; it can penetrate the heart, leading to a questioning of God's faithfulness, the reliability of His Word, or even the very nature of truth itself. The enemy's objective is often to sow discord and disorientation, and deception is his most potent weapon in this regard. When we are led astray by falsehood, we can find ourselves wandering in a spiritual wilderness, unsure of the path forward, and susceptible to further error. The emotional toll is significant, often manifesting as anxiety, disillusionment, and a pervasive sense of unease. The bedrock of faith, built upon the sure promises of God as revealed in the King James Version, can begin to crumble under the weight of persistent, unaddressed deception.

This spiritual disorientation inevitably spills over into our relationships. Trust, that most precious and fragile of commodities, is the bedrock of any healthy connection, whether it be within a family, a friendship, or the broader Christian fellowship. Deception, by its very definition, is a violation of that trust. When a lie is revealed or a hidden truth comes to light, it shatters the existing framework of understanding between individuals. The immediate aftermath is often marked by feelings of hurt, anger, and a profound sense of betrayal. Rebuilding trust after such a breach is a Herculean task, typically requiring a deep and sincere repentance from the one who deceived, along with a long, arduous journey of consistent, truthful action. Without this, the damaged relationship can become permanently scarred, characterized by suspicion and distance. The intimacy that was once enjoyed is replaced by a guardedness, a reluctance to be fully vulnerable, for fear of being hurt again. This can manifest as a constant second-guessing of motives, a perpetual seeking for hidden agendas, which is emotionally exhausting and relational debilitating.

The erosion of trust extends beyond the immediate parties involved in the deception. Within the Christian community, a single instance of significant deception can have ripple effects, creating an atmosphere of suspicion that hinders genuine fellowship from flourishing. If a leader is found to have been dishonest, or if a prominent teaching is discovered to be rooted in falsehood, it can shake the faith of many. Believers may begin to question not only the specific individuals or teachings involved but also the discernment of the leadership and the overall health of the community. This can lead to a regrettable withdrawal from fellowship, a huddling in smaller, more trusted circles, or even a complete departure from the church altogether. The communal damage is substantial, as it hinders the body's ability to function effectively as a unified witness to the world. The enemy delights in such divisions, for a fractured body is a weakened body, less capable of fulfilling its divine mandate.

Furthermore, deception can lead to doctrinal impurity, a subtle yet devastating corruption of the core tenets of our faith. When individuals or groups intentionally or unintentionally introduce falsehoods into biblical teaching, the very foundations of Christian belief can be undermined. This might involve misinterpreting Scripture to support personal agendas, adopting philosophies that contradict biblical worldview, or promoting a watered-down version of the Gospel that appeals to worldly sensibilities rather than calling for true repentance and transformation. The King James Version, with its fidelity to the original languages and its clarity of doctrine, serves as a vital safeguard against such distortions. However, even with such a reliable translation, the human element of interpretation and application can introduce error. When deception enters into doctrinal matters, it can lead entire congregations astray, guiding them away from the liberating truth of Christ and into a spiritual bondage that is far more insidious than overt persecution. The consequences are eternal, as individuals are led to place their faith in something other than the actual and living God.

The ultimate consequence of deception is a departure from God's intended path for our lives and for His church. God's ways are perfect, His truth is life-giving, and His plan for us is one of abundant blessing and spiritual growth. Deception, however, diverts us from this path, leading us into spiritual dead ends and ultimately away from the very source of life. When we are deceived, we are essentially living a lie, operating under false premises, and making choices based on flawed information. This inevitably leads to a misalignment with God's purposes, resulting in a life that falls short of what He intended. It can manifest as a stagnation in spiritual growth, a lack of true joy and peace, and an inability to experience the fullness of life that Christ promised. The Christian life is a journey of increasing sanctification and a deeper walk with God. Deception acts as a potent brake on this progress, hindering our ability to become who we are called to be.

Consider the example of someone who is promised a lucrative investment opportunity that, in reality, is a fraudulent scheme. Initially, they may be excited by the prospect of quick riches, investing their time and resources based on false assurances. As the deception unravels, they face not only financial loss but also the humiliation of being fooled, the anger at the perpetrators, and the disillusionment with their own judgment. This experience can leave them jaded and distrustful, making them hesitant to engage in future legitimate ventures or even to trust their own instincts. The spiritual parallel is clear. When we are deceived about matters of faith, the consequences can be far more devastating than financial loss. We can lose our spiritual inheritance, our sense of God's presence, and our ability to discern truth in the future.

Within the context of the church, deception can manifest in subtle yet destructive ways. A charismatic preacher who deviates from sound doctrine, subtly introducing personal interpretations or even outright heresies, can lead many astray. The allure of their personality and the emotional resonance of their delivery can mask the underlying falsehood. For those who are not vigilant in their study of Scripture, particularly the clear teachings found in the King James Version, it can be challenging to discern the error. The result is a congregation that may be outwardly enthusiastic but inwardly adrift from the foundational truths of the Gospel. This not only harms the individuals within that congregation but also weakens the church's overall witness to the broader community. The trust placed in leadership is paramount, and when that trust is betrayed through deception, the damage is widespread and complex to repair.

The erosion of trust within a community can create a chilling effect on open dialogue and the willingness to be vulnerable. If people fear being judged, manipulated, or misled, they will naturally become more guarded.

This stifles the kind of honest confession and mutual encouragement that are vital for spiritual growth. Instead of a community of mutual support and accountability, it can devolve into a place of polite but superficial interaction, where the real struggles and doubts of faith are hidden beneath a veneer of outward piety. The enemy thrives in such environments, as it prevents the uncovering and addressing of the very issues that hinder genuine spiritual progress. The King James Version, with its emphasis on love, truth, and righteous living, provides a blueprint for an authentic community; however, deception actively works against this ideal.

The impact of doctrinal impurity cannot be overstated. When the core beliefs of Christianity are distorted, the very message of salvation is compromised. For instance, teachings that downplay the seriousness of sin or suggest that salvation is earned through human effort rather than by grace through faith in Christ lead people away from the true Gospel. These distortions, often presented in attractive or intellectually sophisticated ways, can be particularly dangerous. They can create a false sense of security, leading individuals to believe they are right with God when in reality they are far from Him. This is a profound spiritual damage, as it impacts eternal destinies. The Bible remains a steadfast anchor in presenting these vital doctrines with clarity and accuracy, serving as a crucial resource for those who seek to understand and uphold the unadulterated truth.

Ultimately, deception separates us from God's perfect will and His abundant life. When we are living under a cloud of falsehood, whether it pertains to our understanding of God, His Word, or His dealings with us, we are operating outside of His design. This can lead to a life characterized by spiritual barrenness, a lack of true fulfillment, and an inability to experience the transformative power of the Holy Spirit. The Christian journey is meant to be a process of becoming more like Christ, a journey of progressive sanctification. Deception impedes this process, keeping us bound by the lies that have ensnared us. It is a subtle but devastating spiritual captivity, a departure from the freedom and life that are found in unwavering adherence to the truth. Recognizing these profound and far-reaching consequences underscores the urgent necessity of actively pursuing truth, mending the brokenness caused by deceit, and recommitting ourselves to a life of unwavering spiritual integrity and clarity, grounded in the unchanging truth of God's Word, as faithfully preserved in the King James Version.

The profound damage wrought by deception, as we have seen, is not merely a superficial wound. It pierces the very heart of trust, leaving behind a landscape of relational and spiritual desolation. In the aftermath of such betrayal, a natural inclination arises: to cling to the hurt, to nurture the resentment, and to build walls of self-protection around the wounded spirit. However, Scripture offers a pathway through this wreckage, a divinely ordained principle that holds the key to genuine healing and restoration:

forgiveness. This is not a facile dismissal of the wrong done, nor a naive endorsement of continued deceit. Instead, it is a deliberate, often complex, act of releasing the debt owed by the offender, an act rooted in the profound love and sacrifice of our Savior, Jesus Christ.

Jesus Himself modeled this radical forgiveness, even in His darkest hour. As He hung upon the cross, bearing the weight of humanity's sin, His first recorded words were not of accusation or condemnation, but of profound compassion in **Luke 23:34**: "*Father, forgive them, for they know not what they do*" (KJV, 2023). This utterance, spoken amidst unimaginable suffering inflicted by those who had wronged Him deeply, stands as the ultimate testament to the power of forgiveness. It is a call to imitate Him, to extend mercy even when it feels undeserved, to break the chains of bitterness that bind us to our pain. This is the very essence of Christian forgiveness – it is not earned, but freely given, a reflection of God's boundless grace to us.

The Bible consistently underscores the importance of forgiveness as a prerequisite for our own spiritual well-being and for experiencing God's favor. In the Sermon on the Mount, in **Matthew 6:14-15**, Jesus states unequivocally, "*For if you forgive men their trespasses, your heavenly Father will also forgive you. But if you do not forgive men their trespasses, neither will your Father forgive your trespasses*" (KJV, 2023). This sobering declaration underscores the interconnection between our capacity to forgive others and our relationship with God. To hold onto unforgiveness is to build a barrier between ourselves and the very source of love and healing. It allows the poison of resentment to fester within, corroding our spiritual life and hindering our ability to receive the forgiveness that we ourselves so desperately need.

The cycle of bitterness and retaliation, so often the default human response to betrayal, serves only to perpetuate suffering. When we refuse to forgive, we essentially become prisoners of the past, held captive by the actions of another. The deception that wounded us continues to exert its influence, shaping our emotional responses and tainting our present. Resentment, like a slow-acting poison, erodes our joy, clouds our judgment, and can even manifest in physical ailments. It is a constant internal battle, a draining of emotional and spiritual energy that could otherwise be directed toward growth, service, and a deeper communion with God. In this state, the deception has achieved a secondary victory, not only breaking trust but also immobilizing the victim in a mire of negative emotions.

Extending forgiveness, however, is an act of liberation. It is a conscious decision to break free from the emotional entanglement that the deception has created. When we forgive, we are not condoning the behavior of the deceiver, nor are we necessarily forgetting the hurt. Instead, we are choosing to release our claim to vengeance and to place the matter and the offender into God's hands. This act of releasing allows us to reclaim our own emotional and spiritual freedom. It is akin to shedding a heavy burden, allowing us to walk forward with a lighter heart and a clearer mind, unencumbered by the weight of past wrongs. This psychological and spiritual unburdening is crucial for the healing process, allowing the shattered pieces of our trust to begin reassembling, not necessarily into their original form, but into something new and more substantial.

The Apostle Paul, in his letter to the **Ephesians 4:32**, exhorts believers to "*be kind to one another, tenderhearted, forgiving one another, as God in Christ forgave you*" (KJV, 2023). This directive is not a suggestion but a command, rooted in the very nature of our redeemed identity in Christ. Our forgiveness by God, through the atoning sacrifice of Jesus, serves as the model and motivation for our own forgiveness of others. If God, in His infinite holiness, can forgive our rebellion, our sin, our countless betrayals, then surely we, His redeemed children, are called to extend that same grace to those who have wronged us. This divine mandate transforms forgiveness from a mere option into a spiritual necessity. It reminds us that our ability to forgive stems from the forgiveness we have already received, creating a profound cycle of grace.

Within the context of the community, particularly within the church, forgiveness plays an even more critical role. When deception occurs within the Body of Christ, it not only damages individual relationships but also has the potential to fracture the unity of the fellowship. The enemy delights in sowing discord, and broken trust within the church can create an environment of suspicion and division, hindering the witness of the Gospel. Forgiveness, therefore, becomes a powerful tool for mending these communal rifts. It is the catalyst that allows for reconciliation, enabling individuals to move beyond hurt and betrayal towards a place of renewed trust and deeper fellowship. Without a commitment to forgive, the church risks becoming a place where wounds fester and unity is undermined, making it easier for the enemy to achieve his divisive goals.

Consider the profound impact of a leader who has deceived their congregation. The immediate aftermath can be a tidal wave of anger, disillusionment, and a crisis of faith for many. In such a situation, the path of forgiveness is fraught with difficulty. Many will feel that the offense is too great to overlook, that the trust has been irrevocably broken. However, it is precisely in these moments of profound hurt that the biblical call to forgive becomes most urgent. It is not about excusing the leader's actions, but about choosing a path that leads to healing for the community and its individuals. By extending forgiveness, the congregation can begin the process of rebuilding, not necessarily placing the same level of naive trust in that individual again, but fostering an environment where healing and spiritual growth can resume. This process might involve accountability and clear boundaries, but forgiveness is the essential first step in moving past the paralyzing effects of the deception.

Furthermore, seeking forgiveness is equally vital. While this subsection focuses on forgiving those who have wronged us, it is essential to acknowledge that deception can also flow in the other direction. If, in our own actions or inactions, we have contributed to deception or have been the source of another's hurt, the biblical imperative to seek forgiveness is paramount. This involves a humble acknowledgment of our wrongdoing, a sincere apology, and a commitment to making amends. This two-way street of forgiveness—extending it to others and seeking it when we have erred—is essential for maintaining the integrity of our relationships and for fostering a healthy spiritual environment, both individually and corporately.

The process of forgiving someone who has deceived us can be a lengthy and arduous journey. It is not a one-time event, but often a series of conscious choices made over time. There may be moments when the old wounds resurface, when the temptation to revert to bitterness is strong. In these instances, we must continually remind ourselves of the biblical mandate and the example of Christ. Prayer becomes an indispensable tool in this process, allowing us to lay our hurt and anger at God's feet and ask for His strength and His perspective. We can pray for the one who wronged us, asking God to work in their heart and to bring about their own repentance and transformation. This prayerful surrender is a powerful act of faith that continues to loosen the grip of resentment.

The Bible, in its timeless wisdom, offers profound insights into the nature of forgiveness. It speaks of a grace that transcends human frailty, a love that conquers all. When we internalize these truths, we begin to understand that forgiveness is not merely an emotional release but a spiritual discipline that aligns us with the heart of God. It is through this alignment that we find true healing, allowing us to move beyond the brokenness of deception and step into the fullness of life that Christ has promised. The act of forgiving is an active participation in God's redemptive work, a means by which brokenness is transformed into wholeness and bitterness into blessing.

The Apostle Peter, in his first epistle, directly addresses the importance of mutual love and forgiveness within the Christian community. In **I Peter 4:8-9**, Peter writes, "*Above all, keep fervent in your love for one another, because love covers a multitude of sins. Be hospitable to one another without grumbling*" (KJV, 2023). While "covering sins" can be interpreted in various ways, a core understanding relates to extending grace and forgiveness rather than exposing every fault. When deception occurs, the natural tendency is to expose the perpetrator and magnify the sin. However, a mature Christian response involves covering that sin with the grace of forgiveness, not to hide the sin from accountability, but to prevent it from destroying relationships and hindering spiritual progress. This act of "covering" is an act of love that binds the community together, rather than scattering it through judgment and condemnation.

Ultimately, the transformative power of forgiveness lies in its ability to break the cycles of pain and retribution. Deception creates a wound, and unforgiveness becomes the festering infection that prevents healing. By choosing forgiveness, we administer the divine antibiotic, allowing the tissues of trust and relationship to begin to mend. This is not a guarantee that the relationship will return to its previous state, nor is it a mandate to ignore the need for accountability. However, it is the essential step that liberates us from the prison of our own pain and opens the door for the possibility of reconciliation and restoration. It is in this act of release that we truly begin to mend what has been broken.

The aftermath of deception leaves a chasm, a void where trust once resided. Filling this void requires more than just a verbal apology; it demands a tangible, consistent demonstration of trustworthiness. This is where transparency and integrity become the twin pillars upon which rebuilding can occur. Without them, any attempt at restoration is merely building on shifting sands, vulnerable to the slightest tremor of doubt. Transparency, in its purest form, is the willingness to lay bare one's dealings, to ensure that actions are visible and understandable. It means eschewing hidden agendas, secret communications, and deliberately obscured motives. When trust has been broken by deceit, individuals often feel they have been in the dark, manipulated without their knowledge. Reversing this requires a commitment to bringing light into those shadowed corners.

For leaders, especially within faith communities, transparency takes on a heightened significance. The Bible consistently calls for leaders to be above reproach, to exhibit wisdom and discernment that is evident to all. When a leader has fallen into deception, the congregation is left reeling, questioning not only the individual's character but also the very foundation of their spiritual guidance. Rebuilding trust in such a scenario necessitates a radical commitment to openness. This could involve making financial records accessible, clearly articulating decision-making processes, and being forthright about challenges and vulnerabilities. It is about demonstrating that there is nothing to hide, that the leader's heart and actions are aligned with the truth. This openness is not about sharing every personal detail, but about ensuring that the matters entrusted to their care are conducted with an unblemished record.

The Bible, in **I Timothy 3:7**, emphasizes that leaders should have "a good report of them which are without" (KJV, 2023), underscoring the importance of external perception being rooted in genuine internal character, which is best demonstrated through transparent practices. Integrity, the unwavering adherence to moral and ethical principles, is the bedrock upon which transparency builds. It is the internal compass that guides one's actions, ensuring consistency between words and deeds, even when no one is watching. A person of integrity does not bend their principles for convenience or personal gain. When trust has been shattered, regaining it requires individuals to demonstrate, through consistent and principled action, that they can be relied upon. This is particularly challenging in the wake of significant betrayal, where past actions may have seemed to contradict any claims of integrity. Rebuilding this requires a conscious and sustained effort to live out one's values, demonstrating that the deception was an aberration, not the norm, and that a genuine commitment to truth now guides their life.

Proverbs 10:9 tells us, "*He that walketh uprightly walketh surely: but he that perverteth his ways shall be known*" (KJV, 2023). This verse highlights a fundamental truth: those who live with integrity will, in time, be recognized for their reliability, while those who deviate will eventually be exposed. For someone seeking to rebuild trust, this means consistently choosing the path of righteousness, even when it is the more difficult route. It means owning up to mistakes, offering genuine apologies, and making restitution where possible. It is not enough to *say* one has integrity; it must be *demonstrated* through a pattern of behavior that honors truth and ethical conduct.

In the context of the church community, the implications of transparency and integrity are profound. The church is called to be a beacon of truth in a world often characterized by deceit. When deception occurs within its walls, it not only wounds individuals but also damages the church's witness. Rebuilding trust requires a collective commitment to these principles. This means that not only those who have directly caused the breach but also the wider community must embrace openness and ethical conduct. It involves fostering an environment where honest feedback is welcomed, accountability is embraced, and individuals feel safe being vulnerable without fear of manipulation. The Apostle Paul's admonition to the Ephesians to "speak the truth in love" (**Ephesians 4:15**) is a directive that encapsulates both transparency and integrity within a relational context. It implies a willingness to be honest, but also a sensitivity that ensures truth is delivered in a way that builds up rather than tears down.

Consider a situation where financial impropriety has occurred within a church. The members are understandably hurt and suspicious. Rebuilding trust would necessitate a thorough, transparent investigation into the financial dealings, with the findings made openly available to the congregation. This might involve the appointment of an independent committee to oversee the process, ensuring impartiality. Furthermore, new financial oversight policies and procedures would need to be implemented and clearly communicated to ensure transparency and accountability.

The individuals involved would need to demonstrate sincere remorse, offer apologies, and commit to a period of accountability and responsibility. It is through these tangible actions, guided by a commitment to integrity, that the seeds of trust can begin to sprout again. Matthew 24:14-30 emphasizes stewardship and faithfulness in handling the resources entrusted to us by God, reinforcing the seriousness of financial integrity within the church.

Beyond overt acts of deception, the subtle erosion of trust can also occur through a lack of transparency in communication. In relationships, both personal and communal, withholding information, speaking in ambiguities, or habitually exaggerating can create an atmosphere of suspicion. Rebuilding trust in such cases requires a conscious effort to be clear, direct, and truthful in all interactions. It means choosing words carefully, ensuring they accurately reflect reality, and being willing to clarify any misunderstandings. This commitment to clear communication is a vital aspect of demonstrating integrity, showing that one values the other person's understanding and is not attempting to mislead them. The Apostle James issues a stern warning about the power of the tongue, in **James 5:12** stating, *"But above all things, my brethren, swear not, neither by heaven, neither by the earth, neither by any other oath: But let your yea be yea; and your nay, nay; lest ye fall into condemnation"* (KJV, 2023). This simple yet profound instruction underscores the power of straightforward, honest speech in establishing trustworthiness.

The journey of rebuilding trust through transparency and integrity is not a quick fix. It is a long-term commitment that requires patience, perseverance, and a deep reliance on God's strength. There will be moments of doubt, of testing, and of temptation to revert to old patterns. However, by grounding oneself in the timeless principles of truth and honesty, as consistently presented in Scripture, the broken pieces of trust can indeed be reassembled, not necessarily into their original form, but into a stronger, more resilient structure, built upon the solid foundation of God's unchanging character. The Bible, in its enduring message, continually points us toward this unwavering standard, reminding us that our integrity is a reflection of our relationship with the Divine, and thus a crucial element in the restoration of all that has been broken. This commitment to visible, ethical conduct is not merely a strategy for recovery; it is a spiritual discipline that honors God and fosters genuine healing in every sphere of life.

The insidious creep of doctrinal error, often masked by eloquent rhetoric or an appeal to popular sentiment, can leave a congregation spiritually adrift, with its understanding of God and His Word distorted. When the very foundations of belief have been subtly undermined, the imperative to restore doctrinal purity becomes not merely a theological exercise, but a vital act of spiritual preservation. This process begins with an unwavering commitment to the bedrock of our faith: Scripture, with its rich linguistic heritage and enduring translations, serves as an invaluable resource in this endeavor. Its careful rendering of the original languages often preserves nuances of meaning that can be easily lost in more contemporary translations, making it a steadfast guide in discerning truth from error.

The Serpent's Tongue: The Spirit of Deception

The restoration of doctrinal purity necessitates a deep and abiding reverence for biblical exposition. This means moving beyond superficial readings and engaging in diligent, scholarly study that seeks to understand the intended meaning of the text within its historical, cultural, and literary context. It involves a commitment to teaching that is faithful to the entirety of God's Word, not just those portions that are most comfortable or popular. Pastors and teachers bear a profound responsibility to equip the flock with the tools to critically assess the teachings they encounter. This involves training believers to be discerning, to compare what they hear against the unchanging standard of Scripture. As the Apostle Paul urged Timothy (II Timothy 2:15), *"Study to shew thyself approved unto God, a workman that needeth not to be ashamed, rightly dividing the word of truth"* (KJV, 2023). This directive is not for a select few but a call to all who seek to understand God's will, encouraging a proactive approach to spiritual education.

The challenge of doctrinal deviation is often compounded by the fact that errors can be introduced gradually, sometimes so subtly that they are not immediately apparent. Deceptive teachings start with a seemingly minor departure from established doctrine, a new interpretation that sounds appealing, or a focus on aspects of faith that, while not inherently wrong, become skewed when elevated above central truths. Its meticulous translation often provides clarity and precision that guards against the slippery slopes of misinterpretation.

The process of restoring doctrinal purity is not simply about identifying and eradicating error; it is equally about affirmatively cultivating a profound love for biblical truth. This means creating an environment within the church where sound doctrine is not only tolerated but actively cherished and defended. Sermons should be rich in Scripture, with theological concepts explained in clear and depth, and opportunities provided for congregants to ask questions and engage in thoughtful discussion.

The Bible, with its majestic prose, can also serve to instill a sense of awe and reverence for God's Word, reminding believers of its divine origin and authoritative nature. When the Word of God is held in such high esteem, deviations are more readily recognized and rejected. Furthermore, confronting error requires courage and grace. It is rarely a comfortable process, as it can involve challenging long-held beliefs or the pronouncements of respected figures. However, the pastoral responsibility to protect the flock from spiritual harm mandates that truth be spoken, even when it is difficult. This confrontation must always be rooted in love and a genuine desire for the restoration and well-being of individuals and the community. With an emphasis on gentleness and patience in correction, while maintaining a firm commitment to the truth, this approach offers a model for such interactions. As **Galatians 6:1** states, *"Brethren, if a man be overtaken in a fault, ye which are spiritual restore such an one in the spirit of meekness;*

considering thyself, lest thou also be tempted." (KJV, 2023). This balance between firmness on doctrine and tenderness towards individuals is crucial.

One of the primary ways doctrinal purity is compromised is through a departure from the historical, orthodox understanding of the Christian faith, often by prioritizing novel interpretations or subjective experiences over the clear teachings of Scripture, which have guided the church for millennia. When new teachings emerge that contradict these long-established truths, a careful comparison with the Bible can help illuminate the divergence.

The restoration of doctrinal purity also involves a commitment to ongoing discipleship and education. It is not enough to correct an error once; the congregation must be continually nurtured in the truth. This means regularly revisiting core doctrines, explaining their significance, and demonstrating their practical application in daily life.

Moreover, the church must foster an atmosphere where questions are welcomed and critical thinking, grounded in Scripture, is encouraged. A culture that discourages inquiry or penalizes those who raise genuine theological questions can inadvertently create fertile ground for error to take root. When believers feel safe to voice their concerns and seek clarification, the leadership is better positioned to address potential misunderstandings before they solidify into full-blown doctrinal deviations. I am running a few minutes late; my previous meeting is running over.

The task of restoring doctrinal purity is not a passive one. It requires active engagement, diligent study, and a willingness to stand for truth, even in the face of opposition. The legacy of the King James Version, as a translation that has faithfully transmitted the core doctrines of Christianity for centuries, offers both a guide and an encouragement in this vital work. By immersing ourselves in its pages, committed to understanding its teachings with clarity and precision, and by diligently applying its truths to our lives and communities, we can ensure that the church remains a steadfast beacon of God's unchanging Word, a refuge from deception, and a vibrant testament to His saving grace.

The responsibility to maintain doctrinal purity is not solely the purview of the clergy; it is a shared commitment that rests upon all members of the body of Christ. Each believer is called to be a diligent student of God's Word. When deceptive teachings begin to permeate a congregation, it is often through the collective discernment of its members, armed with biblical knowledge, that the error is most effectively identified and resisted. This requires fostering an environment where open discussion about theological matters is encouraged, not as a platform for endless debate or division, but as a means of ensuring clarity and conformity to biblical truth.

The process of restoring doctrinal purity necessitates a careful examination of the historical trajectory of Christian doctrine. The early church councils, the creeds, and the confessions of faith developed over centuries represent a collective wrestling with and articulation of biblical truth. The influence of charismatic personalities can often be a conduit for doctrinal deviation. When a leader or teacher is particularly compelling or popular, their teachings can gain traction even if they are theologically unsound. In such situations, the congregation must be trained to evaluate the message, not the messenger. This requires a conscious effort to separate the individual from the truth of God's Word.

The restoration of doctrinal purity also requires a proactive approach to discipleship. This means ensuring that new believers and young people are thoroughly grounded in the essentials of the Christian faith. Comprehensive Bible studies, systematic theological instruction, and exposure to sound biblical teaching are vital components of this process.

Consider the doctrine of the atonement, a cornerstone of Christian theology. Deceptive teachings might attempt to redefine or diminish the sacrificial, substitutionary nature of Christ's death, perhaps by emphasizing its moral example over its atoning power.

Isaiah 53:5 *"But he was wounded for our transgressions, he was bruised for our iniquities: the chastisement of our peace was upon him; and with his stripes we are healed."* Moreover, **I Peter 2:24** *"Who his own self bare our sins in his own body on the tree, that we, being dead to sins, should live unto righteousness: by whose stripes ye were healed."* (KJV, 2023), offers a clear and powerful testimony to atonement.

Teachings that undermine the authority and sufficiency of Scripture itself must be carefully addressed. If a particular interpretation of Scripture is offered that requires extensive external validation or that subtly suggests the Bible is incomplete or requires reinterpretation through other means, it warrants close scrutiny. Teaching that actively encourages believers to utilize their gift of discernment and assess all teachings against the backdrop of Biblical truths is essential. This cultivates a spirit of intellectual and spiritual humility because God's Word is the ultimate source of truth and wisdom.

The church community must also cultivate a culture of accountability and discernment. This means that pastors and teachers should be open to having their teachings examined by the congregation, not in a spirit of arrogance or defiance, but in a manner that seeks to ensure faithfulness to God's Word. When errors are identified, they should be addressed with prayer and humility. The pursuit of doctrinal purity is an ongoing process that demands vigilance and a deep commitment to God's Word. By diligently studying its pages, promoting sound biblical exposition, and fostering an environment where truth is cherished and defended, the church can effectively guard against deceptive teachings and ensure its witness remains pure and true to the unchanging Word of God. This dedication to doctrinal integrity is not merely an academic pursuit; it is an act of love for God, His Word, and the flock entrusted to our care, safeguarding them from spiritual error and leading them into more profound truth.

The journey of faith, understood through the lens of Scripture, reveals a constant call to engagement. While the restoration of truth is often seen as the responsibility of leadership, the spiritual health of the body of Christ hinges on the active participation of every believer. We are not merely spectators of God's redemptive plan; we are called to be participants, defenders of His truth. This subsection is dedicated to empowering you, the believer, to step into this vital role, to become a warrior for truth in your own life and in the world around you. It is about understanding that discerning truth from error and standing firm in what is biblically sound is not an optional extra, but a fundamental aspect of a mature and engaged faith.

The foundation for this empowerment lies in a deep, personal engagement with the Word of God. It is more than just reading; it is about diligent study, wrestling with the text, and allowing it to shape your understanding and convictions. When you internalize the truths it conveys, particularly those concerning the nature of God, the person and work of Jesus Christ, the role of the Holy Spirit, and the clear mandates for Christian living, you build an inner fortress against deception. This is not about becoming a theological expert overnight, but about cultivating a habit of seeking truth directly from the source. The Apostle Paul's commendation of the Bereans in **Acts 17:11**: *"These were more noble than those in Thessalonica, in that they received the word with all readiness of mind, and searched the scriptures daily, whether those things were of which he spoke were so."* (KJV, 2023). This exemplifies the proactive, investigative spirit that empowers the believer. They did not blindly accept what they heard; they went to the Scriptures to verify. This proactive stance is the bedrock of becoming a warrior for truth.

This warrior spirit is nurtured through the practice of discernment, a spiritual gift and a learned discipline. Discernment is the ability to distinguish between truth and error, between the divine and the counterfeit. It is an ability honed by familiarity with God's Word, prayer, and the counsel of wise, biblically grounded believers. When a teaching or ideology arises that seems to contradict the clear teachings of Scripture, the discerning believer does not immediately dismiss it or wholeheartedly embrace it. Instead, they pause, pray, and consult the Word. This involves comparing the new teaching with Bible doctrines, looking for consistency with the message of Scripture.

To be a warrior for truth means embracing the responsibility to speak truth, even when it is difficult. This can manifest in various ways, from gently correcting a fellow believer who has misunderstood a passage to challenging a deviation from sound doctrine within a church community or even engaging in apologetics in the public square. The key is to do so with grace and love, as instructed in **Ephesians 4:15**: *"But speaking the truth in love, may grow up into him in all things, which is the head, even Christ."* (KJV, 2023). This means that our pursuit of truth cannot be divorced from our commitment to love and edify others. A warrior for truth is not a combative cynic, but a loving advocate for divine revelation.

Consider the practical application of this in a small group setting. If a member introduces a new interpretation of a biblical passage that subtly alters a core doctrine, such as the nature of the Holy Spirit or the exclusivity of Christ for salvation, the warrior for truth within the group would not remain silent. They might say that it is an interesting perspective. So, how does that align with what passages like **John 14:26** say, *"But the Comforter, which is the Holy Ghost, whom the Father will send in my name, he shall teach you all things, and bring all things to your remembrance, whatsoever I have said unto you,' teach us about the Spirit's role?"* (KJV, 2023). They might refer to **John 14:6** where Jesus says, *"I am the way, the truth, and the life: no man cometh unto the Father, but by me."* (KJV, 2023). The goal is not to shame or embarrass, but to collaboratively ensure understanding remains tethered to the Word.

Furthermore, empowering the believer involves equipping them with the tools to critically engage with the vast amount of information and teaching available today, especially in the digital age. The internet, while a powerful tool for good, is also a breeding ground for misinformation and deceptive ideologies. Believers must be taught to approach online content with a discerning eye, to verify sources, and to cross-reference claims with the unadulterated truth of Scripture constantly. This means being wary of overly sensational teachings that appeal primarily to emotion or that seem to contradict the historical, orthodox understanding of Christianity.

The call to be a warrior for truth also extends to our personal lives. It means being uncompromising in our own adherence to biblical principles, even when it requires sacrifice or goes against cultural norms. It means actively seeking to align our thoughts, words, and actions with God's Word. This internal discipline is the first line of defense against spiritual deception. If our own understanding is clouded by sin or compromise, our ability to discern and stand for truth will be significantly weakened.

Passages like **Romans 12:2** are crucial: *"And be not conformed to this world: but be ye transformed by the renewing of your mind, that ye may prove what is that good, and acceptable, and perfect, will of God."* (KJV, 2023). This renewing of the mind, fueled by God's word, is the essence of personal empowerment.

Moreover, the church has a responsibility to foster an environment that allows such empowerment to flourish. This includes providing regular, expository teaching that grounds believers in biblical truth, creating opportunities for discipleship and mentorship, and encouraging open and respectful dialogue about theological questions. When leaders prioritize equipping the congregation with biblical knowledge and the tools of discernment, they are cultivating an army of truth-seekers, not a passive assembly. This investment in the spiritual maturity of individual believers is the most effective strategy for long-term doctrinal health and resilience.

The concept of "speaking truth in love" is paramount. It means that our engagement with those who hold differing or erroneous views must be characterized by compassion and a genuine desire for their well-being. Peter urged believers in **I Peter 3:15** to *"be ready always to answer every man that asketh you a reason of the hope that is in you with meekness and fear"* (KJV, 2023). This readiness involves not only knowing *what* to say, but also how to say it effectively. A warrior for truth understands that their mission is not to win arguments but to win souls. Truth, delivered with love, is a force for transformation.

Consider the doctrine of assurance of salvation. Some teachings might subtly introduce uncertainty, suggesting that one's salvation is contingent on ongoing performance or a subjective feeling. **Ephesians 2:8-9**: *"For by grace are ye saved through faith; and that not of yourselves: it is the gift of God: Not of works, lest any man should boast."* (KJV, 2023). Empowered believers, grounded in these truths, can stand firm against teachings that create anxiety or doubt about their eternal security in Christ. They can gently yet firmly remind others of the finished work of Christ and the promises of God.

The commitment to be a warrior for truth also involves spiritual warfare. The Bible clearly teaches that we are engaged in a spiritual battle against unseen forces of evil that seek to deceive and destroy. **Ephesians 6:10-18**, "sword of the Spirit, which is the word of God" (KJV, 2023), explains the spiritual warfare armor and how it serves as our primary offensive weapon. This means actively employing Scripture in prayer and in our interactions, using its truth to counter the enemy's lies.

This equipping extends to understanding the historical context of biblical interpretation. When new interpretations arise that seem radically divorced from this historical consensus, without compelling biblical justification found within the text itself, the empowered believer can recognize the potential for departure. This does not mean tradition is infallible, but that established truths, grounded in Scripture, provide a strong foundation from which to evaluate novel ideas.

Ultimately, becoming a warrior for truth is a continuous process of growth, learning, and courageous action. It is about embracing the fullness of our identity in Christ, which includes being defenders of His truth. It is about recognizing that our faith is not a private, internal affair but has implications for how we engage with the world and with one another. By immersing ourselves in the Word, cultivating discernment, speaking truth in love, and engaging in spiritual warfare, we actively contribute to the restoration and preservation of truth, ensuring that the light of God's revelation shines brightly in a world often shrouded in darkness and deception. The call is clear: to be not merely hearers, but doers and defenders of the Word.

CHAPTER NINE:
Readiness for his Coming: Eradicating Deceit from our Lives

An event of unparalleled significance shapes the temporal horizon of the Christian life return of Jesus Christ. This eschatological reality, the blessed hope of the Church, casts a long shadow over every aspect of our present existence. It transforms our understanding of what it means to live faithfully, imbuing our daily decisions with eternal weight. Among the most crucial dimensions of this anticipatory life is the eradication of deceit. This is not a minor refinement of character, a superficial polishing of our outward presentation; it is an eschatological imperative, a non-negotiable prerequisite for being found ready when our Lord returns. The Scriptures are replete with exhortations to live lives characterized by truthfulness, sincerity, and integrity; all set against the backdrop of Christ's imminent arrival.

The Apostle Paul, in his first letter to the Thessalonians, provides a stark and powerful articulation of this connection. He writes in **II Thessalonians 2:1-2**, "*Now we beseech you, brethren, by the coming of our Lord Jesus Christ, and by our gathering unto him, that ye be not soon shaken in mind, or be troubled, neither by spirit, nor by word, nor by letter as from us, as that the day of the Lord is at hand*" (KJV, 2023). While this passage directly addresses the danger of being deceived about the timing of Christ's return, it establishes a broader principle: readiness for His coming necessitates a mind and spirit unclouded by deception, whether that deception pertains to temporal matters or to the very essence of truth and holiness. The day of the Lord is the ultimate context for all Christian living. It is the day when every hidden thing will be brought to light, when the character of our lives will be laid bare before the divine tribunal. Therefore, living in anticipation of this day compels us to purge ourselves of every form of falsehood actively, every subtle deviation from truth, and every act of dissimulation.

This imperative to live free from deceit is deeply woven into the fabric of biblical teaching concerning sanctification. Sanctification, the process by which believers are made more like Christ, is intrinsically linked to our preparation for His return. It is a process of purification, a progressive shedding of the old self and the embracing of a new life in righteousness. Deceit, in all its guises – hypocrisy, lying, insincerity, manipulation, and self-deception – is antithetical to this process. It is the very essence of the fallen nature that Christ came to redeem us from. To be ready for Him is to be continually refining our lives, seeking to align our inner disposition, and ensuring that there is no unacknowledged falsehood dwelling within us.

Consider the words of Jesus Himself in **Luke 12:35-40**: "*Let your loins be girded about, and your lamps burning; and ye yourselves like unto men that wait for their lord, when he will return from the wedding; that when he cometh and knocketh, they may open unto him immediately. Blessed are those servants, whom the lord, when he cometh, shall find watching: verily I say unto you, that he shall gird himself, and make them to sit down to meat, and will come forth and serve them. Moreover, if he shall come in the second watch, or come in the third watch, and find them so, blessed are those servants. Moreover, it is known that if the goodman of the house had known what hour the thief would come, he would have watched, and not have suffered his house to be broken into. Be ye therefore ready also: for the son of man cometh at an hour when ye think not.*" (KJV, 2023).

The imagery of girded loins and burning lamps speaks of preparedness, vigilance, and active engagement in service. It is a picture of lives lived with purpose, fully alert and ready for the Master's arrival. Deceit, by its very nature, causes us to lower our guard, to become complacent, and to misdirect our energies. A life of deception is a house left vulnerable, a watchman asleep at his post. The believer anticipating Christ's return must ensure that their spiritual house is in order, free from hidden falsehoods.

The call to eradicate deceit is also a call to embrace authenticity. In a world often marked by superficiality and pretense, Christians are called to radical transparency. This authenticity is not born of a desire for human approval but from an unwavering commitment to the truth of God's Word and the indwelling presence of the Holy Spirit, who Himself is the Spirit of Truth. When we are committed to living truthfully, we are living in alignment with our redeemed identity in Christ. We are presenting ourselves as we truly are before God, acknowledging our weaknesses and relying on His strength, rather than masking our flaws with pretense. This genuine approach to life reflects the character of Christ, who embodies the truth.

The Apostle John's first epistle emphasizes this crucial aspect of our walk as outlined in **I John 2:6**: "*He that saith he abideth in him ought himself also so to walk, even as he walked*" (KJV, 2023). If Christ is the Truth, then walking as He walked means walking in truth, eschewing all forms of deceit. This is not a call to perfectionism, for we are still in the process of sanctification, but it is a call to a relentless pursuit of integrity. It means confessing our sins honestly, both to God and, where appropriate, to one another, rather than covering them up or minimizing their impact. It means speaking with candor and kindness, without ulterior motives or manipulative intent. It means living in a manner that is consistent with our confession of faith, so that our lives bear witness to the reality of the Gospel.

The ramifications of unchecked deceit are profound, both for individual believers and for the broader corporate body of Christ. Deception erodes trust, cripples spiritual growth, and ultimately hinders our ability to bear effective witness to the world. If the Church is to be a beacon of truth in a darkened world, its members must be rigorously committed to living lives unblemished by falsehood. The Apostle Paul's admonition in **Ephesians 4:25** is direct: "*Wherefore putting away lying, speak every man truth with his neighbour: for we are members one of another.*" (KJV, 2023). This interconnectedness within the body of Christ underscores the communal dimension of our pursuit of truth. Deceit within the fellowship is not merely an individual failing; it is a breach in the very fabric of our shared life in Christ, weakening the witness of the entire community.

The eschatological urgency of this matter is further highlighted by passages that speak of the judgment seat of Christ. At this future reckoning, believers will give an account of their deeds, and it is here that the integrity of our lives will be fully evaluated. While the ultimate standard is Christ's righteousness imputed to us through faith, the nature of our earthly walk will still be assessed. Our motivations, our words, our actions – all will be brought into the light. Living in anticipation of this moment fuels the imperative to cleanse ourselves from all filthiness of the flesh and spirit, perfecting holiness in the fear of God (**II Corinthians 7:1**, KJV). A life lived in the shadow of this judgment naturally compels a thorough examination of ourselves, a diligent effort to identify and remove any hidden corners of deceit.

Consider the concept of being found blameless. This is not to suggest sinless perfection, which is unattainable in this life. Instead, it refers to a state of being found not culpable for willful disregard of God's commands, particularly those pertaining to truth and sincerity. It is about living with an earnest desire to please God, actively resisting the allure of falsehood, and cultivating a disposition of unwavering honesty. When we are living with this eschatological awareness, the temptation to compromise the truth, to speak with a double tongue, or to engage in subtle manipulation loses its power. Our focus is fixed on the ultimate accountability, on presenting ourselves to our Lord without shame or regret.

The process of eradicating deceit is an ongoing, Spirit-wrought transformation. It begins with a sincere desire to please God and is sustained by consistent prayer and immersion in His Word. The Bible serves as a constant mirror, revealing the subtle ways deceit can creep into our lives. It calls us to purity of heart, not just outward conformity. For example, **Exodus**

20:16 lists the eighth commandment, "*Thou shalt not bear false witness*" (KJV, 2023), which is not merely a prohibition against overt perjury in a court of law. It extends to all forms of bearing false witness, including gossip, slander, exaggeration, and any utterance that misrepresents reality or misleads another. Living in anticipation of Christ's return means taking this commandment with the utmost seriousness, ensuring that our words are always seasoned with truth and grace.

The eradication of deceit extends to our relationship with ourselves. Self-deception is the most insidious form of falsehood, as it enables us to rationalize our sins, disregard the conviction of the Holy Spirit, and remain comfortable in our spiritual immaturity. When we are genuinely ready for Christ's return, we will be committed to an honest self-assessment, willing to confront our own shortcomings and hypocrisies. We will seek to understand our true motivations, to identify the pride or fear that might drive us to dissimulate, and to surrender these aspects of our lives to the cleansing power of God. The Bible's emphasis on the depravity of the human heart and the necessity of God's intervention in our lives provides a sober and realistic framework for this self-examination. It reminds us that apart from Christ, we are prone to deception, and through His grace, we can truly be set free.

The Apostle Peter echoes this sentiment in his second epistle: **II Peter 1:13:** "*Wherefore gird up the loins of your mind, be sober, and hope to the end for the grace that is to be brought unto you at the revelation of Jesus Christ*" (KJV, 2023). The phrase "girding up the loins of your mind" is a powerful metaphor for preparing our thinking for rigorous and focused engagement. It is about bringing our thoughts into captivity to the obedience of Christ, ensuring that our minds are not allowed to wander into the realms of deceptive speculation or sinful imagination. This mental discipline is essential for maintaining readiness. A mind that is not actively engaged in discerning truth from error, a mind that is susceptible to misleading ideas or allows itself to entertain deceitful thoughts, is a mind that is unprepared for the clarity and holiness of Christ's appearing.

The believer who takes seriously the eschatological imperative to be ready for Christ's return will cultivate a life marked by radical transparency and an unwavering commitment to truth. This is not a burden but a liberating reality, for in living truthfully, we shed the heavy cloak of pretense and embrace the freedom that comes from living in accordance with God's design. It is a call to live with our hearts open, our words honest, and our lives aligned with the divine purpose. As we await the glorious appearing of our great God and Saviour Jesus Christ, let us be found not only watching but also living lives that are a testament to His truth, purified from every shadow of deceit, and ready to meet Him with joy and confidence. This active pursuit of truthfulness is not merely a desirable trait; it is the very essence of readiness, the vital imperative for every follower of Christ. The King James

Version, in its enduring wisdom, continually calls us to a higher standard, urging us to live our lives with our innermost thoughts and our outermost actions, reflecting the pure and unwavering truth of God, anticipating the day when all deception will be banished and His perfect truth will reign supreme.

The Apostle Paul, in his letter to the Ephesians, provides a robust framework for understanding how deceit acts as an impediment to spiritual maturity. In **Ephesians 4:25,** he writes, "*Wherefore putting away lying, speak every man truth with his neighbour: for we are members one of another*" (KJV, 2023). This exhortation is not merely about avoiding outright falsehoods; it is a call to embrace a comprehensive integrity that underpins our very identity as members of the body of Christ. When we engage in deception, whether through outright lying, subtle misrepresentation, hypocrisy, or the willful suppression of truth, we create a fissure within the interconnectedness that defines our spiritual community. This breakage not only impacts our individual journey but also weakens the collective witness of the Church.

Spiritual maturity is a process of becoming more like Christ, and Christ Himself is truth incarnate. Therefore, any deviation from truth, any embrace of falsehood, inherently moves us away from this ultimate goal. Deception introduces an internal dissonance, a disconnect between our outward profession of faith and our inner reality. This dissonance hinders our ability to receive from God and to experience His fullness. Imagine a pipe clogged with debris; water can still flow, but not with the unimpeded force and clarity it is designed for. Similarly, a life marked by deceit, even in seemingly minor forms, obstructs the free flow of God's grace, His wisdom, and His power into our lives. This blockage stunts our growth, preventing us from developing the Christ-like character of true spiritual maturity.

The Bible consistently portrays a direct correlation between truthfulness and spiritual vitality. The Psalms, for instance, often speak of God's delight in those who are upright in heart and whose tongues speak no deceit. When our lives are characterized by honesty, sincerity, and transparency, we create an environment where God's presence can flourish, His voice can be heard, and His purposes can be discerned. Deceit fosters a spiritual fog, obscuring our perception of God's will and making us susceptible to errors and spiritual manipulation. It is like navigating a ship through treacherous waters with a faulty compass; the destination may be clear, but the means of reaching it are compromised, leading to disaster.

Consider the insidious nature of self-deception. This is the most potent barrier to spiritual maturity, as it allows us to remain comfortable in our spiritual stagnation. We can convince ourselves that we are doing well, that our actions are justified, or that our spiritual condition is far healthier than it actually is. This internal dishonesty shields us from the Holy Spirit's conviction, preventing the necessary repentance and reorientation that are crucial for growth. When we deceive ourselves, we are essentially building a wall between ourselves and the very one who can reveal our true state and guide us toward transformation. The Apostle John, in his first epistle, **I John 2:6**, offers a profound insight into this connection: "*He that saith he abideth in him ought himself also so to walk, even as he walked*" (KJV, 2023). Christ's walk was one of absolute truthfulness, even when it led to suffering and opposition. To claim to abide in Him while harbouring deceit is a contradiction. It is akin to claiming to be a disciple of light while still dwelling in darkness. This spiritual incongruity not only hinders our personal development but also weakens our testimony to the world. A believer who is perceived as untrustworthy or insincere will find their witness of Christ's transformative power significantly diminished.

Furthermore, deception breeds a pervasive sense of insecurity and fear. When we are not living in truth, we are constantly vigilant, concerned about being exposed to the truth. This creates an internal tension that saps our spiritual energy and distracts us from our pursuit of God. True spiritual maturity, on the other hand, is characterized by a confident boldness that flows from a clear conscience and a life lived in alignment with God's truth. This confidence is not arrogance; it is the assurance that comes from knowing that one's life is laid bare before God and found to be sincere, even in its imperfections. The pursuit of readiness for Christ's return is therefore inextricably linked to cultivating this inner security through radical honesty.

The practical implications of this are far-reaching. In our relationships, deceit can manifest as gossip, slander, flattery, or a lack of candor. These actions erode trust, foster division, and hinder the kind of open, vulnerable fellowship that is essential for spiritual growth. When we are quick to speak ill of others, spread rumors, or present a false image of ourselves, we actively hinder the spiritual development of both ourselves and those around us. The Bible's emphasis on the power of the tongue and the need for our words to be seasoned with grace serves as a constant reminder of the ethical dimension of truthfulness.

Consider how even seemingly minor deceptions can snowball. A slight exaggeration to make oneself look better, a white lie to avoid confrontation, or a tacit endorsement of falsehood can create a slippery slope. Each act of deception makes the next one easier, gradually eroding our moral compass and dulling our sensitivity to the Holy Spirit's promptings. This gradual decline is a subtle but powerful obstacle to spiritual maturity. We may not realize the extent to which we have compromised our integrity until we find ourselves far from the path of truth, struggling to regain our spiritual footing. This is why the call to eradicate all deceit is so urgent; it is a preventative measure against this gradual spiritual decay.

The concept of readiness for Christ's return is not merely about anticipating an event; it is about cultivating a life that is characterized by the very nature of Christ Himself. Since Christ is truth, a life that is to be found ready for Him must be a life that embraces and embodies truth in its entirety. Deception, in any form, is fundamentally at odds with this expectation. It is like preparing a house for a royal visit by hiding clutter and grime under rugs; the outward appearance may be temporarily improved, but the underlying disarray remains, and it will ultimately be revealed. True readiness involves a thorough cleansing, a willingness to bring everything into the light, and to allow God's truth to transform us from the inside out.

The Holy Spirit, often referred to as the Spirit of Truth, plays a crucial role in this process of eradication. He convicts us of sin, including the sin of deception, and guides us into all truth. When we resist His promptings and choose to remain in deception rather than embracing the truth, we grieve the Spirit and hinder His work in our lives. Spiritual maturity requires a willing and obedient partnership with the Holy Spirit, allowing Him to expose our falsehoods and empower us to live in genuine truthfulness. This involves cultivating a sensitive ear to His voice, a teachable spirit, and a readiness to confess and repent whenever we fall short of His standards.

The Apostle Paul's admonition in **Romans 12:2** is highly relevant here: "*And be not conformed to this world: but be ye transformed by the renewing of your mind, that ye may prove what is that good, and acceptable, and perfect, will of God.*" (KJV, 2023). Conformity to the world often involves embracing its subtle deceptions, manipulations, pretenses, and the pursuit of superficial appearances. Spiritual maturity requires a conscious effort to align our thinking with God's truth, even when it is countercultural. This renewing of the mind is essential for discerning and rejecting the deceptive patterns of our society and for cultivating a life that reflects Christ's integrity.

Furthermore, the process of eradicating deceit fosters a deeper intimacy with God. When we live transparently before Him, acknowledging our weaknesses and relying on His strength, we build a foundation of trust and communion. Deception, conversely, creates a distance, a sense of hiding from God, which ultimately diminishes our experience of His presence and love. True spiritual growth is characterized by an ever-increasing closeness to God, a sense of His nearness and favor. This closeness is a direct result of a life lived in the light of His truth, free from the shadows of falsehood.

The call to put away lying is also a call to embrace vulnerability. It requires us to shed the armour of pretense and to be willing to be seen as we truly are, not just by God, but also by our brothers and sisters in Christ. This vulnerability can be frightening, as it opens us up to the possibility of rejection or judgment. However, it is precisely within this space of genuine vulnerability that authentic community and profound spiritual growth can occur. When we are honest about our struggles, failures, and fears, we create an environment where others can also be honest, leading to mutual encouragement and support in our journey toward Christlikeness.

Remaining entangled in deception is a direct impediment to fulfilling our God-given potential. When we are preoccupied with maintaining false appearances or covering up our shortcomings, we divert energy and focus that could otherwise be directed towards serving God and impacting the world for His kingdom. Spiritual maturity is about becoming the person God created us to be, equipped and empowered. Deceit acts as a self-imposed limitation, preventing us from fully stepping into our calling. By embracing truth, we liberate ourselves from these self-imposed constraints, allowing God's power and purpose to flow through us unhindered.

The urgency of Christ's imminent return is a clarion call to shed every weight, every entanglement, and especially the corrosive influence of deceit, so that when He appears, we may be found not only watching but also living lives that are a true reflection of His own perfect truth and unwavering integrity. This process is not a minor adjustment; it is a fundamental reorientation of our being, a commitment to walk in the light, and a vital component of our preparation for eternal fellowship with our Saviour.

The ultimate accountability that awaits every soul is the final judgment. It is a stark reality, often conveyed with solemnity in Scripture, that will bring all deeds and intentions to light before the divine tribunal. This is not a moment to be approached with casual indifference or a false sense of security built on self-deception or worldly accolades.

Instead, it is the culmination of our earthly pilgrimage, a reckoning where our lives are measured against the immutable standard of God's truth. The Bible leaves no room for ambiguity regarding the fate of those who have actively cultivated deceit in their lives. **Revelation 21:8** provides a sobering declaration of those who will be excluded from the eternal city: "*But the fearful, and unbelieving, and the abominable, and murderers, and whoremongers, and sorcerers, and idolaters, and all liars, shall have their part in the lake which burneth with fire and brimstone: which is the second death.*" This stark enumeration serves as a potent reminder that a life characterized by falsehood, a life that has actively embraced and perpetuated deceit, stands in direct opposition to the perfect holiness of God and the purity of His eternal kingdom.

The truth-teller, conversely, is presented as one whose life is aligned with the divine nature and who, therefore, can face the final judgment with confidence, not in their own merit, but in the completed work of Christ and the integrity of a life lived in response to His truth. Our Lord Jesus Christ himself in **John 14:6** declared, "*I am the way, the truth, and the life: no man cometh unto the Father, but by me*" (KJV, 2023). His very identity is inextricably linked to truth. Therefore, a believer's readiness for His coming is intrinsically linked to their commitment to embodying this truth in every facet of their existence. This commitment extends beyond merely avoiding outright lies; it encompasses a holistic commitment to integrity, honesty, and transparency in our thoughts, words, and actions. It is a deliberate cultivation of a character that mirrors the perfect truthfulness of our Savior.

Consider Daniel's visions, which describe a future judgment where books are opened and individuals are judged according to their deeds. **Daniel 7:9-10** describes the scene: "*I beheld till the thrones were cast down, and the Ancient of days did sit, whose garment was white as snow, and the hair of his head like the pure wool: his throne was like the fiery flame, and his wheels as burning fire. A fiery stream issued and came forth from before him: thousand thousands ministered unto him, and ten thousand times ten thousand stood before him: the judgment was set, and the books were opened.*" (KJV, 2023). These are not merely symbolic accounts; they represent the absolute certainty of divine scrutiny. The "books" here are often interpreted as the records of our lives, encompassing our deeds, our words, and even the silent intents of our hearts. In this moment of divine accounting, every act of deception, calculated falsehood, and every subtle misrepresentation will be laid bare. The believer who has diligently sought to purify their life from deceit, who has striven to speak truth even when it was difficult, and who has lived with an open heart before God, will find that their life, through the grace of Christ, aligns with the standard of divine truth.

The stark contrast between the truth-teller and the deceiver at the final judgment underscores the profound significance of our commitment to authenticity in this life. The Apostle Paul, in his first letter to the Corinthians, reiterates the consequences of unrepentant sin, including deceit. He writes in **I Corinthians 6:9-10**, "*Know ye not that the unrighteous shall not inherit the kingdom of God? Be not deceived: neither fornicators, nor idolaters, nor adulterers, nor effeminate, nor abusers of themselves with mankind, nor thieves, nor covetous, nor drunkards, nor revilers, nor extortioners, shall inherit the kingdom of God.*" (KJV, 2023). While this passage lists various sins, the overarching principle is clear: unrighteousness, which inherently includes dishonesty and deceit, is incompatible with the holy presence of God. The emphasis on being "not deceived" serves as a final warning against the very snare that this section aims to dismantle. The deceiver, often self-deceived into believing their falsehoods have gone unnoticed, will face a reality far removed from their illusions.

The biblical narrative consistently portrays God as the ultimate arbiter of truth and justice. His throne is established in righteousness, and His judgment is always righteous. This means that our own efforts to present a false image, either to others or to ourselves, will ultimately fail. The King James Version, with its rich theological vocabulary, often employs terms like "righteousness," "justice," and "truth" in proximity, highlighting their inseparable connection in the divine character and the divine economy. When we are ready for Christ's coming, we are not just waiting passively; we are actively conforming our lives to this divine standard. This conformity entails a profound commitment to truth, a conscious and ongoing effort to eliminate every trace of deceit from our character and conduct.

The antithesis of the truth-teller, the deceiver, will find no welcome in the eternal kingdom. This is not a matter of God being capricious or unjust; it is a reflection of His perfect nature. Just as light cannot coexist with darkness, truth cannot coexist with falsehood in the absolute purity of God's presence. The deceiver's life, characterized by manipulation, dishonesty, and the distortion of reality, is fundamentally misaligned with the divine order. They have, in essence, chosen a path that leads away from God, the source of all truth. The final judgment serves to confirm this separation, not as a punishment for punishment's sake, but as the inevitable consequence of a life lived in opposition to God's very essence.

This understanding calls for a rigorous self-examination. We must ask ourselves: Are our words always aligned with reality? Are our intentions pure, or do self-serving motives mask them? Do we present an authentic self before God and others, or do we maintain a carefully constructed facade? The temptation to deceive, even in small ways, is pervasive. It can manifest as exaggeration, omission, flattery, or even a silence that tacitly approves of falsehood. The Bible, in its profound wisdom, urges believers to cultivate an inner integrity that permeates every aspect of their lives, ensuring that our speech is not only truthful but also seasoned with grace and wisdom. **James 3:17-18** speaks of the wisdom that is from above: "*But the wisdom that is from above is first pure, then peaceable, gentle, and easy to be intreated, full of mercy and good fruits, without partiality, and without hypocrisy. Moreover, the fruit of righteousness is sown in peace of them that make peace.*" (KJV, 2023). This description of heavenly wisdom is the very antithesis of deceit.

The seriousness of embracing deceit is further amplified when we consider the words of Jesus to the religious leaders of His day, who were masters of hypocrisy and legalistic outward show that masked inner corruption. In **Matthew 23:27**, he called them "*whited sepulchers, which indeed appear beautiful outward, but are inward full of dead men's bones, and of all uncleanness*" (KJV, 2023). This powerful imagery highlights the profound disconnect that deceit creates between outward appearance and inner reality. At the final judgment, this disconnect will be exposed, and those who have prioritized the appearance of righteousness over genuine inner transformation will find their carefully constructed edifice crumbling into dust. The truth-teller, however, whose life is characterized by a genuine inner alignment with God's truth, will stand firm.

Therefore, readiness for Christ's coming is not merely an outward show of piety or a superficial adherence to religious customs. It is a deep, abiding commitment to truth that originates in the heart and permeates every aspect of our lives. It is a life that has been purified from the corrosive influence of deceit, a life that reflects the very character of Christ, who is the embodiment of truth. The Bible consistently emphasizes the importance of the heart and its intentions. **Proverbs 4:23** famously states, "*Keep thy heart with* *all diligence; for out of it are the issues of life."* (KJV, 2023). This verse serves as a foundational principle for understanding how to prepare for the final judgment. Our diligence must be focused inward, ensuring that our hearts are pure and that the "issues of life"—our actions, our words, our attitudes—flow from a source of unwavering truthfulness.

The final judgment is the ultimate affirmation of divine justice and the absolute triumph of truth. For the believer who has striven to live a life purified from deceit, this judgment is not a source of dread but a glorious culmination. It is the moment when our earthly pilgrimage is met with divine recognition of our faithfulness to the truth, not because of our own perfect righteousness, but because of the imputed righteousness of Christ, which we have embraced through faith and demonstrated through a life lived in pursuit of His truth. The deceiver, however, will face the stark reality of a judgment that accurately reflects their chosen path, a path that deliberately turned away from the light of God's truth. The stark pronouncements found within the Bible serve as an enduring testament to the ultimate significance of living a life of integrity, aligning ourselves with the eternal reality of divine truth and justice, and thereby being truly ready for His glorious appearing.

The tapestry of human history is interwoven with threads of truth and falsehood. In our current era, the threads of deception often appear to dominate, creating a dizzying array of illusions that can obscure the bedrock of reality. Within this pervasive atmosphere of untruth, the Christian life is called to be a radical counter-culture, a living testament to the transformative power of God's truth. To be ready for Christ's coming is not merely a passive anticipation; it is an active, deliberate engagement with truth in every dimension of our existence. This engagement propels us into a life that stands in stark contrast to the prevailing norms of a world often content with convenience, compromise, and the subtle art of misleading.

Living in the light of God's truth means more than simply refraining from outright lies. It is a profound and comprehensive commitment to authenticity, integrity, and transparency that permeates our thoughts, our words, and our actions. It is about aligning our inner landscape with the external realities God has established, and it calls for a vigilant rejection of all forms of deception, whether they are grand betrayals of trust or the seemingly minor embellishments that can erode our credibility over time. This counter-cultural stance is not about rebellion for its own sake, but about a faithful allegiance to a higher authority. This divine standard calls us to a life of unwavering truthfulness.

In a world that often celebrates cleverness and strategic ambiguity, the believer is called to embrace a different kind of wisdom – the wisdom that comes from above, which the Apostle James in **James 3:17** describes as *"first pure, then peaceable, gentle, and easy to be intreated, full of mercy and good fruits, without partiality, and without hypocrisy"* (KJV, 2023). This heavenly wisdom is the antithesis of deceit, which is often impure in its motives, disruptive in its effects, harsh in its dealings, and ultimately barren of genuine good fruit. By cultivating this divine wisdom, we become agents of truth, reflecting the very character of God, who is the embodiment of truth itself.

The implications of this commitment are far-reaching, impacting every facet of our daily lives. Consider the marketplace, where the pressure to gain an advantage can often lead to inflated claims, hidden defects, and misleading advertisements. The Christian professional or business owner is called to conduct their affairs with a radical honesty that sets them apart. This means either forgoing a lucrative deal that relies on obfuscation or openly disclosing a potential drawback that others prefer to conceal. It is in these moments of choice, where personal gain stands in opposition to ethical integrity, that our counter-cultural commitment to truth is truly tested and forged. Such integrity, while sometimes costly in the short term, builds a foundation of trust and respect that ultimately honors God and enriches the lives of those around us.

Our interpersonal relationships are another crucial arena for demonstrating this truth. In a culture where flattery is often a currency of social exchange and where feedback can be sugar-coated to avoid discomfort, the believer is called to offer truth spoken in love. This means being willing to confront falsehood or harmful behavior, not with condemnation, but with a genuine concern for the well-being of the other person, mirroring the gentle yet firm approach of Christ. It also means being truthful in our affirmations, ensuring that our praise is sincere and our affections are genuine. The absence of authentic connection, often masked by superficial pleasantries, can leave individuals feeling profoundly isolated and disconnected. The Christian, by contrast, offers a relational authenticity that can be a beacon of hope in a disconnected world.

The very act of living truthfully in a deceptive world makes us a powerful testimony. When our words align with our actions, when our private lives mirror our public personas, and when our commitments are steadfast, we become living advertisements for the reality of God's transforming power. People are often drawn not to abstract doctrines, but to the tangible evidence of changed lives. A life lived in consistent, unwavering truthfulness, even amidst personal cost, speaks volumes about the nature of the God we serve. It demonstrates that there is a reality beyond the fleeting and the fabricated, a reality that offers lasting security and genuine fulfillment.

This counter-cultural pursuit of truth is deeply rooted in our identity in Christ. He Himself declared in **John 14:6**, "*I am the way, the truth, and the life*" (KJV, 2023). To follow Christ is to embrace truth as the very essence of our journey. Our sanctification, the ongoing process of becoming more like Christ, is a process of purification from all that is false and a cultivation of all that is true. This involves a deep introspection, an honest appraisal of our own hearts and motivations, and a willingness to allow the Holy Spirit to expose and remove any hidden deceit. As the psalmist in **Psalm 139:23-24** prayed, "*Search me, O God, and know my heart: try me, and know my thoughts: And see if there be any wicked way in me, and lead me in the way everlasting*" (KJV, 2023). This prayer is the heart of the counter-culture of truth – a plea for divine insight to root out deception from our innermost being.

The Scriptures consistently highlight the corrupting influence of deceit. **Proverbs 12:22** states, "*Lying lips are abomination to the LORD: but they that deal truly are his delight.*" (KJV, 2023). This is not merely a suggestion; it is a declaration of God's perspective. Our faithful adherence to truth is a reflection of our love for Him and our desire to walk in fellowship with Him. When we choose to be truthful, even when it is difficult or unpopular, we are aligning ourselves with God's very nature and demonstrating our readiness for His imminent return. This readiness is a practical, day-to-day discipline.

Consider the pervasive nature of misinformation and propaganda in contemporary society. From political discourse to social media trends, the line between fact and fiction is often blurred. Believers are called to be discerning, to weigh information carefully, and to resist the temptation to spread rumors or unverified claims. This requires a commitment to seeking out reliable sources and verifying information before sharing it. To speak with accuracy and careful consideration. In a digital age where falsehood can travel the globe in seconds, the responsible stewardship of our communication channels becomes a critical aspect of our witness for truth.

Furthermore, the counter-culture of truth extends to our understanding of ourselves. Self-deception is the most insidious form of deceit, for it allows us to harbor falsehoods without even recognizing them. This can manifest as a refusal to acknowledge our own shortcomings, a tendency to rationalize our bad behavior, or a persistent belief in our own inherent superiority. The journey of spiritual growth involves an ongoing confrontation with our own pride and a humble acceptance of our dependence on God's grace. By embracing the truth about our fallen nature and our need for redemption, we open ourselves to the transformative work of the Holy Spirit, who leads us into all truth.

When we actively cultivate truthfulness in our lives, we become a potent force for positive change in the world. Our integrity becomes a compelling argument for the reality of the Christian faith. It is a demonstration that there is a higher standard, a more enduring reality, and a more fulfilling way of life than what the world typically offers. This counter-cultural stance is not about being odd or eccentric, but about being distinct, a people set apart by their commitment to the unvarnished truth of God's Word and the transformative power of His presence.

This commitment to truth is not always easy. It requires courage to speak up when others remain silent, resilience to withstand the pressure to conform to deceptive practices, and a deep reliance on the strength that God provides. There will be moments when honesty costs us something – perhaps a promotion, a social advantage, or even the approval of those around us. However, Scripture assures us that our faithfulness will not go unnoticed or unrewarded. As Jesus Himself in **Matthew 5:10-12** said, "*Blessed are they which are persecuted for righteousness' sake: for theirs is the kingdom of heaven. Blessed are ye, when men shall revile you, and persecute you, and shall say all manner of evil against you falsely, for my sake. Rejoice, and be exceeding glad: for great is your reward in heaven*" (KJV). This promise underscores the ultimate value of living a life that is not only truthful but also rooted in the righteousness that Christ imparts.

The readiness for His coming is therefore inextricably linked to our embrace of truth as a defining characteristic of our lives. It is a call to be a people whose words are dependable, whose intentions are pure, and whose character reflects the perfect truthfulness of our Savior. By consciously choosing to live in the light of God's truth, we not only prepare ourselves for the glorious appearing of our Lord but also become a powerful, counter-cultural witness to a world desperately in need of authenticity and hope. This is not a passive waiting, but an active pursuit of holiness, a relentless dedication to eradicating deceit, and a joyful commitment to embodying the very truth that sets us free.

The pursuit of truth also has implications for our spiritual disciplines. When we pray, we are invited to be open and honest before God, laying bare our hearts without pretense. When we read Scripture, we are to receive its message with humility and a willingness to be challenged and corrected. When we engage in fellowship with other believers, we are called to a level of transparency that fosters mutual accountability and encourages one another on the path of righteousness. Each of these practices, when undertaken with a sincere heart and a commitment to truth, contributes to the ongoing process of spiritual formation, preparing us for Christ's return.

The counter-culture of truth is not an optional extra for the Christian life; it is its very foundation. It is the bedrock upon which genuine faith is built and the light by which our witness shines. To be ready for His coming is to live in such a way that when He appears, He will find us not only waiting, but actively living out the truth that He Himself embodies. It is to be found dwelling in the light, reflecting His glory, and bearing the unmistakable mark of His kingdom – the unshakeable, unwavering power of truth. This makes our lives a vibrant testament, a persuasive argument for the reality of God's love and faithfulness in a world that often feels lost in shadows.

The Word of God is truth, and therefore, to honor the Word is to honor truth itself. The process of eradicating deceit from our lives is not a singular event, a box to be ticked and forgotten; rather, it is a dynamic, lifelong endeavor. It requires a constant, conscious reliance on the indwelling Holy Spirit, the divine Comforter and Illuminator who guides us into all truth

(**John 16:13**, KJV). Without His enabling power, our efforts to shed deception and embrace authenticity would be like a soldier attempting to fight a battle without his armor or his strength. The Spirit empowers us to discern truth from falsehood, to resist the subtle whispers of deceit that can insinuate themselves into our thoughts and motivations, and to speak and act with integrity. This reliance is an active, prayerful posture, a continual surrender to the Spirit's leading, allowing Him to refine our hearts and minds, purging any remnants of falsehood.

Diligence in the study and application of Scripture, particularly the KJV, is the other indispensable pillar of this unwavering commitment. The Bible is not merely a historical document or a collection of moral teachings; it is the living, active Word of God (**Hebrews 4:12** KJV). It is the supreme standard by which all claims to truth, whether from external sources or from within our own hearts, must be measured. Through diligent reading, meditation, and faithful application, we allow God's Word to shape our worldview, purify our thoughts, and align our actions with His divine will. This means more than just intellectual assent; it involves a willingness to be corrected, challenged, and transformed by the truth we encounter. It means wrestling with difficult passages, seeking understanding through prayer and fellowship, and then actively integrating the revealed truths into the fabric of our daily lives. The eradication of deceit is a multifaceted battle, fought on several fronts. It begins in the inner sanctuary of our minds, where thoughts are conceived and intentions are formed. We must be vigilant against deceptive thought patterns, such as rationalization, self-deception, and prideful justification of wrongdoings.

The Apostle Paul in **II Corinthians 10:5** exhorts us to "*bring into captivity every thought to the obedience of Christ*" (KJV, 2023). This requires a conscious effort to examine our thought life, identify and uproot any thoughts that do not align with the truth in Scripture, and replace them with thoughts that are pure, honest, and God-honoring. This is where the Holy Spirit's work is paramount, enabling us to discern the subtle whispers of the adversary that seek to sow seeds of doubt and deception in our minds.

Beyond our thoughts, deceit often manifests in our words. The tongue, **James 3:6**, tells us, is a "*fire, a world of iniquity*" (KJV, 2023). In our interactions, we can fall prey to exaggeration, gossip, slander, half-truths, and outright lies. The commitment to truth calls us to speak with precision, honesty, and kindness. Our words should be seasoned with grace, reflecting the truth in love, always aiming to build up rather than tear down. This may mean refraining from speaking when we lack complete information, admitting when we have erred, and choosing to speak truth even when it is difficult or unpopular.

Our actions, too, must be a testament to truth. Deceit can infiltrate our deeds through dishonest business practices, unfaithfulness in relationships, hypocrisy in worship, and a general lack of integrity in our commitments—the call to readiness for His coming demands that our lives be characterized by transparency and consistency. What we profess in our prayers and our public declarations must be evident in our private dealings and our everyday behavior. When our actions align with our beliefs, when our outward conduct reflects our inner commitment to God's truth, we become powerful witnesses to the transformative power of the Gospel. This integrity is not always the easiest path; it often requires sacrifice and a willingness to forgo personal advantage for the sake of righteousness.

The struggle against deceit is not a solo mission. Our commitment to truth is strengthened and tested within the community of faith. Fellowship with other believers provides opportunities for mutual accountability and encouragement. When we are open about our struggles with deceit and allow others to speak truth into our lives, we create an environment where truth can flourish. When we hide our deceptions from our brothers and sisters, we isolate ourselves and create fertile ground for falsehood to take root.

Consider the profound impact of living a life free from deceit. It builds trust, fosters genuine connection, and brings glory to God. In a world saturated with artifice and manipulation, a life lived in unwavering truthfulness stands out as a beacon of authenticity. It demonstrates that there is a higher standard, a reality beyond the superficial, and a power that can transform lives from the inside out. This is the counter-cultural aspect of our faith, a living testimony to the fact that we serve a God who is Himself the very embodiment of truth.

The process of eradicating deceit, therefore, is a dynamic partnership between the believer and the Holy Spirit, empowered by diligent engagement with God's preserved Word. This partnership embodies our readiness for Christ's return. It means living in such a way that when He appears, we will be found not in a state of hidden deception, but in the bright, unblemished light of His presence. Our lives will reflect His truth, our words will be honest, and our actions will be consistent with our faith. This preparation is not passive; it is an active, ongoing pursuit of holiness —a relentless commitment to the eradication of all that is false —and a joyful embrace of the truth that liberates and transforms.

As we conclude this examination of readiness, let us reaffirm this crucial commitment. When He comes, may we be found, not wrestling with deception, but standing firm in His truth, our lives a testament to His faithfulness, and our hearts prepared to meet Him. This is the ultimate preparation, the truest readiness – to be found dwelling in His light, free from all deceit, and wholly devoted to the One who is Himself the Way, the Truth, and the Life.

Conclusion

Now that I have completely overwhelmed you with information and research on deception, and how it works, I hope that you can see why I chose the Title "***The Serpent's Tongue***." Satan's tongue—his words that hit our brains like fiery darts that torment us- is him bringing all that he has against us in an attempt to deceive us.

However, in order to deceive us, Satan must first plant seeds of doubt into our minds. He knows that if he can remind us of our past or convince us that we are unworthy, then it is easier for him to convince us that everyone else is wrong.

If Satan cannot get you to stop attending a particular church, then his next best option is to convince you that attending that church is associating you with an evil group of people. Then he will ensure that you hear all the rumors and see all the negative Facebook posts. When you hear these actions, you will believe them if he has destroyed your faith.

Satan's Tongue is his greatest asset, and deception is his greatest tool in his toolbox of tricks to use in these last days. In my next book (already ready for publication and will be out within 30 days of this book) is called ***"The Gift of Discernment,"*** you will have all the information you need about using spiritual discernment to recognize the lies spewing from Satan's tongue that are aimed at discouraging us. Discernment is a must-have tool for every Christian in these last days. It is not an option for a spiritual warrior or a prayer warrior. Every pastor and his leadership team should have an active spiritual prayer warrior lifestyle. They should be actively discerning spirits and teaching you about the spirits they are discerning. If your pastor never discusses this topic or tries to make it appear unnecessary when you bring it up, find another church quickly.

Satan is trying to get as many pastors, evangelists, associate and lay ministers, missionaries, and church leadership to accept complacency as a usual way of life. One pastor told me he was not complacent, "Sis, La Wanda, I have just learned to relax in the Holy Spirit and not worry about anything. I do not have to worry or fear; God is taking care of everything. There is no need for me to get upset over these negative political decisions that are occurring. God is going to use all of this to his good. You will see!" That is a perfect example of complacency and deception. When Pastors are no longer shocked at the presence of sin, especially to the point of tolerating it in their churches, they have already become so deceived that they are "backslidden." They are no long in tune with the Holy Ghost. They are accepting and worshipping a counterfeit gospel.

We must remember that Satan is the same as he has always been. He may change his colors or how he presents a topic. He may even change the group of people he uses to implement his hidden agenda, but the agenda says the same, and the tools remain consistent. He had not developed any new tools. Our 21st-century technology may seem like new tools, but it is still the same. Deception is number one, and Complacency is number two in his toolbox.

Remember, the spirit of deception originated in the Garden of Eden, where Satan deceived Eve, persuading her to eat fruit from the Tree of Knowledge of Good and Evil, and continues throughout the entire Bible, culminating in the Book of Revelation. The Apostle Paul begins to warn the Christians about the increasing power of this spirit of deception. Then we reach Revelation, where the Bible concludes with John's letters to the churches about what is to come—increasing deception—as the tribulation period approaches. John warns us of the Spirit of Jezebel and a "lying spirit" that will be unleashed upon the earth in the last days. We are currently living in a time where the greatest amount of fake news, false reports, doctored videos, and AI videos are circulating, deceiving people. The political propaganda during the last two presidential elections, in 2020 and 2024, filled people with so much misinformation that they did not know whom to trust.

What we have to know as Christians is that Satan is going to do everything in his power to stop us from winning souls. This is his final fight, and he is aware of that fact. He knows that he is going to take over and bring in the Antichrist and the Mark of the Beast. When his seven-year reign of terror is over, he will be bound for a thousand years. With this expected doom for his future, he is not going to go down without a fight. He is going to deceive every person possible. If he cannot get you to sin, he will deceive you into thinking that the complacency in your life is not complacency, but instead signs of "getting older" and being tired.

All Satan wants to do is cause you to miss the rapture! He knows that most Christians will not survive the tribulation period. If you will compromise now, then you are not going to stand up to the Antichrist and risk your life. You need to stop listening to the spirit of deception that is

The Serpent's Tongue: The Spirit of Deception

trying to take your soul. You *WILL* take the path of least resistance when that time comes. That is why Satan is working so hard to get the prayer warriors tired, vexed, and complacent. That is why it is working so hard to make Christians feel comfortable doing nothing and not coming to church. He knows this is the easiest way to deceive them. He cannot approach them in the same way he did Eve in the Garden; we would immediately recognize that move. So, Satan sits as a "demonized" (person who is oppressed by spirits) next to you on Sunday Morning and makes them your new BFF. He can use that person to politely and carefully walk you into complacency or into the "work" culture.

I have seen Satan use people in this fashion and completely deceive older Christians in the church who were once "on-fire prayer warriors" who hung onto the horns of the altar with such passion that Satan did not get a chance at any of the young people in the church! Some older people I know say, "Oh no, we will not take the mark of the beast if we are left behind. We know the truth. If I am left, I will know not to take the mark. There is no way Satan can deceive me on that point! If I am left, which I pray I am not, I will spend every waking moment trying to reach every person I can for Christ and bring them to heaven with me!"

Well, I hate to bust your spiritual bubble. However, if you cannot live right and stay rapture-ready with the Holy Spirit here to help you, what are you going to do? The Holy Ghost is holding back evil spirits now—imagine what it will be like when the Holy Ghost is gone and evil is in complete control with no checks and balances and no spiritual interference. I fear that all the lukewarm Christians who feel they have a safety net underneath them, that they will have a chance to give their lives for the gospel, and it will be done, are in for a rude awakening. You need to rethink your "Plan B."

My friend, if you cannot go one day without your pain medications or you have severe health problems that you would not live without medical interventions, medical equipment, and supplies, you will be the first in line to take the mark. No matter how strong you think you are, when the pain gets to the level you cannot tolerate it, you are going to beg for help—but will not be able to receive it without the mark. Regardless of what you think today, you will not suffer the pain and agony. You had better get your heart ready now so you can make it in the rapture. I can say that with conviction, because I am one of those individuals that has health problems that medication is keeping in check. Without the medications, I would be crumpled up in a bed and not able to get up and move, much less drive a car. Daily, I pray to make sure my heart is right. I MUST make it in the rapture. I cannot be left behind. I fear that I would give in due to the pain, since the scripture says that those left behind will pray and beg to die, but death will not come.

Surviving the tribulation period will be a challenge for the brave of heart, the young without health problems, or those in need of medical treatment. So, yes, Satan knows that the ones of us who fit into this category of medication dependency, that he can get us if we are left. Therefore, we must (I know I must) make it in the rapture of the church. I cannot let complacency take hold and leave me behind. I cannot afford to be deceived. My war room prayer each morning is the Jabez prayer. I want to love God and give Him my whole heart, body, and strength.

For our young people, this tsunami of fake news, false information, and blatant lies from evil forces at work in our schools and government has deceived them. They have no idea that the information flooding into their lives through professors and the news media contains information that is contrary to the Bible and that some of the fabricated data and knowledge they share is fake information intended to trap them in an endless cycle of destruction and dependency upon the people who are feeding them these lies.

I want to stir up revival in your hearts today. I want you to feel the need to be reunited with your church family. The COVID Pandemic is over. It is time to get back in church. It is time to refocus and get in your prayer room or war room daily and give God the first fruits of your day—a tithe of your time. It is crucial to begin intercessory prayer for your family and friends. We need to pray the Jabez prayer and ask God to enlarge our coast, to send people across our paths whom we can help, and to send us to those in need so that we can help them. If we pray for others, not selfish or self-centered prayers, God will show us what we can do to help them. God will show us how to lead our families to salvation. If we do not get under a burden for them, no one else will. We must intercede for them before the throne of God daily.

I can hear some of you saying, "Well, what can I do? I am a widow, and I do not have the money to run around visiting people. I definitely cannot cook and take food to someone who is sick. I do not have enough money even to buy food after I pay for my electric, insurance, and medications." You do not have to put money out. God is not going to ask you to take your money for your medications and feed people. However, you can do (at no cost to you) intercessory prayer. It will only cost you some of your time. You can fast and pray for those that you want to see saved and delivered. Your time as a spiritual warrior is more important than money!

As I began examining the current state of affairs in America—both government and churches—I realized that we needed a book on this topic that could spark revival among our pastors. I needed a CALL-TO-ACTION book that would ignite revival in the hearts of parents and pastors as I began to fast and pray. After several weeks of fasting one meal a day, then a three-day complete fast, God gave me some information to share with parents, preachers, and teachers, along with a call-to-action challenge for our pastors and parents. I will be sharing this information in a book called **"Our Future: Uncertain, Hopeful, or Doomed?** This book is expected to be available in the fall or winter of 2025, unless there are delays with the publisher. If you have children in the school system, this book provides valuable information on how to protect them and the activities in which you should be involved. Adding it to this book would have made the book over 500 pages long, and it would not have been relevant to some readers. This will also give us time to make it through the 2024 Presidential Election and see which candidate wins. Some of the strategies in my action plan may need to change if the wrong candidate wins the election.

Therefore, in the interest of keeping this conclusion brief and reasonable, given that this book is already quite lengthy, I would like to remind you that you need to understand the characteristics of deception thoroughly. You need to know the subtle ways that Satan can introduce deception into your life. You also need to pray daily for the gift of discernment to work in your life and grow stronger each day. Put up guards and do not let Satan catch you off guard—he will begin influencing you if you do! Satan's favorite use of deception is to destroy churches, lives, marriages, families, influence governments, schools, and ensure that the next generation is not crippled and prey for the Antichrist. I pray that you will learn Satan's tricks and that this book has helped you to understand how the spirit of deception works. Now, order the next book, **"The Gift of Discernment,"** and make sure you are fully equipped as a spiritual warrior in the last days!

Remember, in this modern, high-tech 21st century, we face a generation where truth is often malleable and spiritual discernment is increasingly elusive. Our modern faith is fraught with subtle distortions, outright falsehoods, and cleverly disguised errors that can lead even the most devout believers astray. Secular humanism and relativistic philosophies, and overt manipulations of false teachers are tools in Satan's hands to deceive this generation and keep us from being rapture-ready.

Know that pride, self-deception, spiritual apathy, complacency, and compromises are the beginning signs that the spirit of deception has moved in and taken up residency in your life or church. I pray that you have learned how to overcome this spirit and not be deceived in these last days.

As we approach the rapture, the spirit of deception will grow stronger and stronger. It will be so powerful that even Christians can be deceived and led away who are staying in the word of God. Deception will be the Antichrist's number one assistant. Without the Holy Spirit in the earth, he will be able to deceive many. Stand in the gap and make up the hedge. Do not allow Satan to deceive you or your family. Put on the whole armor of God each day!

We love and appreciate all of our followers, prayer partners, and fellow pastors. We pray daily for you, asking God to bless you, so that you may have the strength, health, and financial means to be a part of this end-time revival. Get in your war rooms and intercede daily. We will see you at a church near you soon or in the rapture!

With Love and prayers,

La Wanda Blackmon

About the Author

LaWanda Blackmon is a published author in several genres of healthcare. She has four major book series in the genres of Christian Living, collegiate religious textbooks, historical bible-based Christian romance, and Bible prophecy. She has published over 120 healthcare-related books and workbooks, in addition to the 125 religious books for release through 2026.

Her first religious series was *"The Redeeming Love"* Series. Her second series, *"Revelation Made Simple"* (written in 2023 and scheduled for publication at the end of 2024), and the *"Love God's Way"* Christian Romance series were written in the 1980s and 1990s. They will be coming out two per month in 2025 until the entire series has been converted to Kindle eBooks (Paperbacks still available on Amazon too. Each of these books will have new book covers and any necessary updates to information before being listed on Amazon. These books are being published as a series, linking each book to why it is best to *"Love God's Way!"*

LaWanda's first series, *"Redeeming Love,"* was given to her by the Lord, including the titles and outlines of each book. She shares how this series came about. The story is fantastic. This first series was birth in her from the hurt, pain, abandonment, unfair punishment, and betrayal she suffered at the hands of those closest to her. As she laid her hurt and scars at Jesus' feet, he taught her how to love those who had falsely accused her and tried to take her down. As she grew in her spiritual relationship, her love for others, including her enemies, deepened. She was able to forgive each of her accusers as they began to die and call her to ask for forgiveness. In this series, each book addresses the points outlined in *"**Broken: Braced for Favor**"* (2022). Mrs. Blackmon will take you on a journey from Broken to Redeemed as she shows you what it means to have God break you, humble you, and then redeem you as his own! The release dates for each book are in parentheses at the end of the title on the list at the back of this book.

Before she finished the *"Redeeming Love"* series, she was contacted by HFT Publishing and asked to write the series on the book of Revelation. In this series called *"Revelation: Made Simple Series."* The <u>first book</u> she wrote was **"Revelation Made Simple: The Greatest Love Letter to the church from Jesus Christ"** (2022).

The second <u>book</u>, **"Revelation Made Simple: Learn what God wants you to know from this mysterious book that will help you be 'Rapture-Ready!'"** (2023).

The <u>third book</u>, **"Revelation Made Simple: Rapture Ready Study Companion,"** was designed as a companion to the first two books in this series. The key concepts and information from the first two books are presented in a workbook format for those who enjoy taking notes and journaling. It will be out within 90days of the second book.

The <u>fourth book</u> in this series, **"Revelation Made Simple: The Tribulation Period and Our Future Explained,"** is currently in the initial editing phase, with a publication date scheduled for Fall 2025. (The publication date is further out due to the extensive research that is needed will take longer, because Mrs. Blackmon will not be able to travel as much due to her parents' health crisis.

She has begun working on the <u>fifth book</u> on Revelation, **"Revelation Made Simple: The In-Depth Chronological Events of Revelation."** This book will examine the book of Revelation in chronological order, supporting the information with prophecies from the Old Testament. (Anticipated publication date: Spring 2026). Each book builds on the previous one. As you progress through the series, you will be provided with increasingly detailed information to help you become a victorious spiritual warrior as we draw closer to the rapture of the church and the end of the days.

La Wanda has written numerous books that are not part of a series. Now, her Christian Romance books are becoming increasingly popular because they uniquely retell Old Testament stories, converting them into dynamic romance stories. The list of books planned for 2024 publication includes:

Jannes and Jambre: Opposing Moses before Pharaoh

Satan's Seven Seductions

The Gift of Discernment: A Mandatory Gift to Survive in the Last Days

Are you really the Bride of Christ, or are you just dating him for the blessings?

Where are the Warriors? I have left this pea patch for my last time!

Some of the series books will be published as late as 2030. With four books planned for each series per year, plus the non-series book, at least two books will be published in paperback on Amazon each month. As soon as the publisher can convert them to eBooks, the eBooks will follow. There may be a lag in the release dates of the eBooks. Initially, they will all be published in Kindle format. Then later, the best sellers will be published in iBooks and ePub formats.

Author's Credentials and Experience:

Mrs. Blackmon has over 35 years of experience in nursing and has been preaching since she was 16 years old. She became a licensed minister with the Assemblies of God in 1991. She has been ordained for over 15 years. Her heart has always been devoted to medical missions, both domestically and internationally. She loves teaching in ministry and her career as well. Due to their extensive mission work, she transferred into a Non-Denominational Evangelical organization comprised mainly of former Church of God and Assembly of God preachers who needed to broaden their outreach. They continue to be members of an Assembly of God church.

However, since 2019, she has seen a shift in the focus of her ministry. The Holy Spirit has led her to write books for pastors, church leaders, and individuals who desire to be in ministry. As a result, pastors are now calling her the "prophetic voice for Pastors."

Her education includes a two-year registered nursing training program, a double major (Associate of Science), and an Associate of Arts degree. She also holds two Bachelor of Science degrees (in Nursing and Liberal Arts) and two master's degrees (in Nursing and Education). Her doctoral work has been in medical research and education.

Her work experience spans the full spectrum of nursing and nursing leadership, including consulting, nursing professor, and freelance writing. Her passion for education is her greatest asset, as she strives to reach as many people as possible with the message of Jesus each year.

You can reach her at:

La Wanda Blackmon
P. O. Box 712
Brewton, AL 36427-0712
lawanda@minister.com

HFT Publishing, Inc.
P.O. Box 1873
Brewton, AL 36427
bulk orders-fax: 251-248-2709
HFT-Publishing@post.com

Check with Amazon monthly to see if more books have been published for this author. HFT Publishing, Inc. plans to add a YouTube Channel and Facebook marketing for this author. As books and social media accounts are added, the updates will appear on Amazon's Author page for La Wanda.

Mrs. Blackmon's books are and will continue to be produced on a routine schedule. The publisher typically posts monthly. For books included in college and university curricula, they will be provided in hardcover but must be ordered directly from HFT Publishing to receive the educator and non-profit discounts.

Most of La Wanda's nursing books end up being college and university curricula and textbooks across America. Those books are in hardback covers for durability. The other books (novels and religious books) are not published in hardcover due to cost. She wants to keep all books as affordable as possible so that they can reach as many people worldwide as possible.

If you wish to purchase books in bulk for use in your church's Bible study groups or Sunday school classes, please get in touch with HFT Publishing via fax at (251-248-2709) with a written request. List the name of the book(s) and the quantities needed. They will fax you a quote with discounts you cannot receive through Amazon or a Bookstore.

Other Books by this Author

Closer to Jesus Devotional Series: (10-Book Series)

1) (2020) *Getting to know God through the Old Testament: Genesis to Ezra Devotional* (90-day devotional)
2) (2020) *Getting to know God through the Old Testament: Genesis to Ezra Prayer Journal*
3) (2021) *Learning about God through the Eyes of the Old Testament Prophets: Nehemiah to Malachi Devotional* (90-day devotional)
4) (2021) *Learning about God through the Eyes of the Old Testament Prophets: Nehemiah to Malachi Prayer Journal*
5) (2022) *Meeting Jesus through the eyes of the New Testament—Matthew to Romans Devotional* (90-day devotional)
6) (2022) *Meeting Jesus through the eyes of the New Testament—Matthew to Romans Prayer Journal*
7) (2023) *Walking with Power like in the New Testament Churches—Galatians to I John Devotional* (90-day devotional)
8) (2023) *Walking with Power like in the New Testament Churches—Galatians to I John Prayer Journal*
9) (2024) *Preparing to Meet Jesus in the New Testament—II John to Revelation Devotional* (90-day devotional)
10) (2024) *Preparing to Meet Jesus in the New Testament—II John to Revelation Prayer Journal*

Non-Series Books: (5 Books)

 **Jannes and Jambres:** *Opposing Moses before Pharaoh* (2024)

 **Are you truly the Bride of Christ, or are you just dating Him for the blessings?** (2024)

 **Can America come back from COVID-19, election Fraud, & Terrorism?** *Learn What the Future Holds* (2025)

 **What is wrong with the church?** *"One More Night with the Frogs" Syndrome* (2025)

 **Where are the warriors?** *I have left this pea patch for the last time!* (2024)

Check Amazon Monthly to see which books have been added. All books will be converted to Kindle format. Currently, we do not have conversion and publication dates available. The priority is paperback print. The books on contracts with colleges and universities for textbooks will be made available to students in Kindle and hardcover formats. Those texts will be the first ones converted to Kindle eBook format.

Revelation: Made Simple Series: (5-book series)

Revelation Made Simple: *The greatest love letter to the church from Jesus Christ* (2022)

Revelation Made Simple: *Learning What God wants you to know from this mysterious book that will help you to be rapture-ready* (2023)

Revelation Made Simple: *Rapture-Ready Study Companion* (2024)

Revelation Made Simple: *The tribulation and our future explained* (2025)

Revelation Made Simple: *The In-depth chronological events of Revelation* (2026)

La Wanda Blackmon

Redeeming Love Series: (60 Book Series)

Book #	Letter	Book Title
1	**B**	**Broken:** *Braced for Favor* (2020)
2		**Broken:** *Braced for Favor Journal*
3		**Broken:** *Braced for Favor Devotional*
4	**R**	**Redeemed:** *Forgiven and Forgotten (2021)*
5		**Redeemed:** *Forgiven and Forgotten Journal*
6		**Redeemed:** *Forgiven and Forgotten Devotional*
7	**O**	**Opened-Up:** *Stirred Up for Change (2022)*
8		**Opened-Up:** *Stirred Up for Change Journal*
9		**Opened-Up:** *Stirred Up for Change Devotional*
10	**K**	**Knocked Down:** *But not out* (2023)
11		**Knocked Down:** *But not out Journal*
12		**Knocked Down:** *But not out Devotional*
13	**E**	**Enriched:** *Exchange Your Evil Heart for a Good Heart (2024)*
14		**Enriched:** *Exchange Your Evil Heart for a Good Heart Journal*
15		**Enriched:** *Exchange Your Evil Heart for a Good Heart Devotional*
16	**N**	**New Creation:** *Now we are New Through Jesus* (2025)
17		**New Creation:** *Now we are New Through Jesus Journal*
18		**New Creation:** *Now we are New Through Jesus Devotional*
19	**B**	**Begotten:** *We belong to Jesus now* (2026)
20		**Begotten:** *We belong to Jesus now Journal*
21		**Begotten:** *We belong to Jesus now Devotional*

Book #	Letter	Book Title
22	**R**	**Resurrected:** *Our Old Man is New in Christ (2026)*
23		**Resurrected:** *Our Old Man is New in Christ Journal*
24		**Resurrected:** *Our Old Man is New in Christ Devotional*
25	**A**	**Appointed:** *For a Time Like This (2026)*
26		**Appointed:** *For a Time Like This Journal*
27		**Appointed:** *For a Time Like This Devotional*
28	**C**	**Chosen:** *Anointed for this Job (2027)*
29		**Chosen:** *Anointed for this Job Journal*
30		**Chosen:** *Anointed for this Job Devotional*
31	**E**	**Exodus:** *From our Moab to the land of plenty (2027)*
32		**Exodus:** *From our Moab to the land of plenty Journal*
33		**Exodus:** *From our Moab to the land of plenty Devotional*
34	**D**	**Deliverance:** *The Broken Delivered and Set Free (2027)*
35		**Deliverance:** *The Broken Delivered and Set Free Journal*
36		**Deliverance:** *The Broken Delivered and Set Free Devotional*
37	**F**	**Forgiven:** *Mercy and Grace (2028)*
38		**Forgiven:** *Mercy and Grace Journal*
39		**Forgiven:** *Mercy and Grace Devotional*
40	**O**	**Obedience:** *The Obedient Overcome (2028)*
41		**Obedience:** *The Obedient Overcome Journal*
42		**Obedience:** *The Obedient Overcome Devotional*

Book #	Letter	Book Title
43	**R**	**Rejuvenation**: *Restored and Rejuvenated Church (2028)*
44		**Rejuvenation**: *Restored and Rejuvenated Church Journal*
45		**Rejuvenation**: *Restored and Rejuvenated Church Devotional*
46	**F**	**Favored**: *Unmerited Faith and Favor (2029)*
47		**Favored**: *Unmerited Faith and Favor Journal*
48		**Favored**: *Unmerited Faith and Favor Devotional*
49	**A**	**Anointed**: *Adopted and Betrothed (2029)*
50		**Anointed**: *Adopted and Betrothed Journal*
51		**Anointed**: *Adopted and Betrothed Devotional*
52	**V**	**Victorious**: *Living Victoriously in God's Favor (2029)*
53		**Victorious**: *Living Victoriously in God's Favor Journal*
54		**Victorious**: *Living Victoriously in God's Favor Devotional*
55	**O**	**Opportunities**: *Your Divine Purpose (2030)*
56		**Opportunities**: *Your Divine Purpose Journal*
57		**Opportunities**: *Your Divine Purpose Devotional*
58	**R**	**Restoration**: *Restored and Rapture Ready (2030)*
59		**Restoration**: *Restored and Rapture Ready Journal*
60		**Restoration**: *Restored and Rapture Ready Devotional*

The Serpent's Tongue: The Spirit of Deception

Novels Written by La Wanda Blackmon

---

1) **Issac and Rebekah**: *A Divine Love that defies all arranged marriage concepts!*
2) **Jacob, Leah, and Rachel:** *Navigating Two Wives & Two Concubines*
3) **Abraham, Sarah, and Hagar**: *The Love Triangle*
4) **Ahasuerus and Hadassah**: *The Unusual Bride and a King*
5) **Hosea and Gomer:** *The Beauty of Redeeming Love*
6) **King Solomon and the Shulamite Woman**: *A Pure Love That Offers Everything*
7) **King Solomon and the Queen of Sheba**: *A Love from Two Worlds*
8) **Boaz and Ruth**: *Love the Second Time Around*
9) **Samson and Delilah**: *A Love that Destroys*
10) **King David and Michal**: *The Beauty of First Love*
11) **King David and Bathsheba**: *The Unforbidden Love and Murder*
12) **King David and Abigail**: *A Love that Protects*
13) **King David and Abishag**: *A Love that is Patient and Warm*
14) **Elkanah and Hannah**: *The Love of a Second Wife*
15) **Ahab and Jezebel**: *An Unhealthy Love*
16) **King Jehoram and Athaliah**: *A Love that Destroys and Kills*
17) **Lapidoth and Deborah**: *A Love that Lets each other Grow*
18) **Adam and Eve:** *The First Arranged Marriage*
19) **Amram and Jochebed**: *A love that chooses the best route even when it hurts!*
20) **Job and Dinah**: *A Love that Stays Regardless*
21) **Moses and Zipporah:** *A Love that Accepts You Regardless*
22) **Moses and Thabisa**: *A Love that was Fought and Forbidden*
23) **Salmon and Rahab**: *A Love that Protects and Restores*
24) **Abraham and Keturah**: *A Love that Nurtures*
25) **Hur and Miriam**: *A Unique Love (Sister of Moses)*
26) **Zechariah and Elizabeth**: *A Love that Waits*
27) **Mary and Joseph**: *A Love Forged in Faith*
28) **Priscilla and Aquilla**: *A Love that is called for a purpose*
29) **Ananias and Saphirah**: *A love built on deceit*

30) **Zebedee and Salome**: *A Love for Ministry*
31) **Aaron & Elisheba**: *A Love that Serves*
32) **Joanna & Chuza**: *A Love that Disappoints*
33) **Peter & Ahava**: *A Love that Survives*
34) **Pontius Pilate and Claudia**: *A love that disappoints and condemns*
35) **Herod Antipas and Herodias**: *A love that steals, deceives, and cons*
36) **Lot and Ashira**: *A love that lusts for the things of Sodom*
37) **Lot and his two daughters**: Incest—*The Forbidden Love*
38) **Samuel and Eliana**: *A Love for the Chosen One*
39) **Joseph and Asenath**: *A love that heals and restores*
40) **Tamar & Judah**: *A revengeful love*
41) **Noah and Emzara**: *A love that supports*
42) **Jesse and his two wives**: *A Love that resulted in Shame*
43) **King Saul and Abinonah:** *A Donkey Herder's Love*
44) **King Saul and Rizpah:** *A Love that Defies Death*
45) **Heber and Jael**: *The Love of a Warrior Wife*

This author has written a total of 110 religious books at the time this book was written. This will put the dynamic works of this author into the hands of more people than she would ever be able to reach through a pulpit alone.

References

BibleGateway (2023). *Encyclopedia of the Bible* [word and topic searches]. Retrieved on 2-20-2023 from website: www.biblegateway.com/resources/encyclopedia-of-the-bible/ (topic of search).

Hagee, M. (2023). *Spiritual Warfare: Unlock the Supernatural and Access the Promises of God.* Southlake, TX: Breakfast for Seven

Hybel, B. (2008). *Too busy not to pray: Special Edition-20th Anniversary.* Downer Grove, IL: Intervarsity Press.

Jacobs, L. (2012, October 11). *Last days revival or end time apostasy?* Retrieved from https://www.shema.com/last-days-revival-or-end-time-apostasssy-208/

Jing, Z. (2019, June 23). *The last days are here: Are you prepared to meet God? Retrieved from* https://www.holyspiritsspeaks.org/testimonies/prepare-to-meet-God/

Johnson, J. (2023). *The Warrior Bride.* Shippensburg, PA: Destiny Image

KJV. (2023). *The King James Bible online.* Retrieved from: https://www.kingjamesbibleonline.org/ (in search—add scripture needed).

O'Neal, C. (2020). *"Why am I not living a victorious life?"* Brewton, AL: HFT Publishing

O'Neal, C. (2021). *"The Spiritual Warrior."* Brewton, AL: HFT Publishing

Shutterstock (2023). Artwork inside the manuscript. Paid for and licensed from Shutterstock to La Wanda Blackmon. Retrieved from https://www.shutterstock.com

www.ingramcontent.com/pod-product-compliance
Lightning Source LLC
Chambersburg PA
CBHW051900160426
43198CB00012B/1688